THE ENVIRONMENTALIST'S BOOKSHELF

A GUIDE TO THE BEST BOOKS

THE ENVIRONMENTALIST'S BOOKSHELF

A GUIDE TO THE BEST BOOKS

Robert Merideth

G.K. Hall & Co.
New York

Maxwell Macmillan Canada
Toronto

Maxwell Macmillan International
New York • Oxford • Singapore • Sydney

G.K. Hall & Co.
An Imprint of Macmillan Publishing Company   Maxwell Macmillan Canada, Inc.
866 Third Avenue   1200 Eglinton Avenue East, Suite 200
New York, NY 10022   Don Mills, Ontario M3C 3N1

Macmillan Publishing Company is part of the Maxwell Communication Group of Companies

Library of Congress Catalog Card Number: 92–18613

Printed in the United States of America

printing number
1   2   3   4   5   6   7   8   9   10

Library of Congress Cataloging-in-Publication Data

Merideth, Robert
    The environmentalist's bookshelf : a guide to the best books /
Robert Merideth
        p.   cm.
    Includes indexes.
    ISBN 0–8161–7359–1
    1. Human ecology—Bibliography.   2. Bibliography—Best books—
Human ecology.   3. Environmental protection—Bibliography.
4. Bibliography—Best books—Environmental protection.
5. Environmental policy—Bibliography.   6. Bibliography—Best
books—Environmental policy.   I. Title.
Z5861.M45   1992
[GF41]
016.3637—dc20   92–18613
                                        CIP

The paper used in this publication meets the minimum requirements of American
National Standard for Information Sciences—Permanence of Paper for Printed Library
Materials. ANSI Z39.48–1984.∞™

For my parents,
Robert and Patricia

Contents

Acknowledgments

In a sense, this book saw its origins in my eleven years' affiliation with the Institute for Environmental Studies at the University of Wisconsin-Madison, first as a student, then as a member of the staff. For more than two decades the institute has been a leader in interdisciplinary environmental studies through its instructional, research, and outreach programs. Indeed, whether through research on global climate change or the application of remote sensing and land information systems, or through instruction in water resources management or tropical studies, or through daily broadcasts of Earthwatch Radio, the institute provided me with an enriching and stimulating learning environment. There were many individuals within the institute who, over the years, contributed directly or indirectly to this project. I especially would like to thank Becky Brown, Reid Bryson, Jim Clapp, Bill Denevan, Sharon Dunwoody, Mark Hanson, Hugh Iltis, Harvey Jacobs, Erhard Joeres, Ralph Kiefer, Tom Lillesand, Tim Moermond, Dave Moyer, Ben Niemann, Frank Scarpace, Clay Schoenfeld, Jerry Sullivan, and Steve Ventura for all that they have shared with me. Also, I was fortunate to have such colleagues as Dave Musolf, Tom Sinclair, Joanne Mais, Eileen Hanneman, Barbara Borns, Chuck Engman, and Marguerite Traino, who in their various ways made working within the institute a delight. I owe a special thanks to Arthur Sacks, who, as director of the institute, encouraged me in many ways and supported my endeavors over the years, including the beginnings of this book. As a gesture of appreciation to all these friends, I am donating a portion of the proceeds from the sale of this book to the institute's environmental studies library.

There are many persons who have had a direct involvement in the preparation of this book. First, let me thank the 236 respondents to the questionnaire survey who provided lists of their favorite books on nature and the environment, as well as many interesting and useful comments. Let me thank especially two of the respondents who were influential many years ago in my becoming an environmentalist: Marvin Baker, Jr., who, as my major advisor in the department of geography at the University of Oklahoma, first introduced me to the Sierra Club; and Ken Cross, with whom I have shared many thoughts and experiences related to the environment since our days together in high school in Oklahoma City. I must also thank the editors of the National Wildlife Federation and Gale Research Company who produced the various directories from which I was able to find names of environmentalists to whom to send questionnaires. I am indebted to Anne Marie Amantia, Kathleen Courrier, Herb Eleutario, Randy Harrison, Dan Luten, Dave McGinnis, Rick Sepp, and Tom Turner, who provided me with supplemental materials helpful in preparing this book. I am also grateful to Rick Sepp for providing a critical appraisal of the project from the perspective of a biological sciences librarian. Laurie Greenberg and Tom Sinclair worked with me to produce an earlier annotated bibliography at the University of Wisconsin-Madison, and I am grateful to them for their contributions, since the preparation of that report served as a springboard for this project. Kathie Mackie reviewed the entire manuscript and provided many constructive suggestions, for which I extend my deepest gratitude. Let me also thank the editors at G. K. Hall/Macmillan who have taken an idea and crafted it into a book: Catherine Carter, Michael Sander, Elena Vega, and Elizabeth Holthaus.

Finally, I would like to thank my friend and wife, Diana Liverman, with whom I have discovered and discussed many of the books described herein. Without her steadfast support, including her insightful reviews and contributions to various drafts of the manuscript, this project could not have been completed.

THE ENVIRONMENTALIST'S BOOKSHELF

A GUIDE TO THE BEST BOOKS

Introduction

The year 1992 marked the twentieth anniversary of the United Nations Conference on the Human Environment, which was held in Stockholm in 1972. To commemorate this event, the United Nations Conference on Environment and Development was held in Rio de Janeiro, Brazil. As with the twentieth-anniversary celebration of Earth Day in 1990, this gathering of tens of thousands of environmentalists and government officials, including the heads of state of more than 100 nations, renewed our attention to global environmental crises: tropical deforestation; climate change; toxic contamination of land, air and water; and one technological disaster after another.

The year 1992 also marked the thirtieth anniversary of the publication of *Silent Spring* and the twentieth anniversary of *The Limits to Growth*, two books that have had a profound impact on the way we view the environment and our fragile relationship within it.

In *Silent Spring*, Rachel Carson alerted us to the harmful effects of inappropriate and overabundant use of pesticides and helped launch the modern environmental movement. *The Limits to Growth*, written by a team of scientists at the Massachusetts Institute of Technology, warned us about the inevitable global ecological disasters likely to ensue if we do not reduce the accelerating rates of human population growth and natural resources consumption.

In every sense, these two books are environmental classics. In the decades since they were published, they and other books like them have contributed significantly to a level of environmental awareness unprecedented in the history of humankind, as witnessed by the conference in Rio de Janeiro.

There are many other such environmental classics whose authors have become well-known names in the environmental community: Edward Abbey, Lester Brown, Barry Commoner, Paul Ehrlich, Aldo Leopold, Roderick Nash, Henry David Thoreau, and E. F. Schumacher, to list a few.

And there are emerging classics from many new voices who are calling attention to an additional set of issues, such as the linkages between economic development and environmental protection, particularly in developing countries; the disproportionate impacts of environmental pollution and ecological disasters on certain groups of people or regions of the world; the rights of native peoples to preserve their cultural identities and homelands; and such concepts as "ecofeminism," "deep ecology," "conservation biology," and "sustainable development."

The Environmentalist's Bookshelf is a guide to the best of these books on nature and the environment, as determined by a questionnaire survey that was sent to environmental leaders and experts around the world. The guide describes the 500 most recommended books, based on a tally of the responses, and provides selected quotes indicating why the respondents think a particular book is important or meaningful.

This reference was designed to help you, the reader, select the best environmental books from the multitude available. It also provides an overview of the conservation and environmental movement by documenting the individuals and books that have made the movement happen.

There are several types of persons who will find the guide useful:

- concerned members of the general public, especially those involved in local, national, or international conservation and environmental organizations;
- faculty and students at colleges and universities, especially those involved with environmental studies, geography, biology, or related disciplines;
- science teachers and interested students in high schools;
- naturalists and environmental educators at museums, nature centers, and other informal educational settings;
- librarians who work with reference and science collections in public, academic, and government libraries;
- bookstore owners and book dealers who need to select which titles to carry in their environmental and related sections;
- environmental planners, managers, and other professionals.

You are invited to peruse the contents of this guide either by starting at entry 1 and reading straight through to entry 500, or by approaching more selectively through the subject, author, and title indexes.

The Environmentalist's Bookshelf project began in early 1987, growing out of the interdisciplinary work of the Global Sustainability Group in the Institute for Environmental Studies at the University of Wisconsin–Madison. One of the tasks of the group was to compile a listing of essential readings related to the concept of "sustainable development." As a result, I assembled, in collaboration with Laurie Greenberg, Tom Sinclair, and other members of the group, a report called *Global Sustainability: A Selected, Annotated Bibliography*, which includes some 150 titles.

The process of sifting through hundreds of items, trying to determine which were significant and relevant, led me to wonder what were, in a broader sense, the essential books for the environmental community at large. What were the books responsible for shaping thoughts and actions in the past or influencing events in the present—the books that every environmentalist should have on his or her bookshelf?

As I began to research the question further, I found that while a number of individuals had prepared their own lists of favorite books, either in magazine articles or bibliographies, no comprehensive survey had been undertaken to find a consensus on what constituted the "core" environmental literature. (I have summarized the items used in this background research in the appendix, "Sources for Further Reference.")

With that in mind, I mailed a batch of questionnaires in February 1987 to selected individuals whose names I had found through my work with the Global Sustainability Project. I asked them to identify and comment upon the environmental books that had most influenced their thinking and actions, including books they would recommend to students or persons just becoming involved in the environmental movement. The project lay dormant for several years while I worked on other activities, but it was revived in 1991. I mailed the first of several more batches of questionnaires in February of that year.

The names for these later mailings were obtained from a number of sources. The *1990 Conservation Directory*, published by the National Wildlife Federation, was an important reference, especially with its comprehensive listings of state-level environmental groups and governmental offices. I also gathered names from the *Encyclopedia of Associations*, the *Encyclopedia of International Associations*, and the *Research Centers Directory*, all published by Gale Research Company. Finally, I reviewed academic environmental journals to obtain names from the editorial mastheads and from relevant articles. My objective in examining all of these sources was to obtain as much of a cross-sectional representation as possible from various types of environmental and academic groups, as well as to ensure a broad geographic balance.

As a result of these various mailings, I received responses from 236 persons, including scientists, educators, authors, activists, and government officials. Some of these are well known to the public, many are prominent within their professions, and others are experienced but not as well known.

Eighty-two percent of the respondents are from the United States (representing thirty-eight states, the District of Columbia, and the Virgin Islands); 7 percent are from the United Kingdom; and the remainder come from Canada, Mexico, Brazil, Australia, China, Thailand, Russia, Kenya, South Africa, Cyprus, Portugal, Austria, India, Sweden, and Switzerland.

Fifty percent of the respondents are with conservation or environmental organizations; 29 percent are at colleges or universities; 8 percent work with government agencies or government-funded research centers; 7 percent are writers, consultants, or in the private sector; and 6 percent are with schools, museums, nature centers, or other educational institutions.

This group as a whole includes representatives from some 150 environmental associations, 15 environmental journals and magazines, and 3 major foundations funding environmental programs.

A complete listing of the respondents and their affiliations is provided in Part IV.

Using the questionnaire responses, I compiled a database that included the recommended books, as well as the names of respondents who had recommended each book. I also recorded any comments the respondents made about particular books. The list produced from this database included a total of more than 1400 recommended books.

From this master list, I was able to select 100 "core books," 250 "strongly recommended books," and 150 "other recommended books." The distinctions among these categories are based on the number of respondents that recommended each book. For example, a "core" book is one that was recommended by four or more persons; a "strongly recommended" book, by two or three persons; and an "other recommended" book, by one person who provided a substantive comment. In the latter two categories, I cast my "votes" and included some books of my own preference, particularly those published during 1991 and 1992.

Using this organizational system, I prepared a series of short annotations of these 500 most recommended books. Where appropriate, I included the comments and personal observations made by the respondents. Not all books that made it into the top 500 have accompanying quotes. Many respondents simply indicated a book title and author and gave no quote; there are some books that received numerous recommendations but no quotes. Throughout the guide I have included additional books by particular authors that were recommended but did not receive a sufficient number of "votes" to make it into the top 500. For some entries I have broadened the scope a bit and included additional books on the same topic by other authors.

Each of the three categories of books is presented in its own section, and the books in each section are listed alphabetically by the author's last name. Thus, entry 1 is the first alphabetical listing for the "core" books; entry 101, for the "strongly recommended" books; and entry 351, for the "other recommended" books. For the interest of the reader, I have ranked the top forty books (based on the number of respondents recommending each book). The top ten selections are: *A Sand Country Almanac*, by Aldo Leopold (recommended by 100 respondents); Rachel Carson's *Silent Spring* (81); *The State of the World*, from the Worldwatch Institute (31); Paul Ehrlich's *The Population Bomb* (28); Henry David Thoreau's *Walden* (28); Roderick Nash's *Wilderness and the American Mind* (21); E. F. Schumacher's *Small is Beautiful* (21); Edward Abbey's *Desert Solitaire* (20); Barry Commoner's *The Closing Circle* (18); and *The Limits to Growth* (17) by Donella Meadows, Dennis Meadows, Jørgen Randers and William Behrens. (A complete list of the top forty books is provided in the next section; more information on each of the above books can be found in Part I.)

As you can see by reading the comments of the survey respondents, there were various reasons why books were recommended for *The Environmentalist's Bookshelf*. Some books were seen as "eye openers" or influential by certain respondents during their youth or early in their careers. Other books were seen to present radically new ideas or significantly new ways of looking at the world. Some were viewed as essential references, texts, or data sources. Others were selected because they were inspirational and interesting. Some were chosen because they provided an excellent overview or history or because they were massive works of scholarly importance. Others were picked because they were connected with an important event, program, or institution.

Clearly, a great diversity of ideas is presented in these 500 books, which also reflects the broad spectrum of individuals who responded to this survey and of the environmental community in general. While no two environmentalists would likely develop the same list of best books—let alone 236 respondents to this survey—the 500 books listed here represent a best "group" selection.

I believe that books do inspire actions, and that the works of Aldo Leopold, Rachel Carson, Lester Brown, Paul Ehrlich, and the others have made a tremendous difference for the survival of our planet. But there is still much for us to do.

I hope *The Environmentalist's Bookshelf* compels you to search for the books described here, and to discover other important books on nature and the environment that are being published at an ever-increasing rate. And I hope that by using this guide, you become a more informed and active global citizen.

Robert Merideth
State College, Pennsylvania

The Environmentalist's Bookshelf
Top 40 Books

These rankings are based on questionnaire survey responses from more than 236 environmental experts from around the world. The number in parentheses following each title indicates the number of respondents recommending that book. In the case of "ties," books are listed alphabetically by author. More information on each book can be found in Part I.

1. **Leopold, Aldo.** *A Sand County Almanac, and Sketches Here and There.* (100)

2. **Carson, Rachel.** *Silent Spring.* (81)

3. **Brown, Lester R., and staff of Worldwatch Institute.** *State of the World.* (31)

4. **Ehrlich, Paul R.** *The Population Bomb.* (28)

5. **Thoreau, Henry David.** *Walden; or Life in the Woods.* (28)

6. **Nash, Roderick.** *Wilderness and the American Mind.* (21)

7. **Schumacher, Ernst F.** *Small Is Beautiful: Economics as if People Mattered.* (21)

8. **Abbey, Edward.** *Desert Solitaire: A Season in the Wilderness.* (20)

9. **Commoner, Barry.** *The Closing Circle: Nature, Man, and Technology.* (18)

10. **Meadows, Donella H., Dennis L. Meadows, Jørgen Randers, and William W. Behrens III.** *The Limits to Growth: A Report for the Club of Rome's Project on the Predicament of Mankind.* (17)

11. **Berry, Wendell.** *The Unsettling of America: Culture and Agriculture.* (16)

12. **McPhee, John A.** *Encounters with the Archdruid.* (16)

13. **Marsh, George Perkins.** *Man and Nature.* (16)

14. **Thomas, William L., Jr., ed., with Carl O. Sauer, Marston Bates, and Lewis Mumford.** *Man's Role in Changing the Face of the Earth.* (16)

15. **Abbey, Edward.** *The Monkey Wrench Gang.* (14)

16. **World Resources Institute.** *World Resources: 1992–93.* (14)

17. **Myers, Norman, ed., with Uma Ram Nath and Melvin Westlake.** *Gaia: An Atlas of Planet Management.* (13)

18. **Lovins, Amory B.** *Soft Energy Paths: Toward a Durable Peace.* (12)

19. **World Commission on Environment and Development.** *Our Common Future.* (12)

20. **Ehrlich, Paul R., Anne H. Ehrlich, and John P. Holdren.** *Ecoscience: Population, Resources, Environment.* (11)

21. **Eiseley, Loren C.** *The Immense Journey.* (11)

22. **Lovelock, J. E.** *Gaia: A New Look at Life on Earth.* (11)

23. **Miller, G. Tyler.** *Living in the Environment: Concepts, Problems, and Alternatives.* (11)

24. **Odum, Eugene P.** *Fundamentals of Ecology.* (11)

25. **Ward, Barbara, and Rene Dubos.** *Only One Earth: The Care and Maintenance of a Small Planet.* (11)

26. **Daly, Herman, and John Cobb, Jr.** *For the Common Good: Redirecting the Economy Toward Community, the Environment, and a Sustainable Future.* (10)

27. **Devall, Bill, and George Sessions.** *Deep Ecology: Living as if Nature Mattered.* (10)

28. **Lopez, Barry.** *Arctic Dreams: Imagination and Desire in a Northern Landscape.* (9)

29. **Peterson, Roger Tory.** *A Field Guide to the Birds.* (9)

30. **Reisner, Marc P.** *Cadillac Desert: The American West and Its Disappearing Water.* (9)

31. **Vogt, William.** *Road to Survival.* (9)

32. **Adams, Ansell, and Nancy Newhall.** *This Is the American Earth.* (8)

33. **Callenbach, Ernest.** *Ecotopia: The Notebooks and Reports of William Weston.* (8)

34. **Dillard, Annie.** *Pilgrim at Tinker Creek.* (8)

35. **Fox, Stephen R.** *The American Conservation Movement: John Muir and His Legacy.* (8)

36. **Glacken, Clarence J.** *Traces on the Rhodian Shore: Nature and Culture in Western Thought from Ancient Times to the End of the Eighteenth Century.* (8)

37. **McHarg, Ian L.** *Design with Nature.* (8)

38. **McKibben, Bill.** *The End of Nature.* (8)

39. **Hardin, Garrett.** *Exploring New Ethics for Survival: The Voyage of Spaceship Beagle.* (7)

40. **Worster, Donald E.** *Nature's Economy: A History of Ecological Ideas.* (7)

Part I

Core Books

1. **Abbey, Edward.** *Desert Solitaire: A Season in the Wilderness.* New York: McGraw-Hill, 1968. Reprint. Salt Lake City: Peregrine Smith, 1981. 269 pages.

Abbey spent three summers as a park ranger in Arches National Park near Moab in Utah. This book is his elegy for the canyon country that he calls "the most beautiful place on earth." On the one hand, *Desert Solitaire* is a superb natural history that evokes the desert landscape with its rocks, plants, and animals with passion and power. On the other hand, there are chapters with angry and rebellious tones, which rage against the commercialization and development of America's national parks, and against the damming of wild rivers and flooding of extraordinary canyons, such as those of the Colorado River. He mourns the wilderness and remoteness that he first found in Arches, which he saw destroyed by roadbuilding and the promotion of automobile tourism.

"Unabashed and irreverent, tender and delicious, *Desert Solitaire*'s genius schizophrenic style forced me to think more laterally about my own environmental ethic."—Diane Bowen, chair, Loma Prita chapter of the Sierra Club

"A classic. Articulated the concerns of many who shared his anger over the mercenary imperatives that result in industrial tourism."— James R. Conner, chair, Montana chapter of the Sierra Club

"Eloquently speaks for wilderness and the need to 'turn off the key (to our internal combustion machines) and walk on in.' "—Gary Randorf, senior counselor, Adirondack Council

"The 'western environmentalist's manifesto.' It gave us the attitude, the courage, the poetry we needed to become warriors."—Donald Snow, director, Northern Lights Institute

"We need cynics like Abbey who show about the ironies of our relationship to the natural world and challenge us to consider how committed we really are."—Ken Voorhis, director, Great Smoky Mountains Institute at Tremont

Also recommended is Abbey's *The Journey Home: Some Words in Defense of the American West* (Dutton, 1977).

2. **Abbey, Edward. *The Monkey Wrench Gang*.** Philadelphia: Lippincott, 1975. 352 pages.

In describing the exploits and unique style of fictional environmental activists, Abbey, perhaps more than anyone else, influenced thousands of real-world "eco-radicals" and inspired the activities of such groups as Greenpeace and Earth First! Abbey's characters are led by George Hayduke, a veteran of the Vietnam war. Using guerilla-style tactics, they take on developers and other destroyers of the wilderness of southern Utah and northern Arizona. "The watchers on the rim, eating their suppers from tin plates, heard the croon of a mourning dove far down the wash. They heard the hoot of an owl, the cries of little birds retiring to sleep in the dusty cottonwoods. The great golden light of the setting sun streamed across the sky, glowing upon the clouds and the mountains. Almost all the country within their view was roadless, uninhabited, a wilderness. They meant to keep it that way. They sure meant to try. *Keep it like it was*" (p. 77). The story continues in Abbey's follow-up, *Hayduke Lives!* (Little, Brown, 1990).

"I consider this novel to be every environmentalist's antidote to despair, along with its sequel, *Hayduke Lives!* When still another vote goes against us, and I feel utterly impotent about saving the natural world (and ourselves) from our own 'sins' against the earth, I can laugh and cheer on Hayduke and the crowd."—Marcia Bonta, naturalist/writer

"One reading of this book is not enough! Even knowing it was a fictionalized account didn't stop me from recommending it to my friends and my students. Abbey's characters are so extreme, it makes it easy for the rest of us to be moderate and reasonable. I often wonder how many ecoradicals got their inspiration from this book."—Sue Ellen Lyons, president, Louisiana Environmental Educators' Association

"Abbey expressed the frustration of thousands through this work. It is radical because the problem is real!" —Mark C. Wagstaff, executive director, Wilderness Education Association

3.   **Adams, Ansell, and Nancy Newhall.** *This Is the American Earth.* San Francisco: Sierra Club, 1960 (reissued 1992). 89 pages.

Based on an exhibit sponsored by the California Academy of Sciences in 1955, this portfolio contains eighty-three stunning black-and-white images of the North American landscape, with accompanying prose by Newhall. Most of the photographs are by Adams; other contributors include Margaret Bourke-White, William Garnett, Eliot Porter, Edward Weston, and Cedric Wright. This was one of the earlier books in a long series of photographic essay works published by the Sierra Club under the direction of David Brower. As Brower notes in his autobiography, "The most beautiful thing about the book is that now, a quarter of a century after it was written, there is nothing in it that is worn out" (*For Earth's Sake: The Life and Times of David Brower,* Peregrine Smith, 1990, p. 192). Another observer, Stewart Udall, who was Secretary of the Interior during the early 1960s, suggests that perhaps the real beauty of the books was that they let Brower and the Sierra Club effectively influence the passage of favorable wilderness preservation legislation, since the books were often "hand delivered to members of Congress—at times by Brower himself—who would cast the crucial votes on vital issues" (*The Quiet Crisis and the Next Generation,* p. 209; see entry 93).

Other early books in the Sierra Club exhibit format series include: *In Wilderness is the Preservation of the World* (1962), with photos by Eliot Porter and text by Henry David Thoreau; *The Last Redwoods* (1963), photos and text by Phillip Hyde and Francois Leydet; *The Place No One Knew* (1963), photos by Eliot Porter, text by David Brower); and *Time and the River Flowing* (1964), with photos by Francois Leydet and text by David Brower.

4.   **Attenborough, David.** *Life on Earth: A Natural History.* London: Collins, with the British Broadcasting Company, 1979. 319 pages.

Life on Earth is based on three years of travel and research that went into the making of a BBC film series of the same name on the history of nature. Attenborough has had a distinguished career as a naturalist and filmmaker documenting the incredible diversity and wonder of places around the planet. The book is an impressive undertaking; it condenses 300 million years of natural history into some 300 pages, and describes the evolution and coevolution of life on earth. The text is beautifully illustrated with nearly 120 full-page, color photographs.

5.   **Bates, Marston.** *The Forest and the Sea: A Look at the Economy of Nature and the Ecology of Man.* New York: Random House, 1960. 277 pages.

While living for eight years in eastern Colombia and studying jungle yellow fever, Bates was impressed by the unity of the natural world. In this book, he presents a fascinating description of biological communities, from the coral reefs to tropical rainforests (Bates's two favorite environments), as well as lakes and rivers, woodlands, swamps, the desert, and the open sea. He wants us to appreciate the "economy of nature," meaning the intricate relationships among individuals and populations of species. He also wants us to understand the place of our own species in nature. He expresses a deep-felt concern: "In defying nature, in destroying nature, in building an arrogantly selfish man-centered world, I do not see how man can gain peace or freedom or joy" (p. 262).

"Bates popularized some basic information needed to understand tropical forest ecosystems."—Philip M. Fearnside, professor of ecology, National Institute for Research in the Amazon (INPA), Manaus, Amazonas, Brazil

6.   **Bateson, Gregory.** *Steps to an Ecology of Mind.* Northvale, NJ: Aronson, 1988 (orig. pub. 1972). 545 pages.

This is not a book about ecology, but rather about how the human mind perceives, or misperceives, the world. Bateson, with the help of students and colleagues, compiled and edited this collection of his articles published earlier in scholarly journals and popular magazines. They show the breadth and depth of his intellect and wisdom, which includes expertise in the fields of anthropology, biology, psychiatry, evolution, and epistemology. His aim throughout the book is to promote a new manner of seeing the world, of thinking about social and physical processes, and of understanding our own patterns of thought. In the chapter "Roots to Ecological Crisis," he asserts that environmental problems result from a combination of technological advance, population increase, and "conventional (but wrong) ideas about the nature of man and his relation to the environment" (p. 496).

Also recommended is Bateson's *Mind and Nature: A Necessary Unity* (Dutton, 1979).

7.   **Berry, Thomas. *The Dream of the Earth*.** San Francisco: Sierra Club, 1988. 256 pages.

Berry's essays give us a better sense of our own identity as a species and as an integral part of the planet. Many of the essays contain good reviews of the impacts of influential environmental writers and activists.

"An introduction to the Ecological Age as an era in evolution. The elegant, even poetic, style is pure pleasure, making the threat easier to face."—Charles T. McLaughlin, chair, board of trustees, Iowa Natural Heritage Foundation

8.   **Berry, Wendell. *The Unsettling of America: Culture and Agriculture*.** San Francisco: Sierra Club, 1977. 228 pages.

Berry reviews the agricultural history of the United States and provides a cogent critique of the development and status of modern agriculture. In presenting his arguments, he examines the roles of institutions, namely: the federal government, land-grant universities, and scientific research organizations, in addition to the economies of scale of corporate capitalism. He considers environmental problems from the vantage point of agricultural activities and suggests that the linkages between an agricultural crisis and an ecological crisis are more than coincidental.

"Fundamental in terms of shaping attitudes towards agriculture, food, the land, nature, the environment, and human values and community."—John E. Carroll, professor of environmental conservation, University of New Hampshire

"Better than most environmentalists, Berry shows the full interactions within the social/natural interface of agriculture—one of the most important, but neglected, environmental areas. He discusses not only energy and environmental degradation, but the cultural attitudes that have led to many of our environmental crises and the kinds of rootedness, localism, and devotion to place and generations that are needed to help work our way out of our current dilemmas."—Kenneth A. Dahlberg, professor of political science, Western Michigan University

"Berry's work here and elsewhere traces the problems of contemporary civilization to their agricultural roots. His work is a marvelous blend of outrage, clear logic, and compelling prose. It has the solid ring of truth. No one has made the case for agriculture as a calling and craft any clearer. When I first read this book, the onset of the farm crisis was becoming apparent. This book just made sense, especially for a guy who had grown up in Amish country in Pennsylvania."—David W. Orr, professor of environmental studies, Oberlin College

"Berry is today's most eloquent spokesperson for the land and the land ethic. He deserves sainthood."—Gary Randorf, senior counselor, Adirondack Council

9.   **Bertell, Rosalie.** *No Immediate Danger: Prognosis for a Radioactive Earth.* London: Women's Press, 1985. 435 pages.

This is a frightening account of the development, marketing, and operational practices of the nuclear weapons and nuclear power complex. Bertell describes the industry as one cloaked in deceptions and cover-ups about accidents and risks associated with nuclear power, and she strongly condemns the political economy that sustains nuclear power. She urges citizens, particularly women, to become involved in dealing with the threats she sees facing humanity.

"The study reveals that nuclear energy production and nuclear weapons initiate the death crisis of our species. Bertell gives a global analysis of the nuclear energy era. Her book highlights the development of nuclear energy policy as a convenience for superpower military strategies. This is an honest, frank expression on mysterious nuclear programmes. The trend-setting book shall ramble in the world markets to save our biosphere from nuclear holocausts."—G. M. Oza, general secretary, Indian Society of Naturalists, Baroda, India

"Bertell highlights the real causes of the development of nuclear energy and, most importantly, the biological effects of exposure to ionizing radiation as an integral part of the technology. She also denounces the political secrecy which has surrounded the whole process."—Giselda Castro, vice president, Ação Democrática Feminina Gaúcha/Amigos da Terra (Friends of the Earth), Porto Alegre, Brazil

10.　**Beston, Henry.** *The Outermost House: A Year of Life on the Great Beach of Cape Cod.* New York: Holt, 1927. 222 pages.

Henry Beston built a small (20′ × 16′), two-room cottage "at the wrist of the curled forearm" of Cape Cod. He called his beachfront home the Fo' Castle, and equipped it with a fireplace, a two-burner oil stove, oil lamps, a well, and rudimentary furnishings. One autumn he went for a two-week visit, and instead of leaving, remained for a year. He found that the longer he stayed, the more eager he was "to know the coast and to share its mysterious and elemental life" (p. 10). His encounters came through walks along the beach and over the dunes, where he found an interest in the plants, animals, and discarded items from civilization. Although he was in isolation most of the time, with occasional visitors to bring provisions, he felt "a secret and sustaining energy" from his solitude. He lived "in the midst of an abundance of natural life which manifested itself every hour of the day, and from being thus surrounded, [was] enclosed within a great whirl of what one may call the life force" (p. 95). Beston's text is complemented by more than 30 black-and-white photographs by William Bradford.

"A highly personal and exquisitely written view of a year of a beach."—Thomas Urquhart, executive director, Maine Audubon Society

11.　**Blaikie, Piers M., and Harold C. Brookfield.** *Land Degradation and Society.* London: Methuen, 1987. 296 pages.

Blaikie and Brookfield combine two theoretical perspectives to help explain the causes of environmental degradation, particularly in the Third World. The first is "cultural ecology," which looks at the local relationships and interactions of people in the environment; the second is "political economy," which looks at the distribution of resources in society and at the constraints imposed on individuals and groups by political and economic systems. The authors show how people are put into situations where they are forced to degrade their environment, such as by increasing soil erosion, because of land tenure relationships or political or economic structures. But the authors also show that within those structures, people do have some choices and often can adapt and learn to survive despite the constraints. The book also contains good essays on the reasons for degradation of common lands and on the impacts of colonialism on the environment. Some of these themes are discussed also in Blaikie's previous book, *The Political Economy of Soil Erosion in Developing Countries* (Longman, 1985).

12.   **Brown, Harrison S.** *The Challenge of Man's Future: An Inquiry Concerning the Condition of Man During the Years That Lie Ahead.* New York: Viking, 1954. 290 pages.

Brown's basic theme is that "the future course of history will be determined by the rates at which people breed and die, by the rapidity with which non-renewable resources are consumed, by the extent and speed with which agricultural production can be improved, by the rate at which underdeveloped areas can industrialize, by the rapidity with which we are able to develop new resources, as well as by the extent to which we succeed in avoiding future wars" (pp. 66–67). Brown's arguments are very much based on the population and resource availability equations espoused two centuries before by Thomas Malthus (see entry 443). When Brown's book was written, citizens in the industrialized countries were looking forward to a future of unprecedented abundance and opportunity. Brown presented a sobering account by speculating how the world could become—in fact, how the world already was for nearly eighty percent of the people on the planet.

"The first book to address the 'global problematique.' It's definitely on my important environmental books bookshelf."—Stephen Schneider, senior scientist, National Center for Atmospheric Research

"One of many alarmist books, but maybe the best of its time and a personal favorite."—Thomas R. Vale, professor of geography, University of Wisconsin–Madison

13.   **Brown, Lester R.** *The Twenty-Ninth Day: Accommodating Human Needs and Numbers to the Earth's Resources.* New York: Norton, 1978. 290 pages.

Brown, president of the Worldwatch Institute in Washington, D.C. and a prominent thinker and writer on global environmental issues, examines the complex interactions among the world's ecological, economic, and social systems. He describes the dimensions and consequences of ecological stresses from population growth, energy consumption, and food production, and analyses what these mean for the future of our planet. He then argues that human society must learn to adjust its numbers and needs to match the natural capacity of the earth, and reviews several actions and policies that are needed for such an accommodation, such as stabilizing population growth, developing alternative sources of energy and more efficient patterns of energy use, and promoting social and economic equality. The book is directed globally at decisionmakers of all levels of society.

14. **Brown, Lester R., and staff of Worldwatch Institute.** *State of the World.* New York: Norton, 1992 (annual). 256 pages.

Since 1984, Worldwatch Institute has published an annual report on the world's progress toward a sustainable society. Brown and his active group of researchers seem to be continually sifting through and digesting the masses of reports and articles produced each year on global environmental conditions. The result of their efforts is a finely crafted series of reports, a magazine, and other publications that detail such topics as solid waste recycling, renewable energy, deforestation, extinction of species, toxic chemicals, and population. The *State of the World* report grows out of these publications, providing a collection of facts, figures, and anecdotes about what is happening to our planet. It is no wonder that the reference has reached nearly 300,000 readers worldwide and is published in twenty-three languages.

"Keeps us updated on current concerns globally."—Isabelle de Geofroy, information coordinator, TreePeople

"The most comprehensive collection of information and data about the state of the world's environment."—Diane G. Lowrie, vice president, Global Tomorrow Coalition

"The earth's barometer. The book not only tell us what we're doing to the planet, but how to stop doing it and save ourselves."—David E. Blockstein, executive director, Committee for the National Institutes for the Environment

15. **Caduto, Michael, and Joseph Bruchac.** *Keepers of the Earth: Native American Stories and Environmental Activities for Children.* Foreword by N. Scott Momaday. Illustrations by John K. Fadden and Carol Wood. Golden, Co.: Fulcrum, 1990. 209 pages.

Combining the traditions of oral presentation from Native American culture with the structure of contemporary science, this book provides a creative approach to environmental education for children. Caduto and Bruchac have collected a series of Native American stories which relate to the bases of life on earth. Each story is followed by a set of activities, some indoor and some outdoor, connected to that topic. The book is well organized, and the stories and exercises are interestingly presented. Caduto and Bruchac are also authors of *Keepers of the Animals: Native American Stories and Wildlife Activities for Children* (Fulcrum, 1991).

16. **Caldwell, Lynton Keith.** *International Environmental Policy: Emer-*

gence and Dimensions. 2d ed. Durham, NC: Duke University Press, 1990 (orig. pub. 1984). 460 pages.

Caldwell is a leading scholar on environmental policy, having been a principal drafter of the U.S. National Environmental Policy Act (NEPA). He is also a versatile and productive writer. In this book, he provides a detailed and all-encompassing account of how and why nations have cooperated to protect the biosphere. Caldwell takes us on the "Road to Stockholm," as he describes the multinational cooperation which led to the United Nations Conference on the Human Environment in 1972. Then we're off to Nairobi, Geneva, Algiers, Moscow, Rome, New Delhi, Montego Bay, and beyond, as he covers a decade of international environmental conferences, organizations, treaties, compacts, and declarations. His book is well annotated with relevant literature in concerning international environmental science, law, policy, and organization. The revised and expanded version of the book provides up-to-date analyses of recent concerns, such as stratospheric ozone depletion, global warming, and acid rain.

17.   **Callenbach, Ernest.** *Ecotopia: The Notebooks and Reports of William Weston.* Berkeley, CA: Banyan Tree, 1975. 213 pages.

Callenbach imagines an ecological utopia that emerges when Northern California, Oregon, and Washington secede from the United States in 1980. Ecotopia has almost eliminated pollution through recycling, rejection of synthetics, renewable energy, population planning, and public transportation. Social justice has been achieved through forms of communal living, worker control, and gender and racial equality. The story is told from the skeptical point of view of a reporter from a polluted and crime-ridden New York who goes to report critically on the new society, and who finds it increasingly appealing. The book is a powerful and informal means of showing an alternative agenda for appropriate ways of living with nature and each other.

"Lays out the vision of ecodecentralism, the ecological nation, the sine qua non of any future for humanity."—David Haenke, director, Ecological Society Project of the Tides Foundation

Also recommended is Callenbach's *Ecotopia Emerging* (Banyan Tree, 1981).

18.   **Carson, Rachel.** *The Sense of Wonder.* New York: Harper, 1965. Reprint. Berkeley, CA: The Nature Company, 1990. 90 pages.

In this essay, first published in *Women's Home Companion* in 1956, Carson urges parents to teach their children about nature, to satisfy and maintain the natural curiosity that children feel for the world around them. She recalls the visits of her grandnephew, Roger, at her summer home on the coast of Maine and the constant sense of wonder that both she and the boy had as they explored together the nearby forests, bogs, tidal pools, and meadows. She says that becoming a good teacher of the natural world is simply a matter of becoming receptive to what lies around you. She writes that if she were able, her "gift to each child in the world would be a sense of wonder so indestructible that it would last throughout life, as an unfailing antidote against the boredom and disenchantments of later years, the sterile preoccupation with things that are artificial, the alienation from sources of our strength" (p. 43). The book has been reprinted with photographs by William Neill as part of *The Nature Company Classics* series.

"This book is the primer for kids and adults on developing their own environmental ethics and attitudes. When they read how passionately and honestly Rachel Carson feels about our natural world, they can't help but be inspired themselves!"—Nancy Zuschlag, president, Colorado Alliance for Environmental Education

19. **Carson, Rachel. *Silent Spring*.** Boston: Houghton Mifflin, 1962 (25th anniversary ed., 1987). 368 pages.

Silent Spring alerted the world to the dangers of the overuse of pesticides and other chemicals. Rachel Carson described passionately and eloquently an America where the birds no longer sing, where the rivers, soil, and air are polluted, and where children are exposed to toxic chemicals in food and mother's milk. She documented the widespread use of synthetic chemicals, especially DDT, in the eradication of pests, such as mosquitos, fire ants, and gypsy moths. She then associated the use of these "biocides" with decreases in populations of birds and mammals, especially birds of prey who feed at the top of the food chain, and with the acute poisoning of people and ecosystems. Above all, she revealed the long term effects of synthetic chemicals on human health in the form of increased cancer risks, and the ways in which many pests became resistant, requiring the use of yet more chemicals. First serialized in the *New Yorker,* this book had a tremendous impact. Publicity was heightened by the outraged reaction of the chemical industry who denounced Carson as hysterical and unscientific. As scientists and politicians jumped to her defense, the book became the focus of hearings and discussions in legislatures in many countries. In the United States, it became one of the cornerstones of the emerging environmental movement, and played a major role in the shift from a parks-and-conservation perspective to one concerned with pollution. Although some parts of *Silent Spring* are a little outdated, the book still has tremendous relevance. Although the use of DDT has been controlled in the United States, it has been replaced by other toxic chemicals, and is still used widely in other countries.

"I remember when this book was published, my father-in-law, an avid gardener and heavy user of DDT, refused to believe it. My husband and I believed it. It changed our lives and made us environmentalists."—Marcia Bonta, naturalist/writer

"This book is still controversial, but it is nonetheless the volume that catalyzed the movement to control the use of toxic substances."—James R. Conner, chair, Montana chapter of the Sierra Club

"Probably no other book did more than this one to call attention to the damage that man, especially civilized man, was doing to the environment."—Alice L. Fuller, board of directors member, State College Bird Club

"I read the book in China in 1974 when I headed a joint research group of about 150 scientists studying pollution in the western suburbs in Beijing. I got a lot of ideas from the book to improve our project of pollution studies in Beijing, the first project of environmental study in China. My wife and I thought the book was so interesting that we spent about five months translating it into Chinese, and published it in 1977. The version has earned millions of readers in China."—Chengsheng Li, deputy director, Research Center for Eco-Environmental Sciences, Academica Sinica, Beijing, China

"The 'two-by-four upside the head' that America needed to realize the depth of the environmental crisis created by our infatuation with chemicals."—Jack Lorenz, executive director, Izaak Walton League of America

"*Silent Spring* has proven to be timeless. It has set the standard for books of its genre."—Sue Ellen Lyons, president, Louisiana Environmental Educators' Association

"Two reasons it's important: (1) it was the first book to outline a comprehensive ecological theory of pesticides—that's important to people specializing in insecticide/environment problems; and (2) her book was set within a framework that presumed the moral standing of nature—that philosophy was essential to all the environmental activism of the late '60s and early '70s."—John H. Perkins, environmental studies faculty, Evergreen State College

"Made me aware of the growing threat of man-made chemicals to life and their buildup in the food chain leading to devastating impact on certain species."—Russell W. Peterson, president emeritus, National Audubon Society

"The impact of this book is well known; it is especially important because it was written by a scientist about the effect of science on the environment. The title alone says so much; the text serves to support this and leaves you with some fundamental questions about how we live, how we try to control nature, what we are, and what the future holds."—Frederick Sepp, biological sciences librarian, Pennsylvania State University

"Rachel Carson hit a tender spot with this book. The eloquence is still fresh, even though the specifics are outdated. I often wonder whether the negative reaction to her book was the wish of her scientific colleagues not to see, or just because she was a woman. They are so emotional."—John Steinhart, professor of geophysics and of environmental studies, University of Wisconsin–Madison

"Carson, more than anyone else, prodded American society into the environmental movement; her book stimulated the general concern for environmental degradation, whether from pesticides, toxic wastes, or nuclear wastes."—Thomas R. Vale, professor of geography, University of Wisconsin–Madison

"Required reading for any bookshelf. This was perhaps the first book to receive popular acclaim because, apart from anything else, it was well-written, drawing attention to environmental issues."—Roger J. Wheater, director, the Royal Zoological Society of Scotland, Edinburgh

"Obviously, a classic—simply the seminal work with respect to the modern environmental movement."—Michael Zamm, director of environmental education, Council on the Environment of New York City

There are several good biographies of Rachel Carson, including: *Sea and Earth: The Life of Rachel Carson* (Crowell, 1970), by Philip Sterling; *The House of Life: Rachel Carson at Work* (Houghton Mifflin, 1972), by Paul Brooks, Carson's editor and friend; and *Rachel Carson* (Ungar, 1983), by Carol Gartner. Other books that continue the debate initiated by Carson include: Frank Graham's *Since Silent Spring* (see entry 408) a review of the predictions and impact of *Silent Spring* ten years later; *Silent Spring Revisited* (American Chemical Society, 1987), edited by Gino Marco, Robert Hollingworth and William Durhan, which is an alternate interpretation and analysis of Carson's findings; *The Recurring Silent Spring* (Pergamon, 1989), by H. Patricia Hynes, which looks at the contribution Carson made to feminism in science and to the establishment of the U.S. Environmental Protection Agency; and *Rachel Carson: Voice for the Earth* (Lerner, 1992) by Ginger Wadsworth.

20. **Commoner, Barry. *The Closing Circle: Nature, Man, and Technology.*** New York: Knopf, 1971. 326 pages.

We should all memorize Commoner's list of the "laws of ecology":

1. Everything is connected to everything else.
2. Everything must go somewhere.
3. Nature knows best.
4. There is no such thing as a free lunch.

In *The Closing Circle*, Commoner's main argument is that we have ignored these basic laws and as a result have imprisoned ourselves, and all other life on the planet, perhaps inescapably, by using inappropriate technologies. Commoner was at the forefront of the emerging environmental movement in the early 1970s, and he has continued to be an effective spokesperson on issues related to human society, technology and the long-term health of our planet.

"One of the first accounts of unchecked technological development and environmental health hazards."—Michael Belliveau, executive director, and Hannah Creighton, newsletter editor, Citizens for a Better Environment

"Identified and stated the major concepts underlying the cause of environmental problems. His book provided a focal point for further education. Specifically useful are his four 'laws of ecology.' "—Joseph H. Chadborne, president, Institute for Environmental Education

"Points to the crucial role of technology choice in the cause of environmental problems. This was a critical insight. Although some of Commoner's analysis was flawed, his understanding of the role of technology choice was original and is still highly important."—John H. Perkins, environmental studies faculty, Evergreen State College

"This early, thoughtful warning about where our technology choices are taking us introduced Americans to the basic principle of ecology." —Kathleen Courrier, director of publications, World Resources Institute

"Made me rethink certain fundamental sociopolitical issues that govern many of our modern ecological problems."—R. Rajagopal, professor of geography, University of Iowa

"Probably the most important book I've read."—Ann M. Regn, environmental education coordinator, Virginia Council on the Environment

21. **Commoner, Barry.** *Making Peace with the Planet.* New York: Pantheon, 1990. 292 pages.

Commoner declares that our technological society is at war with the natural planet, the "technosphere" versus the "ecosphere." He states that this war "is mutually destructive: nature is devastated and human society suffers, not only because of the devastation, but also because our present, environmentally destructive production systems diminish the opportunities for economic growth, especially in developing countries" (p. 192). But while Commoner faults our blind and ambitious use of technology, he also criticizes the "neo-Luddite" philosophies of certain extreme environmental groups, saying they are counterproductive to finding real solutions. Commoner recommends that we work with technologies that are not "counterecological" and laments that, although such technologies exist, they are little used or promoted. He sees the only way we can hope to make peace with the planet is if we: (1) bring the technosphere into harmony with the ecosphere; (2) redesign the major industrial, agricultural, energy, and transportation systems; (3) develop politically suitable means to bring about long-term environmental quality; and (4) narrow the gap between the standards of living of developing countries and developed countries. In a sense, Commoner is best skilled at presenting a comprehensive picture of how our economic and social systems operate and how energy and materials flow through these systems. He is adept at showing us the buttons that can be pushed to make changes in the way the systems operate and in the sorts of goods and services they produce.

"Shows us that it isn't too late to save the earth using technologies in harmony with the ecosphere and give every human a good life, if we get serious about pollution prevention. But it will be tough, politically, because we will have to control industry."—Michael Belliveau, executive director, and Hannah Creighton, newsletter editor, Citizens for a Better Environment

"Strikes the best balance between the neo-Luddite position, one that claims technology should not exist, and the technological fix position, which says technology is the solution to all problems."—Gary Benenson, associate professor of technology, City College of the City University of New York

22.   **Cornell, Joseph.** *Sharing Nature with Children.* Nevada City, CA: Dawn, 1979. 138 pages.

Anyone who wants to help children learn about the natural world should first read this book. *Sharing Nature with Children* is an easy-to-use guide with descriptions of forty games and exercises for children of all ages. The activities are categorized as "calm/reflective," "active/observational," and "energetic/playful" to fit the mood of the participants. One game, for example, has the children, all blindfolded and in a circle, assume roles of a predator and its prey with the predator and prey having to learn and adjust their respective methods of stalking and avoiding capture. Cornell offers encouragement and a few simple suggestions on how to become a better teacher: (1) teach less and share more; (2) be receptive; (3) focus the child's attention without delay; (4) look and experience first, talk later; and (5) let a sense of joy permeate the whole experience. Even adults can have a great time sharing nature with children!

"A classic about interacting with children and how to 'turn them on' to nature."—Ann M. Regn, environmental education coordinator, Virginia Council on the Environment

"It's so important for children to bond with the earth at a young age—to associate nature with joyful positive experiences. This has more clarity and simplicity than any environmental education book I've used."—Elissa Wolfson, managing editor, and Will Nixon, associate editor, *E Magazine*

"The short lessons, meant to be simple getting-to-know-nature activities, are easily used by teachers and parents alike."—Nancy Zuschlag, president, Colorado Alliance for Environmental Education

23.   **Council on Environmental Quality and Department of State; Gerald O. Barney, study director.** *The Global 2000 Report to the President: Entering the Twenty-first Century.* Washington, DC: U.S. Gov-

ernment Printing Office, 1980. Vol. 1, 47 pages; Vol. 2, 766 pages; Vol. 3, 401 pages.

At the request of the Carter administration, Gerald Barney and a team of researchers undertook the study that produced this report. Their charge was to project current world environmental trends to the year 2000 and to consider the relative merits of computer forecasting programs, or models, used by government agencies to make such predictions. The team found that the agencies' computer models had shortcomings: they sometimes made inaccurate assumptions about real-world processes; there was often a lack of enough data to make reasonable estimates of trends in certain areas; and many of the computer models could not account for or predict "shocks" to the global system, such as political upheavals, economic downturns, or natural or technological disasters. Despite these problems, the report was influential in establishing a debate during the 1980s within government, industry, and academia about global environmental and resource trends. That debate focussed on the report's gloomy, introductory forecast: "If present trends continue, the world in 2000 will be more crowded, more polluted, less stable ecologically, and more vulnerable to disruption than the world we live in now" (p. 1). We are now more than halfway to seeing whether the forecast will be true.

"A work which brought to the minds of policymakers from around the globe the idea that the limits which *The Limits to Growth* [see entry 54] speaks about will get us by the throat if current policies remain the same. A work that stretches the mind of the average person so that they can see the implications of action/inaction on a global scale."— Arthur B. Sacks, special assistant to the dean of the graduate school, University of Wisconsin–Madison

24. **Council on Environmental Quality.** *Environmental Trends.* rev. ed. Washington, DC: U.S. Government Printing Office, 1989 (orig. pub. 1981). 152 pages.

The Council on Environmental Quality (CEQ), together with several other U.S. government agencies, amassed data from numerous sources to highlight environmental trends in air and water quality, toxic substances, land use and conditions, parks, energy production and use, wildlife, solid waste, and many other areas. This report (revised in 1989), in addition to the CEQ's *Environmental Quality* annual reports, provides a useful collection of tables, charts, maps, and text that record key changes in the biophysical environment. Most of the data are from the 1960s and 1970s and, although they are somewhat out-of-date for evaluating current trends, provide important benchmarks from which to measure more contemporary conditions. References to the original sources of the data are provided.

25.   **Cronon, William.** *Changes in the Land: Indians, Colonists, and the Ecology of New England.* New York: Hill & Wang, 1983. 241 pages.

Cronon, a professor of history at Yale University, describes the ecological consequences of the encounter between the European colonists and the native peoples of New England. His book has become a modern classic in environmental history. Cronon contrasts views of nature and property to show how the colonists brought with them a commodified and privatized view of land and resources. But he also argues that the Indians had already begun to transform the landscape through fire and deforestation, and that both Europeans and Indians were mutually changed by the encounter. He also shows how the modern landscape of New England was shaped by its human past.

26.   **Daly, Herman E., ed.** *Economics, Ecology, and Ethics: Essays Toward a Steady-State Economy.* San Francisco: Freeman, 1980 (orig. pub. 1973). 372 pages.

In part an expansion of the 1973 book *Toward a Steady-State Economy*, edited by Daly, this book contains contributions from such notable scholars as Kenneth Boulding, Paul Ehrlich, Nicholas Georgescu-Roegen, Garrett Hardin, and E. F. Schumacher. As the title suggests, the twenty-two essays in the book are centered around three themes. The first set of essays focusses on the biological constraints of ecological systems. The second looks at the value constraints of ethics. And the third portrays economic systems in terms of the interaction of these constraints. Daly's main contribution comes from his critique of neoclassical economics. He characterizes a steady-state economy as being low in consumption, low in birthrates and deathrates, and high in leisure time, durability of goods, recycling rates, and equitable income distribution. He emphasizes the biophysical underpinnings of economics and the driving forces which necessitate a transition to a steady-state economy. He discusses institutional and social changes required for transformation to a sustainable society, as well as the inherent values of a steady-state economy.

"Someone once told me that Herman Daly was a 'one-idea man.' Well, I wish I had ideas like his. The concept of the steady state (or dynamic equilibrium) is a much misunderstood one, yet it represents the essence of the green alternative to expansionism."—Sandy Irvine, associate editor, *The Ecologist,* Newcastle Upon Tyne, England

27. **Daly, Herman E., and John B. Cobb, Jr.** *For the Common Good: Re-directing the Economy Toward Community, the Environment, and a Sustainable Future.* Boston: Beacon, 1989. 482 pages.

With its continued emphasis on market principles, the status quo of economics has become, according to Daly and Cobb, outmoded and institutionally conservative, no longer serving the needs of a world on the verge of social and environmental collapse. The two authors call for a rethinking about the way society produces, values, and distributes goods and services. They propose a package of policies for the "new economics" pertaining to land use, population, agriculture, industry, labor, and taxation and offer strategies on how to implement the policies. They also propose the "sustainable economic welfare" index as a better measure of economic activity than the gross national product (GNP). Such an index, they suggest, reflects more accurately what is happening in the economy, by showing how the benefits of economic growth are distributed among different social groups. It would also show the real costs of economic activity, such as to the environment and long-term sustainability of the planet.

"In this searing critique of 'mainstream' economics, World Bank economist Herman Daly and theologian John Cobb demonstrate how our growth-oriented, industrial economy has led to environmental disaster, and they offer an exciting paradigm for economics, public policy, and social ethics."—Kathleen Courrier, director of publications, World Resources Institute

"The workable greenprint for ecological economics. It shows the only way out, other than destruction and death, for 'civilization.'"—David Haenke, director, Ecological Society Project of the Tides Foundation

28. **Darwin, Charles.** *The Origin of Species by Means of Natural Selection, or, The Preservation of Favoured Races in the Struggle for Life.* Edited by Paul H. Barrett and R. B. Freeman. Volume 15 of *The Works of Charles Darwin.* London: Pickering, 1988 (orig. pub. 1859, John Murray). 478 pages.

"When on board H.M.S. Beagle, as naturalist, I was much struck with certain facts in the distribution of the organic beings inhabiting South America, and in the geological relations of the present to the past inhabitants of that continent. These facts, as will be seen in the latter chapters of this volume, seemed to throw some light on the origin of species—that mystery of mysteries, as it has been called by one of our greatest philosophers" (p.1). Thus, Darwin introduced what was to become one of the most influential, and controversial, books in science. The theory of evolution, which Darwin helped establish with his publication, provides the structure for modern biology. Darwin's primary theoretical contribution was in the explanation he gave for the evolving changes that led to the development of new species. He called the process "natural selection." Darwin reasoned that slight variations randomly occur within populations of a given species and that, over time, changes in the environment (such as geology and climate) would present new conditions to the extent that individuals with certain variations might be more favorably disposed to survive in the new environment, while others would not. Thus, nature would, in a sense, select certain individuals over others, leading to a process of evolving changes from the original species. Darwin's notion of adaptability to new environmental conditions certainly seems relevant to current-day discussions of biodiversity and conservation biology, particularly given the relatively rapid pace at which humans are altering global environmental systems. (See also entry 160 for Darwin's descriptions of his earlier, three-year voyage.)

"Has to be read."—David Hancocks, director, Arizona-Sonora Desert Museum

"A revolutionary explanation of man's development."—Martin W. Holdgate, director general, Jeffrey McNeely, chief conservation officer, and John Burke, head of communications, International Union for the Conservation of Nature and Natural Resources (IUCN)-The World Conservation Union, Gland, Switzerland

"I know that this is a very old book, but by focusing interest on the diversity of life, it sparked interest in all things in nature—especially biological diversity."—Loyal A. Mehrhoff, botanist, Bernice P. Bishop Museum of Natural and Cultural History

"The basis of modern biology and ecology."—Tom Turner, staff writer, Sierra Club Legal Defense Fund

See also: *The Illustrated Origin of Species* (Hill & Wang, 1979), abridged and introduced by Richard E. Leakey. As its title implies, this presents Darwin's text alongside a rich assortment of drawing and photographs that illustrate his key points.

29. **Devall, Bill, and George Sessions. *Deep Ecology: Living as if Nature Mattered.*** Salt Lake City: Peregrine Smith, 1985. 266 pages.

This book, by two environmental activists who are also philosophers, outlines an alternative for our relationship to nature based on a critique of the contemporary anthropocentric, materialistic exploitation of the environment and humans. Deep ecology, according to the authors, is "a way of developing a new balance and harmony between individuals, communities and all of Nature" (p. 7). Acknowledging the influence of Arne Naess (see entry 62), the authors present a mixture of short essays, poems, interviews, and commentaries to illustrate the concepts of biocentric equality, self-realization, diversity, and ecological living that exemplify the deep ecological perspective.

"This is more a collection of essays than a coherent book. Yet it provides an excellent benchmark of the green alternative to the dominant world view. In particular, it traces a lineage of 'deep ecology' thinking from which we can fashion values and understandings that are not simply the more familiar philosophies from the last 300 years with a bit of environmental concern tacked on."—Sandy Irvine, associate editor, *The Ecologist,* Newcastle Upon Tyne, England

30. **Dillard, Annie. *Pilgrim at Tinker Creek.*** New York: Harper's Magazine Press, 1974. 271 pages.

Dillard writes in her opening essay, "I propose to keep here what Thoreau called 'a meteorological journal of the mind,' telling some tales and describing some of the sights of this rather tamed valley, and exploring, in fear and trembling, some of the unmapped dim reaches and unholy fastnesses to which those tales and sights so dizzyingly lead" (p. 11). Indeed, Dillard has been compared to Thoreau and Emerson as a transcendentalist, as a spiritualist, and as a person of enhanced senses. She seems to perceive beyond what most people see, hear, or feel, and her writings show a deep reflection inward as well. For Dillard, Tinker Creek in Virginia's Blue Ridge country is a universe, partially explored, and mostly unmapped. Her book won the Pulitzer prize in 1975 for general nonfiction.

"Annie Dillard has a writing style and a way of looking at the natural world that has sparked my interests, raised questions, and encouraged me to explore in ways previously unthought of. A must for any naturalist."—Ken Voorhis, director, Great Smoky Mountains Institute at Tremont

Also recommended is Dillard's *Teaching a Stone to Talk: Expeditions and Encounters* (Harper, 1982).

31. **EarthWorks Group. *50 Simple Things You Can Do to Save the Planet.*** Berkeley, CA: EarthWorks Press, 1990. 96 pages.

The major assumption of this book is that there really are simple things you can do to save the planet. You might make just a small contribution, but it does add up. For instance, you can: stop the amount of junk mail you receive; drive less (and bike, walk, or use mass transportation more); buy products with less packaging; eat "lower" on the food chain; and recycle as many materials as possible. For each of the "50 simple things," the guide gives a background summary on the problem being addressed, a list of facts related to the problem, a few recommended actions, and sources of more information on the topic. You might not be able to do everything at once, but you can certainly start with just one of the ideas—and then try to modify your lifestyle even more over a period of time. For additional tips, see *The Next Step: 50 More Things You Can Do to Save the Earth* (Andrews and McMeel, 1991) by the EarthWorks Group.

32.   **Ehrlich, Paul R.** *The Population Bomb.* rev. ed. New York: Ballantine in association with Sierra Club, 1971 (orig. pub. 1968). 201 pages.

Ehrlich's concern is the idea of global population on the verge of exploding, brought about by a rapid population growth rate, particularly in the developing countries. He stresses the connection between this growing population and a negative impact on the environment, and cites the population growth as a cause of the famines and disasters occurring during the 1960s in many parts of the world. Ehrlich calls for family planning and promotion of the concept of zero population growth (ZPG). "The birth rate must be brought into balance with the death rate or mankind will breed itself into oblivion. We can no longer afford merely to treat the symptoms of the cancer of population growth; the cancer itself must be cut out" (p. xii). This was one of the first neo-malthusian treatises to have a major impact on the study of human-environment relationships. The critics of Ehrlich's message come from two approaches: (1) those who suggest that human ingenuity is capable of ensuring unlimited resources and can come up with solutions to population growth (and, in fact, population is seen as a resource and not a problem from this viewpoint); and (2) those with a Marxist or socialist critique stating that the unequal distribution of resources is the main cause of environmental degradation, and that rapid population growth is a symptom, rather than the cause, of environmental degradation. Ehrlich and his wife, Anne Ehrlich, address these and other critiques in their recent book, *The Population Explosion* (see entry 175). Ehrlich has had a tremendous impact on the thinking of environmentalists, both in the area of population and in the field of conservation biology.

"Not all of his predictions have come true, but the book called attention to the problem of overpopulation, and incited people to ask the right questions."—James R. Conner, chair, Montana Chapter of the Sierra Club

"*The Population Bomb* was the first comprehensive study I read about human population growth. It alerted me to the horrors of this ultimate environmental degradation and made me a convert to the cause of zero population growth (and negative population growth!)"—Sue Ellen Lyons, president, Louisiana Environmental Educators' Association

"Real issues confrontation at the most basic level. Highlights the urgency at human level, thus making it clearly identifiable to all readers."—John D. Rogers, librarian, the Conservation Trust Resource Bank and Study Centre, Reading, England

"Defined the driving force behind environmental degradation, all other things being equal. Sounded a warning that needed to be heard."—Arthur B. Sacks, special assistant to the dean of the graduate school, University of Wisconsin–Madison

"Ehrlich awakened contemporary concern for human population growth as an environmental issue; as a stimulant to thought and action, this was the most influential book since *Silent Spring* [see entry 19]."—Thomas R. Vale, professor of geography, University of Wisconsin–Madison

"The most influential polemic on overpopulation—the fundamental environmental problem."—Charles Walcott, executive director, Cornell University Laboratory of Ornithology

33. **Ehrlich, Paul R., and Anne H. Ehrlich. *Extinction: The Causes and Consequences of the Disappearance of Species.* New York: Random House, 1981. 305 pages.**

Focusing on practices and policies that destroy plant and animal species, the Ehrlichs give a historical and evolutionary perspective on species extinction. Although the notion of species preservation has been promoted for some time, this book was an important precursor to others that helped define the field of "conservation biology" as it began to take shape during the 1980s. The book looks at a number of topics, including the ethics of nature preservation, the economic and ecological value of plant and animal species, and the role of human activities in promoting extinction. The authors also suggest actions and policies that might slow the rate of species extinction and might encourage better the preservation and protection of plants and animals on this planet.

34. **Ehrlich, Paul R., Anne H. Ehrlich, and John P. Holdren.** *Ecoscience: Population, Resources, Environment.* 3d ed. San Francisco: Freeman, 1977 (orig. pub. 1970 as *Population, Resources, Environment*). 1051 pages.

This classic textbook provides a comprehensive overview of population-resource-environment interrelationships. The authors state several basic assumptions that guide the overall content of the book: (1) the planet is overpopulated (when the book was first published in 1970, the world's population was 3.5 billion; now in the early 1990s, it has swelled to 5.2 billion); (2) a large population size and a high rate of population growth are major hindrances to solving human problems; and (3) demand for resources and food from a large, rapidly growing population means more environmental degradation. The book reviews in detail the physical and biological systems of the earth, discusses population and natural resources (both renewable and nonrenewable), and describes relevant social, economic, and political change. It also reflects on an "apprehension about the course of humanity," and attempts to provide the reader with sufficient background information to initiate remedies to global environmental problems. Although the authors present population as the dominant factor affecting the environment, they cover a number and variety of other environmental problems, and, in fact, were among the first to look at the impacts of nuclear war on the environment.

"The first comprehensive and detailed analysis of the world's crisis of overpopulation and the resulting demands on the environment."—R. Maitland Earl, chair, International Society for the Prevention of Water Pollution, Alton, England

"A gold mine of information. The single best synthesis of the whole range of environmental problems."—Stephen Schneider, senior scientist, National Center for Atmospheric Research

35. **Eiseley, Loren C.** *The Immense Journey.* New York: Vintage, 1957. 210 pages.

This is a series of essays on the experience of nature and human origins by an anthropologist who writes like a poet. Eiseley uses fossils, rivers, and animals to stimulate his musings on evolution and the meaning of life. Many essays take a minor incident such as a swim in a river, an encounter with a bird or frog, or the observation of a bone or rock, and use it to illustrate deep and enduring ideas about the human relationship to nature and the long history of life on earth. The imagination and prose of some essays are breathtaking, and convey a real sense of wonder and discovery.

36. **Fox, Stephen R.** *The American Conservation Movement: John Muir and His Legacy.* Boston: Little, Brown, 1981. Reprint. Madison: University of Wisconsin Press, 1985. 436 pages.

Written in a biographical style—about the life of John Muir, founder of the Sierra Club—Fox's book focuses on the people involved in shaping the conservation movement in the United States. The book is readable and enjoyable, with many anecdotes. Fox shows that Muir, a preservationist, was one of the more intriguing figures in American history. His views that nature should be preserved untouched by humans, especially contrasted with those of his contemporary, Gifford Pinchot, a more utilitarian conservationist who believed that nature should be used by humans, but in a renewable and managed fashion. Included is a list of Muir's fourteen books, as well as a bibliography of articles and books about Muir.

"Required reading for those who want to understand the environmental movement."—James R. Conner, chair, Montana chapter of the Sierra Club

"The best and most clear-eyed history of the conservation movement in the United States, avoiding the piety that too many such histories fall into."—Joseph Kastner, author

37. **Fox, Warwick.** *Towards a Transpersonal Ecology: Developing New Foundations for Environmentalism.* Boston: Shambala, 1990. 380 pages.

A remarkable overview of the deep ecology movement, particularly of its rapid growth and development during the 1980s; includes an excellent summary of the writings of the major proponents of deep ecology.

"The most recent and possibly the most lucid book on deep ecology ideas. Discusses and critiques the ideas that have floated around deep ecology circles, then reviews the origins and intent by examining those of formulator Arne Naess. Gets a little lost in philosophical gobbledygook, but it's an excellent reference on deep ecology for those past the introductory stage."—Annie Booth, doctoral student, Institute for Environmental Studies, University of Wisconsin–Madison

"Links deep ecology and personal growth movements." —Bill Devall, author/teacher, Humboldt State University

38.   Glacken, Clarence J. *Traces on the Rhodian Shore: Nature and Culture in Western Thought from Ancient Times to the End of the Eighteenth Century.* Berkeley: University of California Press, 1973. 763 pages.

This monumental work documents Western views of the human relationship to nature from the fifth century B.C. to the eighteenth century A.D. Using a tremendous range of original sources, Glacken seeks to understand the origins and dynamics of three ideas: (1) the earth as designed by God for people; (2) the influence of environment on human nature and culture; and (3) people as geographic agents of the transformation of the earth. He traces these ideas from the Greeks through the rise of Christianity, science, and natural history using the work of most of the great Western philosophers and writers. For example, he documents in great detail the emergence of concepts of the dominion and control over nature associated with Christianity and Baconian mechanistic science, and the origins of concern about the environmental impacts of human activities in the work of Montesquieu and Buffon. Although some may find the density and detail of this volume overwhelming, the index and chapter outlines are excellent and can be used as a guide to in-depth understanding of specific topics and writers only superficially discussed in more popular literature.

39.   Hardin, Garrett. *Exploring New Ethics for Survival: The Voyage of Spaceship Beagle.* New York: Viking, 1972. 273 pages.

Most people associate Hardin with his essay, "The Tragedy of the Commons," which appeared in the December 13, 1986 issue of *Science* magazine. In this essay, Hardin argued that uncontrolled use of shared resources (especially by a growing population) is a recipe for environmental degradation. He believes that population is the major cause of environmental problems and that humans are basically selfish and will consume all they can. Thus, he believes that society needs to impose regulations over the individual to obtain a socially desired result, such as population control. He maintains that there are some individual freedoms, such as parenthood, which society can restrict to preserve the whole. As with all of Hardin's writings, this book is provocative and many of his assertions and recommendations generate immense debate. But Hardin makes us face these tough issues, perhaps more than we might otherwise, and that seems to be a substantial first step toward finding solutions.

"Introduced me to the deeper moral and ethical dimensions of our dilemma of growth. Hardin's rigorous logic in pulling apart language to reveal how it can be misused in argument deeply impressed me and changed the way I evaluate the written word."—Marvin W. Baker, Jr., associate professor of geography, University of Oklahoma

Also recommended: Hardin's *Population, Evolution and Birth Control* (Freeman, 1969); *Stalking the Wild Taboo* (Kaufman, 1973); and *Naked Emperors: Essays of a Taboo Stalker* (Kaufman, 1982).

40. **Hays, Samuel P.** *Beauty, Health, and Permanence: Environmental Politics in the United States, 1955–1985.* New York: Cambridge University Press, 1987. 630 pages.

————. *Conservation and the Gospel of Efficiency: The Progressive Conservation Movement, 1890–1920.* Cambridge, MA: Harvard University Press, 1959. 297 pages.

As a political historian, Hays is interested in the processes of political decisionmaking and the manner in which power is distributed in government, especially concerning the environment. In *Conservation and the Gospel of Efficiency,* he focuses on the conservation movement to describe the changes in the political process that were occurring at the turn of the century. He suggests that the notion of wise management of natural resources was part of a broader reform movement in this country, in which well-educated engineers, scientists, and policymakers were convinced that government could be used as a tool to help create a technological utopia, a society in which resources were efficiently managed, extracted, and distributed. This was also the approach taken by Theodore Roosevelt and Gifford Pinchot (see entry 287). In *Beauty, Health, and Permanence,* Hays succinctly describes the change in attitudes that led to a transition from the "conservation movement" to the "environmental movement." He then provides an extended political history of the modern environmental era, one characterized by a concern for scenic wilderness (including protection of flora and fauna), regulation of pollutants and harmful substances, and an interest in long-term sustainability of the planet's capacity to support life. Together, these two books provide a substantial contribution to the understanding of the conservation and environmental movements during two important periods in the history of the United States.

41. **Jackson, Wes, Wendell Berry, and Bruce Colman, eds.** *Meeting the Expectations of the Land: Essays in Sustainable Agriculture and Stewardship.* San Francisco: North Point, 1984. 250 pages.

Is it possible to maintain a highly productive agricultural system and yet avoid the negative environmental and social side effects? This collection of essays examines this question, advocating what the authors refer to as "new" or "sustainable" agricultural practices, such as farming without chemicals and recycling organic waste into fertilizer. Citing destructive consequences of conventional agricultural methods in the United States, they call for a reexamination of food policy and farming techniques. Collectively, the essays address the ecological, economic, cultural, and political aspects of agriculture and its application to modern society. Contributors of the essays come from a variety of backgrounds and provide examples of sustainable agriculture from both the United States and Latin America.

"An important statement on the issue of sustainability of agriculture and steps towards stewardship."—Stephen R. Gliessman, director, Agroecology program, University of California–Santa Cruz

42. **Krutch, Joseph Wood.** *The Voice of the Desert: A Naturalist's Interpretation.* New York: William Sloane Associates, 1954. 223 pages.

Krutch invites us into the special world of the cactus wren, the saguaro, the kangaroo rat, and the tarantula spider. He beckons us to share and appreciate "his country," where wild flowers bloom in profusion during April, where the midday summer sun forces a dormancy upon all creatures, where the tension between survival and extermination is delicately balanced, and where striking beauty and unforgiving harshness cloak the same landscape.

"In a way, I suppose Krutch comes closest to speaking directly to our present circumstance. It was about the year 1965 that I remember discovering Krutch's writings, and they were at that point very helpful to me. He never wrote a single outstanding classic the way Leopold and Thoreau did, but his gentle, mature, humane, and wise books deserve to be remembered just as long."—Donald E. Worster, Hall professor of American history, University of Kansas

43. **Leopold, Aldo.** *A Sand County Almanac, and Sketches Here and There.* Introduction by Robert Finch. Illustrations by Charles W. Schwartz. New York: Oxford University Press, 1949 (special commemorative ed., 1987). 226 pages.

Nestled among the jack pine and scrub oak near the Wisconsin River sits "the shack." This weathered old farm building became the inspirational retreat for a man who could not live without wild things. It was on this land, located in one of the "sand counties" of central Wisconsin, that Aldo Leopold crafted his poetic chronicle of a land too poor for farming, but so rich in nature's economy. *A Sand County Almanac* is a delightful collection of stories about the land and life that Leopold—scientist, conservationist, and philosopher—saw with such vivid detail: the peenting and twittering display of the male woodcock at dusk; hunting grouse when the tamaracks are a "smokey gold;" arising early in the morning to sit outside with coffeepot and notebook, recording the vocalizations of his property's "tenants." Like no one else, his recall of natural wonders has awakened and inspired so many. To read Leopold, to understand his message, is to heighten one's senses and sensibility. Perhaps Leopold's best-known essay, or at least the concept presented in that essay, concerns what has become known as "the land ethic." Within this philosophical concept, Leopold articulated best the idea of respect and reverence for the land that has influenced subsequent generations of conservationists. In another essay called "The Round River," he writes: "Conservation is a state of harmony between men and land. By land is meant all of the things on, over, or in the earth. Harmony with the land is like harmony with a friend; you cannot cherish his right hand and chop off his left. That is to say, you cannot love game and hate predators; you cannot conserve the waters and waste the ranges; you cannot build the forest and mine the farm. The land is one organism" (pp. 189–190). Leopold died on April 21, 1948, helping to fight a grass fire on a neighboring farm. This book had been accepted for publication by Oxford University Press one week earlier.

"Leopold is the twentieth-century heir to Emerson and imbues environmental ethics with a scientific and pragmatic basis. His work flows from Schweitzer and Bailey, two theologians."—J. William Futrell, president, Environmental Law Institute

"These essays set forth a philosophy of natural resource conservation couched in terms of a man-to-land ethic. It has been the prime stimulus to the growing awareness of the need to come to terms with our environment."—John A. Gustafson, treasurer, American Nature Study Society

"The classic! If government officials read and understood this book, our planet would be safe and sane."—David Hancocks, director, Arizona-Sonora Desert Museum

"Easily the most important book ever published on natural resource conservation and the value of individual involvement in resource management, care, and protection. I hand out dozens of copies a year as gifts and quote Leopold often in my talks and articles."—Jack Lorenz, executive director, Izaak Walton League of America

"No one has captured the ecological world view more concisely and clearly than has Leopold. For me he was a revelation at age twenty-two."—David W. Orr, professor of environmental studies, Oberlin College

"This book made me more aware of the wonder, variety, and beauty of nature and enhanced my ability to enjoy and appreciate such assets."—Russell W. Peterson, president emeritus, National Audubon Society

"A work that shows that speech is possible across disciplines, that the integration of science and art can be achieved with meaning and power and beauty. A work that provides a vision of responsible action, that brings ethics into both daily life and the world of science. A landmark in every respect."—Arthur B. Sacks, senior special assistant to the dean of the graduate school, University of Wisconsin–Madison

"If anyone has an interest in environmental affairs, sooner or later they come to know this book and the 'land ethic;' it's an environmentalist imperative. For this reason and others, the book has been instructive and meaningful. I was surprised to read that the land ethic was preceded by an Aldo Leopold who 'never heard of passing up a chance to kill a wolf.' Since that reading, I've come upon numerous examples of this change in values in others, and acknowledged that different trails may eventually lead to the same place."—Frederick Sepp, biological sciences librarian, Pennsylvania State University

The best of Leopold's remaining unpublished essays and materials has been assembled and edited recently by Susan L. Flader and J. Baird Callicott in *The River of the Mother of God and Other Essays by Aldo Leopold* (University of Wisconsin Press, 1991). Flader is also author of *Thinking Like a Mountain: Aldo Leopold and the Evolution of an Ecological Attitude toward Deer, Wolves, and Forests* (see entry 186); and Callicott is editor of *Companion to A Sand County Almanac: Interpretative and Critical Essays* (University of Wisconsin Press, 1987), and author of *In Defense of the Land Ethic: Essays in Environmental Philosophy* (State University of New York Press, 1988). The most recent and exhaustive biography of Leopold is Curt Meine's *Aldo Leopold: His Life and Work* (see entry 256), while a more personal biography can be found in *Aldo Leopold: The Professor* (Palmer, 1987) by one of Leopold's students, Robert A. McCabe.

44. **Lopez, Barry.** *Arctic Dreams: Imagination and Desire in a Northern Landscape.* New York: Scribner's, 1986. 464 pages.

This is an exciting account of Lopez's visit and fascination with the land, wildlife, and people of the Arctic. He is a master of detail; he sees with a keen eye and writes with a poet's heart. In one passage, he describes the colors of icebergs he is observing from the deck of a ship: "At the waterline the ice gleamed aquamarine against its own gray-white walls above. Where meltwater had filled cracks or made ponds, the pools and veins were a milk-blue, or shaded to brighter marine blues, depending on the thickness of the ice. If the iceberg had recently fractured, its new face glistened greenish blue—the greens in the older, weathered faces were grayer. In twilight the ice took on the colors of the sun: rose, reddish, yellows, watered purples, soft pinks" (p. 207). In other sections, Lopez introduces the Native Americans who are bound closely to their traditional ways of survival within the Arctic's ecosystem, and yet are being changed by an invading culture from the south. With additional reports about the birds, mammals, plants, and other life that frequent this area, Lopez provides a beautiful picture of an enduring land.

45. **Lopez, Barry.** *Of Wolves and Men.* New York: Scribner's, 1978. 309 pages.

What can be more intense than the fascination and fear we humans feel for the wolf? Is there some innate bond we have with *Canus lupus*? In *Of Wolves and Men,* presented in four sections, Lopez explores the intimate and distant relationships we have had with this amazing creature. He reviews the natural history of the wolf, including its physiology and behavior. He then presents numerous accounts "of wolves and men" from the folklore, myths, and legends from Native American, European, and other cultures into whose consciousnesses the wolf has crept. This is an intriguing book—a closer look at why we are frightened of the wild beast, and yet feel a sense of awe for such a magnificent animal.

"Lopez's feel for wilderness and its inhabitants is contagious in this book. It's a very readable and sincerely written work."—Meredith Taylor, chair, Wyoming chapter of the Sierra Club

"It's unlikely that this book will appear often on the survey of best environmental books but it is meaningful to me. Having read too much literature that reported on wolf behavior, I found that Lopez provided some intriguing thoughts. First, that the wolf society parallels human society more closely than people would realize. Second, that 'the reasons for wolf behavior are not completely clear to any-one—not biologists, Eskimos, hunters, or writers know why wolves do what they do.' Personally, I hope this never changes."—Frederick Sepp, biological sciences librarian, Pennsylvania State University

46.   Lorenz, Konrad Z. *King Solomon's Ring: New Light on Animal Ways.* New York: Thomas Y. Crowell, 1952. 202 pages.

There is a famous series of photographs by *Life* magazine photographer Nina Leen that shows Lorenz in his later years, a trail of ducklings following right behind the "papa duck" as he takes a swim. This illustrates perfectly the fact that the imprinting studies that Lorenz conducted earlier in this century are classics in the field of animal behavior studies. In this book, he offers numerous anecdotes based on his investigations and interactions with animals, particularly birds and fish. The stories are lively, often humorous, and very informative.

"A tale of animal stories which led to the science of ethology. Must reading for prospective animal behaviorists."—Charles Walcott, executive director, Cornell University Laboratory of Ornithology

47.   Lovelock, J. E. *Gaia: A New Look at Life on Earth.* New York: Oxford University Press, 1979. 157 pages.

Many scientists have found Lovelock's book to be interesting because it presents a theory that the earth's systems consist of close linkages between the biota, atmosphere, and oceans. Others have favored the book because it can be interpreted as a somewhat romantic notion of the earth as a being—the mother Gaia. In either case Lovelock, who is an independent scientist in England, has presented very clearly and concisely the ideas that he and Lynn Margulis, a professor of biology at the University of Massachusetts, have published in scientific papers during the previous decade (see entry 292). These include the idea that life created the earth's existing atmosphere and that the earth system adjusts to changes in a self-regulating fashion. In the book, Lovelock reinforces and lends some scientific evidence to the notion that the earth is a fragile system in which humans are just a single part. It presents a very innovative and daring hypothesis that has provoked much discussion and influenced a lot of research during the past decade. Lovelock continues his discussion of the Gaia hypothesis and the reaction to that hypothesis in *The Ages of Gaia: A Biography of Our Living Earth* (Norton, 1988), and offers advice on how we might care for patient Earth in *Healing Gaia: Practical Medicine for the Planet* (Harmony, 1991).

"The author advances a hypothesis to explain the biosphere as a self-organizing, self-maintaining, homeostatic system. Although some aspects of the hypothesis have been questioned, there has been broad acceptance amongst environmental scientists of the plausibility of the general proposition. Lovelock's synthesis is truly a seminal work that provides, at the least, a point of departure for investigating the earth as a biogeochemical system with properties that may be described as 'organismic'."—Lynton Keith Caldwell, Arthur F. Bentley professor emeritus of political science, Indiana University

"A brilliant, gracefully written essay on the emerging revolution in geosphere-biosphere interactions."—William C. Clark, professor, John F. Kennedy School of Government, Harvard University

"One *must* have some body of imaginative ideas about nature. This is Lovelock's most recent statement of views that I don't fully share, but greatly respect."—F. Kenneth Hare, provost emeritus and professor emeritus of geography at Trinity College at the University of Toronto

48. **Lovins, Amory B.** *Soft Energy Paths: Toward a Durable Peace.* San Francisco: Friends of the Earth International, 1977. 231 pages.

Lovins looks at energy use and its technological applications in modern, industrialized societies that are characterized by relative economic wealth, excessive consumption of energy and other resources, and social disintegration. Lovins is codirector of the Rocky Mountain Institute in Snowmass, Colorado, and in this book points out the fallacies and environmental risks in the practices of excessive energy consumption and the absence of effort to identify alternatives. He describes a transition to "soft technologies" such as solar and other renewable energy sources, that will require institutional, political, economic, and social changes in order for them to be implemented.

"There may be no environmentally benign technology for producing energy, but Lovins showed that there are alternatives to coal and nuclear power that are economically sound and less harmful to the environment."—James R. Conner, chair, Montana chapter of the Sierra Club

"This must be on everyone's list—one of the best—it keeps escaping my library as it's lent again and again."—Jane Sharp, former president, Conservation Council of North Carolina

49.   **McHarg, Ian L.** *Design with Nature.* Garden City, NY: Natural History, 1969. 197 pages.

Lewis Mumford writes in the book's introduction that he would put *Design with Nature* "on the same shelf that contains as yet only a handful of works in a similar vein, beginning with Hippocrates, and including such essential classics as those of Henry Thoreau, George Perkins Marsh, Patrick Geddes, Carl Sauer, Benton MacKaye, and Rachel Carson" (p. viii). McHarg eloquently characterizes how the placement of cultural features over the landscape can be done with a sense of harmony. His vision of juxtaposition of the human world within the natural world is clear and thoughtful. His book is, perhaps, most renowned for its discussion of the "overlay method" for planning. This is a process whereby multiple "layers," or maps, of environmental and socioeconomic data are overlaid to reveal a combination of characteristics about the land that no single layer alone can do, and to show which areas are best suited for which types of land use. The overlay method that McHarg popularized now forms the theoretical basis for today's computerized geographic information systems, which are revolutionizing the capabilities of local and state governments to develop and monitor land use plans. McHarg has had a tremendous impact on the architectural and planning community, both in this country and around the world.

"Systematic approach to ecological land use planning incorporating natural and cultural features of particular landscapes. Offers a developmental vision incorporating environmental protection, human settlements, and economic development needs within a sound ecological framework."—William G. Berberet, former dean of the College of Liberal Arts at Willamette University

"McHarg develops not only an elegant and valuable methodology of overlays to show the contextual setting, limitations, and opportunities for land use planning and landscape architecture (at various scales), but links this with the need for participatory decisionmaking processes and planning for dealing with local and/or regional land use issues."—Kenneth A. Dahlberg, professor of political science, Western Michigan University

"McHarg presents a rational argument that progress can continue without sacrificing the quality of the environment."—Jack Greene, National Wildlife Federation

"A seminal and beautifully written expression of what was then a fundamentally fresh approach to urban design that values the importance of ecosytem protection."—Paul Relis, executive director, Community Environmental Council, Inc.

"A common-sense approach to land use planning that utilizes nature systems studies. This book has influenced my career since my sophomore year in college."—Kristie Seaman, education director, Sanibel-Captiva Conservation Foundation

50. **McKibben, Bill.** *The End of Nature.* New York: Random House, 1989. 226 pages.

First published in the *New Yorker* magazine, McKibben's book elaborates on the powerful notion that there is no part of the planet that has not been transformed by human actions: not the depths of the ocean, nor isolated atolls, nor the interior of Antarctica. Through the global circulation of the atmosphere and oceans, and through direct and indirect transport by humans, the products and residues from our industrialized society have managed to reach places that heretofore were considered remote "wilderness" and completely "natural." McKibben uses the examples of global warming and the hole in the ozone layer to show how humans have transformed and threatened the planet. In a manner similar to Frederick Jackson Turner's discussion of the concept of the end of the "frontier" in North America and its influence on the American consciousness, McKibben reflects on the concept of the end of the natural world and its meaning for human society worldwide. He does not know if we have the will to reduce our impacts on the planet, given the levels of comfort and patterns of consumption that individuals would have to forego. But he does retain some optimism: "this could be the epoch when people decide at least to go no further down the path we've been following—when we make not only the necessary technological adjustments to preserve the world from overheating, but also the necessary mental adjustments to ensure that we'll never again put our good ahead of everything else's" (pp. 213–4).

"It is the natural successor to *Silent Spring* [see entry 19]."—Philip Neal, general secretary, National Association for Environmental Education, Walsall, England

"Redefining the value we attach to nature at the eleventh hour—a warning that may be too late."—Thomas Urquhart, executive director, Maine Audubon Society

51. **McPhee, John A.** *Encounters with the Archdruid.* New York: Farrar, Straus, 1971. 245 pages.

In searching the library database for books by John McPhee, one is amazed at the length of the list and at the diversity of topics: basketball, oranges, Scottish culture, canoes, plate tectonics, Alaskan wilderness, and the Swiss army, to name a few. McPhee seems to have an immense and far-ranging curiosity about people and places in the world. He also has the tenacity to focus his attention on a particular topic until he has seen it from every angle and described it in vivid detail. *Encounters with the Archdruid* is a special book about David Brower, former director of the Sierra Club. McPhee characterizes the "encounters" between Brower and three of his foes: a developer, a water engineer, and a mineral specialist. For example, he discusses how he persuaded Floyd Dominy, dam builder extraordinnaire for the Bureau of Reclamation, to take a raft trip down the Colorado River with Brower, and describes the debate they had regarding the utility and fate of America's wild rivers. McPhee shows the tension and humor, the antagonism and humaneness, the opposite points of view between a staunch defender of the wilderness and those who want to convert the natural resource into a commodity. This is certainly one of McPhee's best biographies.

"Through the literary skills of John McPhee, this book is more like a novel in its readability and ecological overtones, as it describes the confrontations between David Brower and three antagonists during journeys in three wildernesses. I found it a lively book assisting students in their understanding of issues of environmental crisis."— James A. Fowler, former chair, Michigan Natural Areas Council

52.   Marsh, George Perkins. *Man and Nature.* Edited by David Lowenthal. Cambridge, MA: Belknap of Harvard University Press, 1965 (orig. pub. 1864. Reprint. *The Earth as Modified by Human Actions: a New Edition of Man and Nature.* 1874.) 472 pages.

Marsh was a lawyer and politician who later became a diplomat for the United States government. His first posting was as U.S. Minister to Turkey in 1848. He spent much of his time travelling through other parts of the Mediterranean basin—Greece, Egypt, and Palestine—where he saw first-hand the detrimental impacts of human overuse of the land. He had observed similar changes in the landscape in his home state of Vermont, where flocks of sheep had denuded the slopes of the Green Mountains. Thus, he became concerned about timber clearing, agriculture, animal grazing, and water diversions. He saw that combined with the physical geography (topography, climate, vegetation) of certain landscapes, these contributed to an increasing decline in natural resources. Although Marsh's book was an important early call for restrained use and wiser management of natural resources, Preston James, the historian of geography, writes that "Marsh's warning was sounded in a country with seemingly endless resources, and at a time when the need for conservation programs had yet to be formulated" (*All Possible Worlds: A History of Geographical Ideas*, Odyssey, 1971, p. 196).

"About the first explicit statement of concern over depletion of material (economic) resources."—Daniel B. Luten, professor emeritus of geography, University of California—Berkeley

"The first, and still most, illustrative and comprehensive writing on how humans change the environment and what this does to humans in return."—Tom McKinney, agricultural researcher, Rocky Mountain Institute

"This book has been described by Lewis Mumford as . . . 'the fountainhead of the conservation movement,' and by Stewart Udall as . . . 'the beginning of land wisdom.' It was the first to show clearly the relationships of human populations and their environmental impacts; it was a primary influence on John Muir, Teddy Roosevelt and Aldo Leopold. Its insights are profound and most valuable for modern times. Lowenthal noted: 'Few books have had more impact on the way men view and use land.' "—Charles H. Southwick, professor of biology, University of Colorado

53. **Matthiessen, Peter.** *Wildlife in America.* rev. ed. Introduction by Richard H. Pough. Drawings by Bob Hines. New York: Viking, 1987 (orig. pub. 1959). 304 pages.

Matthiessen's book is both fascinating and depressing at the same time. It is fascinating because of its engaging reporting of the historical accounts of the American wilderness, describing the great currents of wildlife flowing across the landscape and through the skies. The depressing aspect lies in its stark depiction of the reality of the senseless, and often brutal, destruction of most of the wild creatures that were native to North America, including many that have become extinct, such as the passenger pigeon and the Carolina parakeet. But Matthiessen also tracks the rise of the conservationist movement and the efforts of individuals and groups to halt the loss of animal species on the land and in the adjacent seas. The book contains a sampling of some of the best wildlife paintings and illustrations available, including photographs and drawings, which emphasize what the decimation of wildlife was like.

54. **Meadows, Donella H., Dennis L. Meadows, Jørgen Randers, and**

William W. Behrens III. *The Limits to Growth: A Report for the Club of Rome's Project on the Predicament of Mankind.* New York: Universe, 1972. 205 pages.

Rapid population growth, widespread malnutrition, depletion of resources, and a deteriorating environment. These were the major global trends forecast in the early 1970s by a research team at the Massachusetts Institute of Technology (MIT), under the auspices of the Club of Rome. The team used a computer simulation model called World 3, a process the researchers called "system dynamic analysis," pioneered by Jay Forrester at MIT. The amazing and distressing findings of the research were published in 1972 for general readership and prompted an immediate debate on the long-term prospects of the planet. In *The Limits to Growth,* the MIT team first introduces us to the basic premises underlying their research program. They used the graphic results of their computer simulations to document trends in population, resource use, and the economy, and go on to describe the dynamic characteristics of exponential growth and the physical limits imposed on growth by a finite planet. Finally, the authors evaluate the relation of technological advance to physical constraints, showing various levels of population and consumption expected under different conditions. Although the computer programs used in the original study are outdated, the book had an impact in the early 1970s because of the novelty of computers at that time. And the ideas presented in this book still seem as valid today as they were two decades ago. A twentieth anniversary update, *Beyond the Limits: Envisioning the Future with World 3* (Chelsea Green, 1992), has been prepared by Donella Meadows, Dennis Meadows, and Jørgen Randers, which updates the forecasts and reviews the events and activities that have occurred since the publication of *The Limits to Growth,* in addition to reassessing the earlier predictions.

"This book made a huge impression on my thinking about the finiteness of the earth and the impossibility of continuing current rates of resource exploitation."—Marvin W. Baker, Jr., associate professor of geography, University of Oklahoma

"Opened my eyes to the long-term impact of geometric growth and to the need for computerized modelling of the many interacting forces at work."—Russell Peterson, president emeritus, National Audubon Society

"This was as important a book for the 'scientific' approach to environmental problems as was Rachel Carson's *Silent Spring* [see entry 19]

for the popular environmentalist approach. It was the first major attempt to look at global problems of environment and resources through simulation modelling. It served as a catalyst for concern about global environmental problems in general and for the vast strides that have since been made in analyzing and modelling these problems."—D. Scott Slocombe, School of Urban and Regional Planning, University of Waterloo, Ontario, Canada

A related and subsequent book by the Club of Rome, *Mankind at the Turning Point* (Dutton, 1974), by Mihajlo Mesarovic and Eduard Pestel, describes a more complex global simulation model developed by the authors and its forecasts. A critique of *The Limits to Growth* study is found in *Models of Doom* (Universe, 1973). An objective evaluation of several global models used to forecast trends for policymakers is provided in the U. S. Office of Technology Assessment report, *Global Models, World Futures, and Public Policy: A Critique* (U.S. Government Printing Office, 1982).

55. **Miller, G. Tyler, Jr.** *Living in the Environment: An Introduction to Environmental Science,* 6th ed. Belmont, CA: Wadsworth, 1990. 680 pages.

This is one of the most widely used textbooks on environmental studies. It is big and comprehensive, with good references and examples, and has a lot of data. The text covers such topics as ecology, demography, food supply, pollution, the use of environmental resources, and environmental economics and politics. It also includes opinion essays by leading environmentalists.

"A spectacular introductory text for environmental studies courses. It has an amazingly comprehensive coverage of environmental topics from the world view of the ecological paradigm. Also, it includes detailed charts, maps, graphs, and tables that contain a wealth of additional data."—William G. Berberet, former dean of the College of Liberal Arts at Willamette University

"The standard, introductory college-level text to the environment. This should be must reading for every teacher from middle-year high school through college."—Dennis W. Cheek, coordinator of curriculum development, Science, Technology and Society Education Project, New York Department of Education

"Quite the best book to put in front of students on these issues. Well-planned, fully documented and regularly updated. I have used varous editions of this for over twelve years."—Ian Douglas, professor of geography, University of Manchester, England

Also recommended is Miller's *Resource Conservation and Management* (Wadsworth, 1990).

56.   Mowat, Farley. *Never Cry Wolf.* Boston: Little, Brown, 1963. 175 pages.

Mowat has vowed never to let facts interfere with the truth. In this popular book, he reveals the misinformed and contradictory decisions made by scientists and bureaucrats in the Canadian Wildlife Service, particularly regarding that agency's policies on "predator control." As a young biologist for the service in the late 1950s, he was sent to the Keewatin Barrens in the Arctic to study the purported carnage being inflicted upon deer herds by roving packs of wolves. He spent two summers and a winter studying the behavior and diet of wolves, caribou, deer, rodents, and other fauna, and showed that wolves were not the cause of the problem. The story he presents in *Never Cry Wolf* is both a personal tale of one man's encounter and fascination with the wildlife and wilderness of the Arctic, and a scathing critique of human selfishness and government ineptitude.

57.   Muir, John. *My First Summer in the Sierra.* Boston: Houghton Mifflin, 1911. 354 pages.

Having settled "the bread problem" by agreeing to accompany a shepherd and his flock into the Sierra Nevada in exchange for provisions, Muir began his long-desired trek into the mountains, toward the headwaters of the Merced and Toulomne Rivers (in the area now encompassed by Yosemite National Park). As the snows melted on the higher elevations and the sheep progressed toward the mountain meadows, Muir was able to pursue his studies of the wilderness, taking eight- or ten-mile sidetrips from the temporary encampments along the way. This book contains the daily records of his encounters, observations, and activities during the four-month journey, from June through September of 1869. Environmental writer Tim Palmer, who more than a century later also spent time travelling around the Sierra, said of Muir's writings, "Although flowery by today's standards, his descriptions of the mountains and his emotional response to them have never been equaled" (*The Sierra Nevada: A Mountain Journey,* Island, 1988, p. 9).

58.   Muir, John. *Our National Parks.* Boston: Houghton Mifflin, 1901. 380 pages.

Muir observed that, "thousands of tired, nerve-shaken, overcultured people are beginning to find out that going to the mountains is going home; that mountain parks and reservations are useful not only as fountains of timber and irrigating rivers, but as fountains of life" (p. 1). Thus, he offers to those in the rat race of the early 1900s a guide to the special areas sure to restore mental and physical health. Muir describes the four national parks that had been established by 1900: Yellowstone, General Grant (later renamed Kings Canyon), Sequoia, and Yosemite. He dotes heavily on Yosemite, with six of the book's thirteen chapters describing Yosemite's forests, wild gardens, animals, birds, fountains, and streams. He also devotes a chapter to the thirty national forest reservations in the western United States, many of which later became national parks. There is an interesting account of his meeting with Ralph Waldo Emerson and companions in Yosemite. Muir describes, with some frustration, his futile attempts to take Emerson into the back country of the Sierras, and laments that Emerson seemed "too late in the sundown of his life" and was too "restrained by his handlers." Muir wrote sarcastically: "His party, full of indoor philosophy, failed to see the natural beauty and fullness of promise of my wild plan, and laughed at it in good-natured ignorance, as if it were necessarily amusing to imagine that Boston people might be led to accept Sierra manifestations of God at the price of rough camping" (p. 132). Muir is a spirited and engrossing writer and this book is one of his best.

59. **Muir, John.** *The Yosemite.* Notes and introduction by Frederic R. Gunsky. Garden City, NY: Doubleday, 1962 (orig. pub. 1912). 225 pages.

This is Muir's "guidebook" to his favorite place on earth. He has written with such enthusiasm and eloquence that the reader is often compelled to visit the magical valleys and majestic peaks of the heart of the Sierra Nevada of which he writes. The notes by Gunsky in this particular edition are meant to clarify the text and to bring the reader up-to-date on what has happened in the Yosemite since Muir's death (which occurred soon after the book was published). A notable change, in fact, was the flooding of Hetch Hetchy valley from a dam across the Toulomne River. A set of photographs of the area taken in the late 1890s by Joseph N. LeConte is also included. A special illustrated edition of *The Yosemite*, with photographs by Galen Rowell, is also available (Sierra Club, 1992).

"Muir wrote eloquently and movingly about Yosemite National Park and staked out the high moral ground for wilderness preservation."—Kevin Proescholdt, executive director, Friends of the Boundary Waters Wilderness

60.   Mumford, Lewis. *The Myth of the Machine*. Vol. 1, *Technics and Human Development*. New York: Harcourt, 1967. 342 pages.

————. *The Myth of the Machine*. Vol. 2, *The Pentagon of Power*. New York: Harcourt, 1970. 496 pages.

A concise history in two volumes, by one of the greatest thinkers of the twentieth century, which concerns the history of human development and technological development, as well as the relationship between the two. Donald L. Miller writes in his biography, *Lewis Mumford: A Life* (University of Pittsburgh Press, 1989) that *The Myth of the Machine* "arose from Mumford's sobered view of the age in which he had lived. It is a search for an answer to what he considered the central question of the century: why had technological progress brought with it such catastrophic ruin?" (p. 520).

"Mumford was influential for me partly because I encountered his work when I was ready to think about causes and alternatives to our present course. His thought is encyclopedic, his vision utterly clear, and, I think, wise. The story Mumford relates in these two volumes and his other (extensive) works, weaves human institutions, technology, art, economics, and social life into a pattern. Grand theory we are told, is out. But with Mumford one can see the topography of modern life and its pathologies whole. His discussion of organic social forms is brilliant."—David W. Orr, professor of environmental studies, Oberlin College

"The best historical account of the human impact on the environment."—Theodore Roszak, professor of history, California State University–Hayward

61.   Myers, Norman, ed., with Uma Ram Nath and Melvin Westlake. *Gaia: An Atlas of Planet Management*. Garden City, NY: Anchor/Doubleday, 1984. 272 pages.

Open the Gaia atlas and you will find a bounty of detailed and colorful diagrams, maps, and photographs. The illustrations definitely grab one's attention and prove to be an effective means of communicating environmental facts and concepts. The atlas is organized around several themes, including land, ocean, elements, evolution, humankind, civilization, and management. Each theme is considered from the perspectives of "potential," "crisis," and "management."

Some seventy environmentalists and futurists prepared chapters and essays that address the various themes from these three perspectives, and the generous use of visuals helps to highlight this abundant textual material. Some of the themes, and many new ideas, appear in the more recent *Gaia Atlas of Future Worlds: Challenge and Opportunity in an Age of Change* (Doubleday, 1990), written by Myers.

"I find the pictures speak to people of many different cultures in a way text cannot do."—Dennis L. Meadows, professor of environmental studies, University of New Hampshire

"It has to be the most readable and complete directory to the environment published so far. Excellent illustrations."—Philip Neal, general secretary, National Association for Environmental Education, Walsall, England

"The first truly global environmental treatise that is problem-solving-oriented. Framed in a non-Western way, it displays the problems and solutions visually, like an atlas."—Paul Relis, executive director, Community Environmental Council, Inc.

62. **Naess, Arne. *Ecology, Community, and Life Style: Outline of an Ecosophy.*** Translated and revised by David Rothenberg. Cambridge University Press, 1989. 223 pages.

Naess, a Norwegian philosopher, gave up his faculty position in 1969 to work toward helping the world avert ecocatasrophe. In 1973, he introduced the term "deep ecology" in an article entitled, "The Shallow and the Deep, Long-range Ecology Movements," that appeared in the journal *Inquiry.* Naess characterizes shallow ecology as that involving fights against pollution and resource depletion while still maintaining the health, affluence and security of a relatively privileged few. Deep ecology, on the other hand, involves an alternative worldview, rejecting the "man-in-nature" viewpoint in favor of equalitarianism with all other species. He builds a moral framework upon a foundation of ecological theory, creating what he calls an "ecosophy." His ecosophy acknowledges the uniqueness of humankind, but recognizes that all of nature is tied together. This leads to a discussion about the nature of economic and political systems vis-à-vis the role of deep ecologists.

"A thought-provoking book relating our attitudes and lifestyle to the environment. A good, mind-disturbing text."—M. Pugh Thomas, director, Environmental Resources Unit, University of Salford, Salford, England

63.	**Nash, Roderick.** *Wilderness and the American Mind.* 3d ed. New Haven, CT: Yale University Press, 1982 (orig. pub. 1967). 425 pages.

This study of the American view of wilderness sees the confrontation with nature and awe of wild places as the essence of American culture and civilization. Nash traces the history of wilderness perception and philosophy from the classical Greeks to the romantic and transcendental views of Henry Thoreau. The political struggle for wilderness preservation is depicted in the fights to save the Hetch Hetchy valley in California from being flooded, and the Alaskan landscape from the impacts of oil exploration and extraction, as well as in the development of a wilderness ethic with the writings of John Muir and Aldo Leopold. *Wilderness and the American Mind* was based on Nash's doctoral dissertation at the University of Wisconsin, and since its publication in 1967 has been one of the most important histories and guidebooks of the American conservation movement.

"A scholarly treatment of the social and psychological concepts of nature as transformed over time in America."—Diane Bowen, chair, Loma Prita chapter of the Sierra Club

"An intellectual history of the American conservation movement and environmental movement."—J. Baird Callicott, professor of philosophy and of natural resources, University of Wisconsin–Stevens Point

"Essential to understanding the philosophical foundation of the National Wilderness Preservation System."—James R. Conner, chair, Montana chapter of the Sierra Club

"The best history of American attempts to appreciate and preserve wilderness."—Frank J. Popper, chair, department of urban studies, Rutgers, the State University of New Jersey

64.	**National Wildlife Federation.** *Conservation Directory.* Washington, DC: National Wildlife Federation, 1992 (annual). 398 pages.

This directory is perhaps the most comprehensive source available for names, addresses, and telephone numbers of conservationists and environmentalists in the United States. It lists relevant congressional committees, members of congress for all states, federal and state conservation and environmental agencies, and national and state nongovernmental organizations. The directory provides a description for each agency and organization, including mission statement, size and budget, and publications. There is also a listing of addresses and telephone numbers for national wildlife refuges, forests, parks, and seashores. The section on conservation and environment organizations of foreign governments is rather brief. The directory has one index listing names of individuals and another listing the 1200 or so newsletters and other publications produced by each agency and organization. For information on additional directories, see also entries 190 (on international organizations) and 475 (United States).

65.   Odum, Eugene P. *Fundamentals of Ecology.* 3d ed. Philadelphia: Saunders, 1971. 574 pages.

This textbook is favored by many in the biological sciences. Eugene Odum is a prominent name in the field of ecology and his pioneering research on ecological systems has had an important influence in helping people to think about and understand the impacts of pollution. The concepts of ecological functions and processes characterized by Odum, including how materials and energy flow through "ecosystems," perhaps more than any other concept began to show people how pollution could both disperse and accumulate in the environment and how humans, as integral parts of the ecosystem, could be affected. *Fundamentals of Ecology* presents the concepts and theories of ecology in terms of systems, describes and compares the characteristics of several types of ecoystems (freshwater, marine, estuarine, and terrestrial), and concludes with a review of ecosystems theory and analysis, resource protection, pollution control, human health, and well-being.

"A classic statement for the field. Probably cited more than any book in the field of ecology for its seminal insights."—Dennis W. Cheek, coordinator of curriculum development, Science, Technology, and Society Education Project, New York Department of Education

66.   Odum, Howard T. *Environment, Power, and Society.* New York: Wiley-Interscience, 1971. 331 pages.

Howard Odum's book, like that of his brother Eugene (see entry 65), was an early and important work on the flow of energy and materials in environmental systems. He uses systems dynamics and modelling to show the cause-and-effect linkages and pathways between various components of the natural world, and between humans and their environment. He even characterizes systems of "energetics" and the role of power for various types of human societal processes: economics, law, and religion. To illustrate the technical concepts he presents in the text, he provides numerous "network diagrams" that show the flow of such theoretical energies and materials. The book is a bit complex in certain parts, and therefore is probably most useful to advanced students in ecological sciences.

67.   Office of Technology Assessment. Various Reports. Washington, DC: U.S. Government Printing Office.

The Office of Technology Assessment (OTA) was created in 1972 to help the U.S. Congress anticipate and plan for the impacts of technological change on society. To carry out this mission, OTA conducts, at the behest of a twelve-member bipartisan congressional committee, detailed and objective analyses of many complex technological issues. The results of these studies appear in a series of balanced and insightful reports that can be very useful to citizens wanting information on particular topics. For example, a report called *Technologies to Maintain Biological Diversity* (March 1987), outlines basic concepts and concerns related to biological conservation, including the advantages and disadvantages of various technological means used to preserve biological diversity. The report also provides some history of federal legislation and international agreements related to conservation and summarizes its findings, recommendations, and policy options to Congress on the maintenance of biological diversity.

A selection of other OTA reports which may be of importance to some environmentalists includes: *Building Energy Efficiency* (May 1992); *Complex Cleanup: The Environmental Legacy of Nuclear Weapons Production* (February 1991); *Changing By Degrees: Steps to Reduce Greenhouse Gases* (February 1991); *Beneath the Bottom Line: Agricultural Approaches to Reduce Agrichemical Contamination of Groundwater* (May 1990); *Coping with an Oiled Sea: An Analysis of Oil Spill Response Technologies* (March 1990); *Facing America's Trash: What Next for Municipal Solid Waste* (October 1989); *Catching Our Breath: Next Steps for Reducing Urban Ozone* (July 1989); *Pesticide Residues in Food: Technologies for Detection* (October 1988); *Field-Testing Engineered Organisms: Genetic and Ecological Issues* (May 1988); and *Technologies to Sustain Tropical Forest Resources* (March 1984). A catalog listing these and other reports can be obtained from the U.S. Congress, Office of Technology Assessment, Washington, DC 20510.

68.   Olson, Sigurd. *The Singing Wilderness.* New York: Knopf, 1956. 244 pages.

As Olson says in his introduction, "The singing wilderness has to do with the calling of loons, northern lights, and the great silences of a land lying northwest of Lake Superior" (p. 5). Olson's books contain some of the best nature writing available and *The Singing Wilderness* is his best known work. In it he depicts and north country and its seasonal changes with beauty, reverence, and awe, and paints a vivid picture for the reader of the natural world there. Complementing the text are back-and-white line drawings by Francis Lee Jacques. Olson's will always be the clearest voice from the north woods.

"In this, Olson's first book, he describes in beautiful prose the natural history and value of the Quetico-Superior wilderness and the area along the Minnesota-Ontario border."—Kevin Proescholdt, executive director, Friends of the Boundary Waters Wilderness

69. **Ophuls, William.** *Ecology and the Politics of Scarcity: Prologue to a Political Theory of the Steady State.* San Francisco: Freeman, 1977. 303 pages.

Ophuls's basic claim is that contemporary ecological crises require immediate societal and technological changes to counter the negative trends. He suggests that by the time these various crises reach their peaks at some point in the future, it will be too late to do anything about them. In this book, Ophuls first defines scarcity in terms of the ecological crises we face in population, food, mining, pollution, energy, and technology. He then outlines historical trends in politics and economics that contributed to these crises, and offers a paradigm for a shift toward a sustainable state, proposing such ideals as "ecological self-restraint" as a means for reaching that goal. His bibliographic essays at the end of each chapter are very useful and interesting. Ophuls and A. Stephen Boyan, Jr. have since written an update, *Ecology and the Politics of Scarcity Revisited: The Unravelling of the American Dream* (Freeman, 1992).

"Puts environmental issues into a broad geopolitical context."—Alan Miller, professor of psychology, University of New Brunswick, Fredericton, Canada

"A thorough, carefully developed work showing how American political values and institutions are poorly adapted to a future in which resources that can be exploited freely are scarce rather than in excess."—Richard L. Perrine, professor of civil engineering, University of California–Los Angeles

70. **O'Riordan, Timothy.** *Environmentalism.* 2d ed. London: Pion, 1981 (orig. pub. 1976). 403 pages.

"Environmentalism is as much a state of being as a mode of conduct or a set of policies," suggests O'Riordan in his opening (p. ix). In this book, he reviews the various perspectives taken by those who embrace "environmentalism." He characterizes the debates between growth and no-growth advocates, and reviews the frameworks used to measure environmental quality and human attitudes about the environment. He gives a thorough review of environmental politics and law, and suggests that "environmentalism as a vehicle for social reform is fuelled by two complementary anxieties" (p. 301), which are the realization of scarcity of resources and the uncertainty about the future. He concludes with a discussion of environmentalism and its role in a new global world order.

"This older book helps us to understand the way in which the environmental movement is set is a context of changing political attitudes."—Ian Douglas, professor of geography, University of Manchester, England

"The key comprehensive work on the development and state of concern for the environment from a wide variety of perspectives: philosophical, economical, planning, law, political, and institutional. Excellent bibliography. Noteworthy is the book's coverage of both North American and English (and to some extent other nations') environmental issues and initiatives."—D. Scott Slocombe, School of Urban and Regional Planning, University of Waterloo, Ontario, Canada

71. **Osborn, Fairfield.** *Our Plundered Planet.* Boston: Little, Brown, 1948. 217 pages.

Osborn had a distinguished career in service to a number of conservation organizations. He was a member of the board of trustees of the New York Zoological Society during the 1920s and 1930s, becoming president in 1940. He later was a cofounder of The Conservation Foundation and served as its president from 1948 to 1962. He was also active in the American Forestry Society, the Council of the Save-the-Redwoods League, and the International Committee for Bird Preservation, all of which kept him at the forefront of the conservation movement for many years. Osborn expresses in this book his deeply felt concerns about the plight of humanity and the rapid depletion of the resource bases upon which all life depends. "Man must recognize the necessity of cooperating with nature. He must temper his demands and use and conserve the natural living resources of this earth in a manner that alone can provide for the continuation of civilization" (p. 201).

"One of the first books concerned with world population and resources. Inspiring."—Raymond F. Dasmann, professor emeritus of environmental studies, University of California–Santa Cruz

72.   Peterson, Roger Tory. *A Field Guide to the Birds*. 4th ed. Boston: Houghton Mifflin, 1980 (orig. pub. 1934). 384 pages.

————. *A Field Guide to Western Birds*. 3rd ed. Boston: Houghton Mifflin, 1990 (orig. pub. 1941). 432 pages.

Peterson is certainly one of the world's greatest painters of wildlife, and his field guides for bird identification are an institutional feature of the environmental movement. He developed the "Peterson System" of bird identification, a simple, easy-to-use method of bird identification that uses a few key and easily visible field marks to distinguish between species. This was a revolutionary change from field guides that had been used previously, and Peterson's guides have enjoyed widespread success.

"The field guide devised by Roger Tory Peterson was a great assist to birdwatchers and the more people became interested in birds, the more they became environmentally aware. Birds also are indicators of environmental health."—Alice L. Fuller, board of directors member, State College Bird Club

"Although not the first field guide, Peterson's guides since the first one was issued in 1934 have led the way to public enlightenment about the natural world. This was the essential catalyst to the subsequent environmental movement."—John A. Gustafson, treasurer, American Nature Study Society

"Introduction of the first Peterson 'field guide' opened up a new world for lay persons interested in the world around them. One no longer had to be a professional to identify birds—this sparked a great interest in birds and later in other biological fields. With interest comes concern."—Loyal A. Mehrhoff, botanist, Bernice P. Bishop Museum of Natural and Cultural History

"Environmentalism without an understanding of nature is hollow. The birdwatcher's bible was introduced many of us to a personal association with nature."—David E. Blockstein, executive director, Committee for the National Institutes for the Environment

"The revolutionary book that, in turning bird-watching from a pastime of the elite into a preoccupation of millions, created a working core and heart of the American environmental movement."—Joseph Kastner, author

Although personal preferences for field guides differ among the North American birding community, most bird-watchers have on their bookshelves the Peterson guides as well as two other field guides with different presentational styles: *Field Guide to the Birds of North America* (National Geographic Society, 1987), and *Birds of North America: A Guide to Field Identification* (Western, 1983), by Chandler S. Robbins, Bertel Bruun, and Arthur Singer.

73. **Porritt, Jonathon.** *Seeing Green: The Politics of Ecology Explained.* Foreword by Petra Kelly. New York: Blackwell, 1984. 252 pages.

Porritt, who as a teacher in 1975 was inspired by magazine articles to join the Ecology Party in Great Britain, has written a history and analysis of the green political movements. He reviews the "green literature," providing a synthesis of books and articles over the previous decade on green politics. Porritt, now director of Friends of the Earth International, suggests that a basic characteristic of the green movement is an awareness of the different impacts of ecological devastation on the poor versus the affluent. He also believes that the economics on which industrial capitalism is based, which he says has benefitted a relatively small number of people, is neither able to sustain society's need nor protect the planet: "There can be no clearer demonstration that those who are working for a better planet must simultaneously devote themselves to working for social justice" (p. 98).

"Describes green politics as the rediscovery of old wisdom made relevant in a very different age."—Giselda Castro, vice president, Ação Democrática Feminina Gaúcha/Amigos da Terra (Friends of the Earth), Porto Alegre, Brazil

74. **Reisner, Marc P.** *Cadillac Desert: The American West and Its Disappearing Water.* New York: Viking, 1986. 582 pages.

Although many books have been written on water in the American West, Reisner captured the imaginations of many young environmentalists through his spirited history of water development in California, Arizona, and other parts of the region. Reisner, who worked as a writer for the Natural Resources Defence Council, combines a thoughtful interpretation of previous literature with numerous interviews to show how political power and economic growth transformed the western landscape. Beginning with the exploration of the West by

John Wesley Powell, *Cadillac Desert* documents the thirsty growth of cities like Los Angeles and the extravagant use of water by agribusinesses. Reisner is unashamedly critical of the developers, dam builders, and public agencies like the Bureau of Reclamation and Corps of Engineers, who showed little concern for either environment or equity in the race to exploit rivers like the Colorado and to tame them with dams. The book is enlivened with stories about the individuals who fought for and against the engineering of the western waters.

"'Reclaiming' the West required power and money, toward which water ran uphill. No one who reads this book will ever forget the names Floyd Dominy and William Mulholland. Or speak of them with reverence."—James R. Conner, chair, Montana Chapter of the Sierra Club

"A tremendous amount of research has been turned into an absorbing account of an issue (water development) that has not yet been addressed rationally, or even with some degree of sanity."—Shannon A. Horst, director of public awareness, Center for Holistic Resource Management

"This brings home the seriousness of water problems in the West, how we got here, and (the best part of the book) where we go from here."—Meredith Taylor, chair, Wyoming chapter of the Sierra Club

An additional and highly recommended history of water resources development in the American West is Donald Worster's *Rivers of Empire: Water, Aridity, and the Growth of the American West* (Pantheon, 1985).

75.   **Rolston, Holmes, III.** *Environmental Ethics: Duties to and Values in the Natural World.* Philadelphia: Temple University Press, 1988. 391 pages.

Rolston acknowledges the moral obligation of humans to nature. In a series of essays, he describes a philosophy which outlines human duties to sentient life, or organic life, to endangered species, and to ecosystems. He also presents an "ethic of the commons" and an "ethic for commerce" and, in a notable exercise, lists a set of questions to help determine the scope of one's sense of "residence" in the environment.

"Traditionally, ethicists have examined the obligations of human beings to one another. Rolston examines the obligations of mankind to the natural world."—James R. Conner, chair, Montana chapter of the Sierra Club

Also recommended is Rolston's *Philosophy Gone Wild: Essays in Environmental Ethics* (Prometheus, 1986).

76.   Roszak, Theodore. *Where the Wasteland Ends: Politics and Transcendence in Post-Industrial Society.* New York: Doubleday, 1972. 492 pages.

This is a passionate critique of the narrow focus of the scientific world view, industrialism, urbanism, and capitalism, and is a call for spiritual renewal and alternative lifestyles based on decentralized, deurbanized, small-scale communities. Roszak argues that technology, objectivity, reductionism and quantification have alienated people from nature and each other, resulting in pollution, loneliness, and artificialness. He uses the poetry of Blake, Wordsworth and Goethe to express his disquiet with regard to technological society and to communicate his alternative vision.

"A brilliant, emotional polemic on the horrors of technocratic thinking."—Alan Miller, professor of psychology, University of New Brunswick, Fredericton, Canada

77.   Sale, Kirkpatrick. *Dwellers in the Land: The Bioregional Vision.* San Francisco: Sierra Club, 1985. 217 pages.

Sale describes a "bioregion" as "any part of the earth's surface whose rough boundaries are determined by natural characteristics rather than human dictates, distinguishable from other areas by particular attributes of flora, fauna, water, climate, soils, and landforms, and by the human settlements and cultures those attributes have given rise to" (p. 55). He uses the concept of the bioregion as a framework for analyzing human-nature interactions. He also suggests that, conceptually, the bioregion is the scale at which most of these interactions might naturally occur, through which a stable, self-sustaining, and self-regulating ecological system might best support human life.

Also recommended is Sale's *Human Scale* (Seeker and Warburg, 1980).

78.   Sax, Joseph L. *Mountains without Handrails: Reflections on the National Parks.* Ann Arbor: University of Michigan Press, 1980. 152 pages.

Sax offers a good summary of the debate about the use and role of national parks and wilderness areas. Preservationists such as Edward Abbey (see entry 1) want these areas to remain unspoiled (meaning no roads, accommodations, or other facilities) and, in essence, off-limits to the citizens who are unable to leave behind the comforts of civilization. The other side of the debate, of course, is that the parks are part of the public domain and should not be merely refuges for an elite group of hardy backpackers. After analyzing the nature of the debate and the arguments of "preservationists" and "automobile tourists," Sax presents a compromise view that while parks should have areas of undisturbed wilderness, and that their role should be to entice people out of their automobiles, there should be areas where all persons, whether novices to the outdoors, elderly, or infirmed, can experience the natural world without great difficulty. While the conflicting demands imposed on parks and wilderness areas remains a problem for those who are charged with protecting and managing these areas, Sax's book does help the reader understand the forces and motives involved.

"Abbey called attention to industrial tourism. Sax explained what our national parks could be if industrial tourism were replaced with contemplative recreation."—James R. Conner, chair, Montana chapter of the Sierra Club

79. **Schell, Jonathan.** *The Fate of the Earth.* New York: Knopf, 1982. 244 pages.

The devastating and terrifying effects of nuclear weapons, and the ways in which nuclear war could lead to the extinction of the human race are graphically and humanely described in *The Fate of the Earth*. Schell uses accounts of the Hiroshima atomic bomb, government reports, and interviews with scientists to establish what the aftermath of nuclear war has been and could be. He sets the nuclear dilemma within the context of humanity's mastery over nature and its ability to destroy nature, and thereby its ability to destroy the human species as well. In the last part of the book, he examines the political conditions and theories that have produced the arms race, such as the concept of deterrence, and then presents a number of ways in which humanity could escape the threat of nuclear annihilation. First appearing in the *New Yorker*, *The Fate of the Earth* became a best seller, contributing to the widespread democratization of knowledge and the debate about nuclear weapons and the arms race.

"Vividly connects military policy with environmental issues."—Eric

Katz, assistant professor of philosophy, New Jersey Institute of Technology

"Peers into the terrifying abyss of extinction and presents a vision for recapturing our futures."—Giselda Castro, vice president, Ação Democrática Feminina Gaúcha/Amigos da Terra (Friends of the Earth), Porto Alegre, Brazil

80.   **Schneider, Stephen.** *Global Warming: Are We Entering the Greenhouse Century?* San Francisco: Sierra Club, 1989. 317 pages.

Schneider, a senior scientist at the National Center for Atmospheric Research in Boulder, Colorado, documents the debate about global warming, from both the scientific and political perspectives. As a researcher and an influential contributor to policymaking at the national and international levels as well, Schneider offers a unique perspective on the global warming issue, as only someone in the center of the debate can do. He describes how the climate models have been used to study global warming by forecasting what the effects of temperature increases and other impacts might be. He also discusses how scientists have debated these issues and tried to communicate their importance to policymakers, the media, and the public. Schneider is very much concerned that the average citizen should be able to participate in these debates, and not feel shut out because the issues are "too scientific." Perhaps the best contribution of his book is his advice on how citizens can stay involved and not get lost in the complexity of the debate.

"In addition to giving a great deal of data on global warming and the greenhouse effect, the most notable part of the book is the way it shows the impact a technical expert can have in influencing public policy, and the problems of doing so. Discusses very well the limits of what a scientist should and should not say. Very clear on making a separation between scientific evidence and personal values."—Gary Benenson, associate professor of technology, City College of the City University of New York

81.   **Schumacher, Ernst F.** *Small Is Beautiful: Economics as if People Mattered.* New York: Harper, 1973. 290 pages.

Schumacher criticizes classical economic theory with its emphasis on materialism and economic growth, and proposes an alternative based on smallness and permanence. He suggests that the cultivation and the expansion of needs is the antithesis of wisdom. He contends that production and economic growth do not necessarily result in a high quality of life. Schumacher discusses the constraints of land, materials, and energy on sustained economic growth and notes that the Third World has special problems of unemployment, lack of food, education, and health. He proposes that intermediate technologies and regional educational programs can help solve these problems. "I have no doubt that it is possible to give a new direction to technological development, a direction that shall lead it back to the real needs of man, and that also means: *to the actual size of man.* Man is small, and, therefore small is beautiful" (p. 159).

"A most fundamental work, now known throughout the world, by perhaps the most important resource economist who ever lived."—John E. Carroll, professor of environmental conservation, University of New Hampshire

"This book made—to a broad audience—the all-important point that the primary goal of economic development should be to wipe out poverty without exhausting natural resources, and it gave birth to the 'appropriate technology' movement."—Kathleen Courrier, director of publications, World Resources Institute

"It is the economical answer to so many of our problems and gives a clear idea of how to cope with the world's crises."—António Eloy, director, Associação Portuguesa de Ecologistas/Amigos da Terra (Friends of the Earth), Lisbon, Portugal

"While not strictly a book on nature and environment, I consider it like a 'perestroika' of the conventional and established economic thinking with its associated ramifications on the environment and natural resources."—Apichai Sunchindah, program officer, Swiss Development Cooperation, Bangkok, Thailand

82. **Sears, Paul B.** *Deserts on the March.* 4th ed. Norman: University of Oklahoma, 1980 (orig. pub. 1935). 264 pages.

Sears had moved to Oklahoma in 1927 to serve as chair of the department of botany at the University of Oklahoma. Soon thereafter, though, as historian Angie Debo noted, "it was was the sight of the dry wind scooping up the Oklahoma soil that drove his pen" (*Oklahoma: Foot-Loose and Fancy Free,* University of Oklahoma Press, 1949, p. 78). Sears wrote *Deserts on the March* to explain the causes of the destruction of the North American semiarid grasslands, and to alert people to the loss of topsoil from a whole region and the great dust storms that resulted. Although somewhat restricted in its analysis, particularly concerning the political economy of the region, the book was nonetheless an important contribution to the small but growing body of literature about the human impact on the world's environment. Another recommended book on the topic is Edward H. Faulkner's *Plowman's Folly* (Grosset & Dunlap, 1943).

"This 1935 volume was the first analytical, practical, and also philosophical approach to an ecological disaster: the Dust Bowl."—Sharon F. Francis, coordinator, New Hampshire Natural Resources Forum

83. Seuss, Dr. *The Lorax.* New York: Random House. 70 pages.

This is the story of a "Once-ler," who arrives by wagon and settles in the beautiful land of "Truffula trees," which is inhabited by a group of creatures who are dependent on the fruit of the trees. The Once-ler soon learns that he can produce and successfully market "Thneeds" using certain parts of the trees. He begins to chop down all the trees in the land, and the Thneed factory spews out so many pollutants into the air and water that the native creatures are forced to leave. Soon there is nothing but a barren landscape, devoid even of the very Truffula trees that the Once-ler used to make Thneeds. *The Lorax* is a creative and powerful story about the exploitation of natural resources, loss of biodiversity, and local economic collapse, all wrapped up in the world of Dr. Seuss's entertaining storytelling and enchanting characters.

"This book brought environmental concerns and environmental ethics to children and in the process to many adults."—Warren Gartner, president, Environmental Education Association of Indiana

"A profoundly religious tale of sin and the possibility of redemption through trees, the truth."—David Haenke, director, Ecological Society Project of the Tides Foundation

"As close to being a perfect children's book as anything we've read."—Elissa Wolfson, managing editor, and Will Nixon, associate editor, *E Magazine*

"This story about the destruction of natural resources and consequent pollution is excellent for all ages."—Nancy Zuschlag, president, Colorado Alliance for Environmental Education

84. Shiva, Vandana. *Staying Alive: Women, Ecology, and Survival in India.* London: Zed, 1989. 234 pages.

The author offers a non-Western, feminist perspective on development, science, and natural resource management. She indicates in her introduction: "This book has grown out of my involvement with women's struggles for survival in India over the last decade. It is informed both by the suffering and insights of those who struggle to sustain and conserve life, and whose struggles question the meaning of a progress, a science, a development which destroys life and threatens survival" (p. xiv). Shiva analyzes the historical roots of development and science to demonstrate how both women and the more humane aspects of these disciplines have been overlooked in these areas. She illustrates these analyses with historical accounts of forest management in India, the world food crisis, and contamination of the earth's water, and offers an alternative paradigm that incorporates more humane and rational management of natural resources.

"Clearly shows the fallacious thinking which pits economics, growth, and development against people and the environment."—William Ellis, editor, TRANET

"A powerful argument for ecofeminism—and for the Third World perspective on the meaning of development."—Susan E. Place, assistant professor of geography, California State University–Chico

"Great book, great writer—a remarkable woman!"—John Revington, director, Rainforest Information Centre, Lismore, New South Wales, Australia

85. **Soulé, Michael E., ed. *Conservation Biology: The Science of Scarcity and Diversity*.** Sunderland, MA: Sinauer, 1986. 584 pages.

Paul and Anne Ehrlich suggest that "the idea that natural systems and species are among the valuable common resources of an interdependent world is an idea whose time has come" (*Extinction: The Causes and Consequences of the Disappearance of Species,* p. 299; see entry 33). Michael Soulé has been at the forefront of the emerging field of conservation biology, which is dedicated to the idea of preserving the abundance and diversity of life on our planet. Soule and his writings have helped define the direction of research and practice for the discipline. This book expands upon the articles prepared by a number of conservation biology experts that first appeared in *Conservation Biology: An Evolutionary-Ecological Perspective* (Sinauer, 1980), edited by Soulé and Bruce A. Wilcox. It includes papers from a conference held at the University of Michigan in 1985 on topics ranging from population genetics to philosophy and ethics. Soulé and Kathryn A. Kohm are editors of an additional related book, *Research Priorities for Conservation Biology* (Island, 1989).

86.   **Stegner, Wallace.** *Beyond the Hundredth Meridian: John Wesley Powell and the Second Opening of the West.* Introduction by Bernard DeVoto. Boston: Houghton Mifflin, 1954. 438 pages.

Stegner portrays the history of the nineteenth-century American West through the persona of John Wesley Powell—scientist, writer, explorer of the West, and master of the federal bureaucracy. Though Stegner focuses on Powell, this is not necessarily as much a biography as it is a vivid analysis of the governmental policies that Powell and his contemporaries promoted. Powell was a proponent of technological management of the arid environments in the West, through dams, irrigation projects, and other efforts. Stegner writes about Powell's legacy: "All the great river systems—Missouri, Columbia, Colorado, Rio Grande, Sacramento-San Joaquin, and every tributary branch and twig—have been surveyed and mapped in even greater detail than he intended. Blue river lines are strung with the irregular blue beads of reservoirs or projected reservoirs, and the storage dams, as well as the map symbols that record them and the topographic base map on which they are superimposed, are part of the heritage that Powell left" (p. 353). For Powell's own account of his life and adventures, see entry 290.

"Understanding the American West begins with understanding John Wesley Powell, and there is no better biography of Powell than Stegner's."—James R. Conner, chair, Montana chapter of the Sierra Club

87.   **Stone, Christopher D.** *Should Trees Have Standing? Toward Legal Rights for Natural Objects.* Foreword by Garrett Hardin. Los Altos, CA: Kaufman, 1974. 102 pages.

In April 1972, the U.S. Supreme Court issued its ruling against the Sierra Club in a case in which they tried to prevent a developer from building a ski development in the Mineral King Valley in the Sequoia National Forest. The Sierra Club had claimed that the recreational facilities proposed by the developer would adversely affect the aesthetics and ecology of the area. A district court had granted a preliminary injunction, but the Ninth Circuit Court of Appeals reversed that decision, saying that the club lacked standing because it had not alledged any adverse affects on the organization or its members. On appeal to the U.S. Supreme Court, the majority opinion upheld the court of appeals' ruling. Justice William O. Douglas, however, wrote a strong and widely-quoted dissent, saying that "contemporary concern for protecting nature's ecological equilibrium should lead to the conferral of standing upon environmental objects to sue for their own preservation," and he then referred to Stone's article, "Should Trees Have Standing?" published in the *Southern California Law Review*. This book is a reprint of Stone's article, in which he elaborates on moral and legal arguments about judicial standing for natural objects. It provides an ample foundation for the text of the Supreme Court's ruling on the Sierra Club v. Morton case, which is provided as an appendix.

"Ethical dilemma about plants and animals unable to speak for themselves; it causes the reader to reflect and react."—Lori Colomeda, education director, Schuylkill Center for Environmental Education

"A serious essay proposing that in our legal system some natural objects that have value in perpetuity be accorded legal 'rights' in the same sense as corporations under our system."—Richard L. Perrine, professor of civil engineering, University of California—Los Angeles

"A fascinating piece of work that forces one to reevaluate the commonly-held anthropocentric beliefs regarding value of life."—R. Rajagopal, professor of geography and of civil and environmental engineering, University of Iowa

88. Thomas, Lewis. *The Lives of a Cell.* New York: Viking, 1974. 153 pages.

This is a short book, a collection of essays, that discusses the nature of information and the means that have arisen among living organisms for communicating and understanding, such as through chemical signals, body movements, sounds, or langauge. Thomas even describes the flow of information at the cellular level and makes comparisons at the organismic, group, community, and global scales.

"Lewis Thomas's intellectual links with natural phenomena are penetrating and wondrous at the same time."—Joseph H. Chadbourne, president, Institute for Environmental Education

Also recommended is Thomas's *The Medusa and the Snail: More Notes of a Biology Watcher* (Viking, 1979).

89. **Thomas, William L., Jr., ed., with Carl O. Sauer, Marston Bates, and Lewis Mumford. *Man's Role in Changing the Face of the Earth.*** Chicago: University of Chicago Press, 1956. 1193 pages.

In 1955, a group of distinguished academics gathered in Princeton, New Jersey, to assume a major scholarly undertaking: to look at the activities of humans, both historically and prospectively, in influencing environmental changes. The conference was sponsored by the Wenner-Gren Foundation for Anthropological Research, and produced an assemblage of sixty-five detailed and well-referenced papers on the subject—nearly 1200 pages in printed text! The conference reflected the multiple approaches used by those in different discplines to describe an integrated view of human modification of the earth. In addition to the editors and collaborators (Thomas, Sauer, Bates and Mumford), some notable participants were Edgar Anderson, Harrison Brown, Kenneth Boulding, F. Fraser Darling, Clarence Glacken, Luna Leopold, Fairfield Osborn, Paul Sears, Arthur N. Strahler, C. W. Thornthwaite, Edward Ullman, and Abel Wolman. The book is divided into three sections: "Retrospect" provides an examination of historic influences on the earth, focussing on the agency and attitudes of humans in shaping those influences; "Process" describes the means of environmental change such as deforestation and soil erosion; and "Prospect" looks at the future for human beings on earth, including a view of the limits to population growth, and of the limits of raw materials and nonrenewable energy sources. (see also entry 92 for a more recent product of scientific collaboration.)

"I read this massive collection while still in graduate school. It made me realize for the first time the full scope and utter pervasiveness of man as ecological dominant—not only in this century, but well in the past as well."—Marvin W. Baker, Jr., associate professor of geography, University of Oklahoma

"Probably the first 'environmental' book, in the current sense of word. This was my principal reference for my own book *Environmental Conservation* [see entry 161], first published in 1959."—Raymond F. Dasmann, professor emeritus of environmental studies, University of California–Santa Cruz

"A classic book that has received relatively little attention—a more thorough documentation of the theme first developed by Marsh [in *Man and Nature;* see entry 52]."—Charles H. Southwick, professor of biology, University of Colorado–Boulder

90.   **Thoreau, Henry David.** *Walden.* With essays by E. B. White and Max Lerner. Philadelphia: Courage, 1987 (orig. pub. 1854, Tickenor and Fields). 207 pages.

This is the book that has inspired so many naturalists and back-to-earth advocates. In *Walden,* Thoreau demonstrated that living simply and frugally had both personal and social virtue. "I went to the woods because I wished to live deliberately, to front only the essential facts of life, and see if I could not learn what it had to teach, and not, when I came to die, discover that I had not lived . . . I wanted to live deep and suck out all the marrow of life, to live so sturdily and Spartan-like as to put to rout all that was not life, to cut a broad swath and shave close, to drive life into a corner, and reduce it to its lowest terms, and if it proved to be mean, why then to get the whole and genuine meanness of it, and publish its meanness to the world; or if it were sublime, to know it by experience, and be able to give a true account of it in my next excursion" (p. 60). His message is interpreted by some as anti-urban, or anti-industrial. The spirtual notions of transcendentalism found in this book have influenced the writings of generations of nature writers. Although this is a classic it is not easy to read, given the older and denser style in which it was written. But it is worth the effort.

"This book was the first and foremost influence on my own environmental ethic. A profoundly spiritual experience with nature courtesy of the mind and metaphor of Thoreau."—Diane Bowen, chair, Loma Prita chapter of the Sierra Club

"Caring for the world we live in goes back to another century with this remarkable interpreter of the natural world."—Alice L. Fuller, board of directors, State College Bird Club

"One of the first and most well-known discussions of man's relationship with nature."—Warren Gartner, president, Environmental Education Association of Indiana

"This book has awakened the conservation consciences of generations of movers and shakers—a classic that still speaks to the human relationship with the natural environment as well as to society."— John A. Gustafson, treasurer, American Nature Study Society

"Lest I forget basics, I must add Thoreau. He is a young man's writer who can bemuse us when we get gray! His influence is so pervasive, he probably gets left off lists like this one. He must be included. His perspective, not without its ambiguities, is fundamental to the ecological world view. His critique of materalism is essential reading."—David W. Orr, professor of environmental studies, Oberlin College

"As a book reviewer and fishing writer, I dip into this once or twice a year. The insights, Thoreau's sense of humor, and the simplicity and directness of the writing have remained enjoyable for me during the last twenty years."—John Rowen, books editor, *Albany Report* for the Environmental Planning Lobby

"My first introduction to nature writing through the public school system. The first to reveal philosophy of nature and all the things we should be listening to in nature's messages."—Kristie Seaman, education director, Sanibel-Captiva Conservation Foundation

"For whatever reasons, this is one of the 'environmental' books that is first read or comes to mind. At the time, I questioned but understood Thoreau's behavior and desire, i.e. a young man turning away from civilization for a more natural life in the woods. Despite his egotism and verbosity, it is imagery more than text—a simple life in a cabin by a tranquil pond—that stays with me and is known to many who have never read *Walden*."—Frederick Sepp, biological sciences librarian, Pennsylvania State University

"This one has so influenced my whole life that I am volunteering to rescue Walden, which the state manages as a swim-recreation park. The goal is to get Walden into sanctuary status, as a monument to Thoreau. Thoreau really began the conservation ethic by his prophetic thinking."—Mary P. Sherwood, chair, Walden Forever Wild

"I'd have never become a citizen, were it not for this book. Plus, it converted me from shallow predator to complicated philosopher, and gave me the will to write. This book said it's OK to love nature with all your heart."—Donald Snow, director, Northern Lights Institute

"Someone who looked at nature in a special way—up close and personal."—C. Dart Thalman, former director, Quebec Labrador Foundation/Atlantic Center for the Environment

"Still the most influential and meaningful North American book, because of the way it sets up the relationship between the individual (American) and nature as a moral nexus."—Peter Timmerman, researcher, Institute for Environmental Studies, University of Toronto, Ontario, Canada

"Thoreau anticipated and articulated contemporary concern for environment in terms of the aesthetic resource (wild nature) and in terms of the philosophical bases for a nature-humanity relationship."—Thomas R. Vale, professor of geography, University of Wisconsin–Madison

91. **Timberlake, Lloyd.** *Africa in Crisis: The Causes, the Cures of Environmental Bankruptcy.* London: Earthscan, 1985. 232 pages.

Timberlake is a senior writer with the International Institute for Environment and Development in London. In this book, he describes the African famine in the mid-1980s and argues that this is the result of inappropriate economic, agricultural, and environmental policies and practices, which have created social groups and geographical areas at the margins of survival. In other words, he believes that these groups and areas have become more vulnerable to environmental stresses or extremes, such as droughts, and are more likely to suffer severe consequences. Claiming that technical solutions alone will not resolve these problems, Timberlake emphasizes the need to address the socioeconomic and political factors that are the driving forces behind environmental degradation. He states that equitable access to arable land, irrigation supplies, fertilizer, and credit are all necessary to halt this degradation. *Africa in Crisis* was the winner of the 1985 World Hunger Media Award. Another important book by Timberlake and Anders Wijkman is *Natural Disasters: Acts of God or Acts of Man?* (Earthscan, 1984), which examines the role of human activities in exacerbating the impacts of environmental extremes.

92. **Turner, B. L., II, William C. Clark, Robert W. Kates, John F. Richards, Jessica T. Mathews, and William B. Meyer, eds.** *The Earth Transformed by Human Action: Global and Regional Changes in the Biosphere over the Past 300 Years.* New York: Cambridge University Press, 1990. 713 pages.

Inspired by such previous works as *Man's Role in Changing the Face of the Earth* (see entry 89) and George Perkins Marsh's *Man and Nature* (see entry 52), a number of prominent scholars have comprehensively reviewed the ways in which human activity has altered the earth system. This book is structured into four sections. The first section looks at the major forces of global change during the past 300 years: population and long-term population change; technological change; institutions, social organizations, and cultural values; the location of production and consumption; and urbanization. The bulk of the book looks in detail at changes in the components of the biosphere: land; water; oceans and atmosphere; biota; and chemicals and radiation. A third section includes excellent regional case studies of environmental changes in different parts of the world: the long-term perspective in China; tropical frontiers in Amazonia, Borneo and the Malay Peninsula; the highlands of Caucasia and East Africa; the plains of Russia and the United States; the basin of Mexico; and areas of other countries in Europe. A final section reviews theories and explanations regarding human use of the earth. *The Earth Transformed* is a weighty volume, with a plentiful number of excellent maps, tables, and figures to supplement the text.

"The book gives the most comprehensive analysis of the existing state of environment and sources of its dynamics. An attempt to make linkages between social and natural sciences was made."—Olga Bykova, Institute of Geography, Russian Academy of Sciences, Moscow

93. **Udall, Stewart L.** *The Quiet Crisis and the Next Generation.* rev. ed. Salt Lake City: Peregrine Smith, 1988 (orig. pub. as *The Quiet Crisis.* New York: Holt, Rinehart, 1963). 296 pages.

In the early 1960s, environmental problems were still very much a "quiet crisis." Through this historical account of Americans who fought to protect the environment, Stuart Udall helped give environmentalism a stronger voice with which to call for better management and preservation of our air, land, and water. As Secretary of the Interior during the Kennedy and Johnson administrations, Udall saw clearly the vastness of America's natural wealth, and the certain destructiveness of an industrial society consuming that wealth. He details this conflict, a conflict that has existed since the first colonization of the new world, by describing the thoughts and endeavors of Jefferson, Thoreau, Muir, Powell, the Rossevelts, and many others. The book is well written and provides an excellent overview of the roots of modern environmental activities. In the revised edition, Udall describes events, individuals, and organizations that were important during what he calls the "Age of Ecology," the period from 1962 to 1988. This includes Rachel Carson, David Brower, Paul Ehrlich, Barry Commoner, Ralph Nader, William Zahniser of the Wilderness Society, and the Environmental Defense Fund. He looks at their contributions to the ecological movement, as well as the impact of Earth Day in 1970. Finally, he offers his reflections on the Reagan legacy of the 1980s, and discusses its influence both on the environment and on the environmental movement.

"A thoughtful, popular 1960s introduction that contributed the concept of 'crisis' to the environmental crisis."—J. Baird Callicott, professor of philosophy and of natural resources, University of Wisconsin–Stevens Point

94. **Vogt, William.** *Road to Survival.* Introduction by Bernard Beruch. Illustrations by Stuart E. Freeman. New York: Sloan, 1948. 335 pages.

Vogt was a field naturalist with the National Audubon Society and editor of *Bird Lore* magazine during the mid-1930s. He began work on conservation in Latin America in 1939, and eventually became chief of the Conservation Section of the Pan-American Union, where he published a series of books on the population and natural resources of Latin American countries. From 1951 to 1961, Vogt served as director of the Planned Parenthood Federation of America and then became secretary of The Conservation Foundation. His experiences, particularly his work in Latin America, influenced his attitudes about the causes of environmental deterioration around the world. He saw rapid population growth as a prime threat to the resource base of society, and much of his writings thus reflect a neo-malthusian perspective.

95.   **Ward, Barbara, and Rene Dubos.** *Only One Earth: The Care and Maintenance of a Small Planet.* New York: Norton, 1972. 225 pages.

Commissioned by the United Nations Conference on the Human Environment held in Stockholm in 1972, this book was one of the first to stress the interconnectedness and joint dependency of all human societies on the globe—the idea that each shares with the other this tiny planet whirling in the void of space. Ward and Dubos, two important figures in the global environmental efforts of the period, address the environmental concerns in developed countries, such as pollution, and the problems of developing countries, such as water supply and sanitation. The book concludes with recommendations for cooperative monitoring and research on global environmental issues, and for a global rather than national approach to environmental problems, health problems, and avoidance of war.

"This small book summarizes the biospheric concept of the planet Earth and its ecologic and socioeconomic interdependencies. A large international group of corresponding experts contributed to the preparation of the book. It is significant as having set the tone of the 1972 United Nations Conference in Stockholm."—Lynton Keith Caldwell, Arthur F. Bentley professor emeritus of political science, Indiana University

"This eloquent book looked to the future—the greenhouse effect, the Los Angelization of the planet—and became a touchstone in the debate on how economic development and population growth tax natural resources."—Kathleen Courrier, director of publications, World Resources Institute

"I read this book as an undergraduate student and found it to be both terrifying and challenging. It gave me the feeling that I really must try and do something with my life that would help others understand and solve global environmental problems."—Diana M. Liverman, associate professor of geography, Pennsylvania State University

Also recommended are Ward's *The Home of Man* (Norton, 1976) and *Progress for a Small Planet* (Norton, 1979).

96.   **Western Regional Environmental Education Council.** *Project WILD Aquatic Education Activity Guide.* Boulder, CO: WREEC, 1987. 239 pages.

———. *Project WILD Elementary Activity Guide.* Boulder, CO: WREEC, 1985 (orig. pub. 1983). 278 pages.

———. *Project WILD Secondary Activity Guide.* Boulder, CO: WREEC, 1985 (orig. pub. 1983). 288 pages

With an emphasis on wildlife, these activity guides (one for elementary students, another for secondary students) are touted by the WREEC as "an interdisciplinary, supplementary environmental and conservation education program." The guides contain a wealth of indoor and outdoor projects and appear to be a lot of fun, even for adults! Supplements to each guide were published in 1985, which contain new and updated materials. An aquatic education activity guide was also published in 1987 to help children explore the variety of aquatic habitats.

"An excellent training and teaching tool used in all fifty states to explain connection of wildlife and habitats through well-designed activities that appeal to all ages. I've used it to train volunteers, resort recreation leaders, the general public, and teachers."—Kristie Seaman, education director, Sanibel-Captiva Conservation Foundation

97.   **Wilson, E. O., ed.** *Biodiversity.* Washington, DC: National Academy, 1988. 521 pages.

According to the World Wide Fund for Nature, nearly 1, 000 species of plants and animals, mostly in tropical forests, become extinct each year. And that rate of extinction is rising rapidly. How do we begin to protect the diversity of biological species, let alone identify and understand them, in the face of such immense onslaught by human actions around the world? At the National Forum on Biodiversity held in Washington, D.C. in 1986, some of the world's leading experts on biological conservation gathered to discuss exactly those issues. This book contains the collected wisdom of more than sixty of those experts. Their articles are arranged around such themes as: human dependence on and the value of biodiversity; threats to biodiversity; ways of monitoring and protecting biodiversity; the roles of science and technology in maintaining biodiversity; restoration ecology; proposed policies; and future prospects. The book was one of the earliest to offer such a range of discussion on the topic, and was instrumental in helping to give identity to the emerging field of conservation biology.

"The best broad collection of essays on this topic, suitable for an educated audience with expertise outside of biology. The topic is critical to understanding our current situation."—Dennis W. Cheek, coordinator of curriculum development, Science, Technology, and Society Education Project, New York Department of Education

98. **World Commission on Environment and Development.** *Our Common Future.* New York: Oxford University Press, 1987. 400 pages.

This is the report of the World Commission on Environment and Development (WCED), chaired by Gro Harlan Bruntland of Norway, which was established in 1983 to examine global environment and development issues, and to propose long-term strategies for global cooperation in establishing policies that expand and sustain global natural resources and manage them more effectively. The report pays particular attention to issues of population, food security, species loss, genetic resources, energy, and human settlements. It argues that environmental protection and economic development *are* compatible and that inequities in the global distribution of wealth and resources are at the root of much environmental degradation. The senior government ranking of the various WCED participants meant that the commissioners had access to the highest levels in their governments and that they could, in fact, speak for their governments. This has perhaps been the reason why the report had a greater impact than other similar reports produced by international committees.

"Accepting the growing consensus on environment problems, this international group effort suggested politically realistic solutions and triggered a debate just about everywhere except the United States."—Kathleen Courrier, director of publications, World Resources Institute

"The first truly international statement of the notion of sustainable development."—F. Kenneth Hare, provost emeritus, Trinity College, University of Toronto, Canada

"Built on the foundation of the World Conservation Strategy and made an immensely valuable contribution to refocussing the attention of world leaders on the need for a 'global agenda for change'."—Martin W. Holdgate, director general, Jeffrey McNeely, chief conservation officer, and John Burke, head of communications, International Union for the Conservation of Nature and Natural Resources (IUCN)-The World Conservation Union, Gland, Switzerland

"The book contains a thorough analysis of the driving forces of the environmental changes and, that being especially important, marks the path of sustainable development."—Olga Bykova, Institute of Geography, Russian Academy of Sciences, Moscow

"It offers the basic message that we all live on the same planet which is at a critical juncture in terms of its future and we can either all work together now for our common good and survival or else there is not much future to look forward to."—Apichai Sunchindah, project officer, Swiss Development Cooperation, Bangkok, Thailand

"This book was written by a commission and does not possess the tightly-integrated reasoning that one expects from a single-authored book. Its impact on the thinking of the world has been enormous, however, and it deserves to be listed for that reason alone. It clarifies two vital points: (1) development that does not preserve the integrity and viability of ecosystems cannot be successful; and (2) environmental protection efforts that leave half the world in miserable poverty are bound to fail."—Lester W. Milbrath, director, Research Program in Environment and Society, State University of New York at Buffalo

99.   **World Resources Institute, in collaboration with the United Nations Environment Programme and the United Nations Development Programme.** *World Resources: 1992–93.* New York: Oxford University Press, 1992 (biennial). 385 pages.

The biennial World Resources report provides a rich concentration of environmental information distilled from a vast array of sources worldwide. At the core of the report are nearly fifty data tables describing conditions of the people and environment in 146 countries. The masterful compilation and organization of this morass of statistics is impressive. Supplementing the data tables are about a dozen documentary chapters that synthesize the "raw numbers." These chapters summarize what is happening to the various components of the environment. And by highlighting numerous environmental successes and failures around the world, the report provides beginner guidelines on how citizens and governments can address the prospects of the global environment. (See also entry 346 for a description of the World Resources Institute's *The 1992 Information Please Environmental Almanac.*)

100. **Worster, Donald E.** *Nature's Economy: A History of Ecological Ideas.* Cambridge: Cambridge University Press, 1985 (orig. pub. as *Nature's Economy: A History of the Subversive Science.* San Francisco: Sierra Club, 1977). 404 pages.

Donald Worster describes himself as an "intellectual historian" interested in the origin of contemporary conceptions of ecology. As demonstrated by this book and others that have followed, he is also a creative scholar, a talented writer, and an artisan, who has deftly woven a colorful and detailed fabric from seemingly thousands of historical threads. Worster wants the reader to understand better how ecology has become what it is by showing the development of "science" within the context of "society." He describes the five distinct periods in which ecological thought underwent significant transformation, from the ideas of the eighteenth century to the ideas of this century. He traces the notions of Gilbert White and the "arcadian" views of nature, discusses the "imperial and reasoned" perspectives of Carl Linneaus, engages the romantic approach of Henry David Thoreau, and presents the revolutionary ecology and pessimistic views of Charles Darwin and Thomas Malthus. Worster then cites the notions of abundance, distribution, and succession of the biologists of the early 1930s, including the development of the "land ethic" by Aldo Leopold, and reviews the emergence of "the new ecology" based on the flow of energy and materials through the ecosystem. Finally he looks at the intellectual and conceptual connection ecology has made with philosophy, sociology, politics, and religion. His descriptions are rich with details about the words and work of key ecologists and naturalists. The book is a wonderful way to dive into the past—and then to plunge ahead into the future.

"This volume changed my way of thinking about how ecological theory has evolved over time. Especially it drove home the truth that scientific thought can never be separated from the culture and society that nurtures its practitioners at any given time."—Marvin W. Baker, Jr., associate professor of geography, University of Oklahoma

Part II

Strongly Recommended Books

101.   **Alexander, Christopher, Sara Ishikawa, and Murray Silverstein.**
A Pattern Language: Towns, Buildings, Construction. New York: Oxford University Press, 1977. 1171 pages.

Combining elements of psychology, sociology, and philosophy with architecture, this book offers a "language" for articulating designs for human-used spaces. We should strive, the authors urge, to create a harmony between ourselves and our environment, paying close attention to both the smallest details and the overall context for such spaces as personal rooms, gardens, homes, offices, and public spaces. The aim of the suggestions in this book is for us to grow healthy and to protect our spaces.

"Nature also includes humans; environments are also built. *A Pattern Language* sketches the essential elements of these organic extensions of the biosphere. We learn much of nature from how we as a species fit in."—Peter Bane, publisher, *The Permaculture Activist*

102.   **Allen, Paula Gunn.** *The Sacred Hoop: Recovering the Feminine in American Indian Traditions.* Boston: Beacon, 1986. 311 pages.

Allen's essays are written from a different perspective than those generally found in Native American literature—the perspective of a woman.

"While we critique 'Western' views of human relations to nature, we often don't pose workable alternatives. This book presents an alternative view that has functioned for several thousands of years, i.e. the Native American view, specifically Laguna Pueblo. While examining this perspective the author also demonstrates a tie to the suppression of the valuing of females and feminine principles and the abuse of nature. Written by a Laguna woman, it is very readable and thought provoking."—Annie Booth, doctoral student, Institute for Environmental Studies, University of Wisconsin–Madison

103.　　**Altieri, Miguel.** *Agroecology: The Scientific Basis of Alternative Agriculture.* Boulder, CO: Westview, 1987. 227 pages.

As defined by Altieri, alternative agriculture is any approach to farming that attempts to provide sustained yields through the use of ecologically sound management technologies. Alternative agriculture as such has been the domain of small farmers in underdeveloped countries as well as "organic" farmers of Europe and the United States. This book provides ample documentation on successful systems of alternative agriculture, based on extensive field research and case studies undertaken by Altieri and a number of other agricultural ecologists. The book looks at the historical and theoretical frameworks of agricultural ecology, describes the methods for designing and evaluating alternative agricultural systems, reviews and compares various examples of agroecological systems around the world, and examines the necessary steps toward a more widely established use of sustainable agriculture.

104.　　**Anderson, Edgar.** *Plants, Man, and Life.* Boston: Little, Brown, 1952. 245 pages.

This is an early and interesting account of the relationship between plants and humans, and the role plants have played in human cultural, economic, and aesthetic life. Undoubtedly, more recent work has been done on plant biogeography, ethnobotany, plant genetics, and the political economy of plant production. But Anderson's book was a good foundation for later work in those areas.

"An outpouring of natural enthusiasm for plants, their beauty, their utility as food sources, their threats from human activity, and their scientific challenge."—Orie Loucks, professor of zoology, Miami University, Ohio

105.　　**Anderson, Lorraine, ed.** *Sisters of the Earth: Women's Prose and Poetry About Nature.* New York: Vintage, 1991. 426 pages.

Anderson has assembled a collection of some ninety poems and essays that illustrate the diversity and strength of feminist voices and perceptions about nature. The focus of the book is mainly on writers in the United States, and includes extracts from the works of Mary Austin, Emily Dickinson, Annie Dillard, Ursula LeGuin, Susan Griffin, Joy Harjo, Margaret Murie, Marge Piercy, Alice Walker, and Ann Zwinger. Contains an annotated bibliography of additional readings.

106. **Arvill, Robert.** *Man and the Environment: Crisis and the Strategy of Choice.* 5th ed. London: Penguin, 1983 (orig. pub. 1967). 432 pages.

A comprehensive assessment of the impact of humans and human activities on the air, land, water, and biotic resources of Great Britain.

"A classic work and a keynote book, both dated and timeless. Like all classic works, should be read by all with a particular interest in a topic."—M. Pugh Thomas, director, Environmental Resources Unit, University of Salford, Salford, England

107. **Austin, Mary.** *The Land of Little Rain.* Boston: Houghton Mifflin, 1903. Reprint. Albuquerque: University of New Mexico Press, 1974. 280 pages.

Having left the midwest to settle in the Owens Valley of California, Austin became enchanted with the arid lands there. And although her life was filled with much hardship, she became a prolific writer—and one of the most enduring of her era. In this collection of fourteen essays, she conveys her deep fondness for and understanding of the way of life in the desert and mountains of southeastern California, and displays an empathy for the people living there.

108. **Bailey, Liberty Hyde.** *The Holy Earth.* New York: The Christian Rural Fellowship, 1943 (orig. pub. 1915, Macmillan). 117 pages.

Bailey, who served as dean of the New York State College of Agriculture in Ithaca from 1903 to 1913, charts in this slim book a philosophical and religious outline for human interactions with the land. He presents several notions about agriculture and society that are still relevant to modern-day debates.

109. **Barbier, Edward B.** *Economics, Natural Resource Scarcity and Development.* London: Earthscan, 1989. 223 pages.

Barbier discusses conventional and alternative economic approaches to natural resource scarcity, particularly their relevance in light of contemporary environmental degradation. He develops an alternative approach through economic analyses of environmental degradation in three cases: Amazonian deforestation, the global greenhouse effect, and upper watershed degradation in Java. Based on these analyses, he explores "economics for sustainable development."

110.   **Barnaby, Frank, ed.** *The Gaia Peace Atlas.* Foreward by Javier Pérez de Cuéllar. New York: Doubleday, 1988. 271 pages.

During the 1980s, many scholars and policymakers discussed and explored the interconnections between environment and peace. This volume offers a collection of views on the issues related to these interconnections, from noted politicians, scientists, and environmental and peace activists. The authors discuss the roots of conflict and peace, the social and environmental costs of defense and military spending, and efforts to achieve peace and justice around the world. The book also includes extensive recommendations on how to achieve and maintain a sustainable society. For related and in-depth discussions on the connections between peace and the environment, see Arthur Westing's *Warfare in a Fragile World: the Military Impact on the Human Environment* (Taylor & Francis, 1980), as well as other books published by the Stockholm International Peace Research Institute.

111.   **Bass, Rick.** *Winter: Notes from Montana.* New York: Houghton Mifflin, 1991. 162 pages.

Literally on the "last road in the United States" near the Canadian border, Bass chronicles the first year he and his wife spent on their homestead in the remote Purcells Mountains of northern Montana. "I felt like I'd waited all my life to peel off my city ways, city life, and get into the woods—molting, like an insect or a snake" (p. 160). Bass is a talented writer and has established himself in the new generation of American nature writers.

112.   **Bent, Arthur Cleveland.** *Life Histories of North American Birds.* New York: Dover Books.

This is one of the most comprehensive (and affordable) collections of descriptions of North American birds to be found. Although prepared between 1919 and 1948 by one of America's foremost ornithologists, the collection is still of great use to professional and amateur ornithologists, as well as naturalists in general. The eighteen books in the series, each describing a group of bird families (four books are published as two-volume sets) were originally published as research bulletins of the U.S. National Museum of the Smithsonian Institution.

113. **Berger, John J.** *Restoring the Earth: How Americans are Working to Renew Our Damaged Environment.* Foreword by Morris K. Udall. New York: Knopf, 1985. 241 pages.

During the past decade or so, the science of ecological restoration has certainly taken hold as a viable management tool to help remedy damaged ecosystems. Although there is some debate whether restored ecosystems can ever be the same as original ecosystems, the techniques of ecological restoration do offer some hope for areas destroyed or altered by human actions. Berger's book is an account of about a dozen case studies in which individuals and organizations have attempted to restore forests, wetlands, prairies, fisheries, croplands, rangelands, mined lands, toxic waste sites, rivers and lakes, and other ecological sites. He details the problems and successes that the projects have encountered, and urges the spread of restoration projects through local or regional restoration assemblies.

Related books include: *Environmental Restoration: Science and Strategies for Restoring the Earth* (Island, 1990), edited by Berger; *Restoration Ecology: A Synthetic Approach to Ecological Research* (Cambridge University Press, 1987), edited by William R. Jordan III, Michael E. Gilpen, and John D. Aber; *Rehabilitating Damaged Ecosystems* (CRC Press, 1988), edited by John Cairns, Jr.; and *Biological Habitat Reconstruction* (Belhaven, 1989), edited by G. P. Buckley.

114. **Berkes, Firket, ed.** *Common Property Resources: Ecology and Community-based Sustainable Development.* London: Belhaven, 1989. 302 pages.

The product of several conferences held during 1986, this collection of papers is by biologists, geographers, economists, political scientists, and others, and attempts to address many of the social, economic, and political aspects of managing common resources. The various authors provide an overview of the institutional arrangements for resource management, rights to use, and human ecology and psychology. Several chapters critique conventional notions of resource management. There are case examples of village fisheries' rights in Japan, lobster fishery developments off the coasts of Mexico and Maine, and irrigation water rights issues in the Philippines. In addition, several authors explore the diverse social and cultural concepts of common property and resource management, with case studies from Mali, India, and the South Pacific.

In many ways, the book provides contemporary viewpoints to the discussion about how to manage common property sustainably, best articulated some twenty years ago by Garrett Hardin in his classic essay, "The Tragedy of the Commons" (see entry 39). Another collection of papers on the same topic is *The Question of the Commons: The Culture and Ecology of Communal Resources* (University of Arizona Press, 1987), edited by Bonnie J. McCay and James M. Acheson.

115. **Berry Wendell.** ***The Gift of Good Land.*** San Francisco: North Point, 1981. 281 pages.

These are essays that continue the thoughts presented in *The Unsettling of America* (see entry 8), in which Berry urges adoption of the holistic perspective of agriculture and of economy. According to this perspective, the natural and cultural components in these areas are integrated and sustained by each other, rather than consumed. These twenty-four essays are additional evidence of Berry's wisdom, insightfulness, and keen ability to view with equal clarity both the parts and the whole of the agricultural system.

"Provides a basic education on the land and what it needs to be healthy, and on the people who care for it."—Shannon A. Horst, director of public awareness, Center for Holistic Resource Management

116. **Berry Wendell.** ***Home Economics.*** San Francisco: North Point, 1987. 192 pages.

This is a collection of fourteen essays, dedicated to his friend Wes Jackson, that again extends Berry's dialogue about the human relationship with the land, about how that relationship in modern times has become artificial and distant. In one essay, he describes and refutes the "Six Agricultural Fallacies" (pp. 123–132): (1) that agriculture may be understood and dealt with as an industry; (2) that a sound agricultural economy can be based on an export market; (3) that the "free market" can preserve agriculture; (4) that productivity is a sufficient standard of production; (5) that there are too many farmers; and (6) that labor is bad.

117. **Black, John N.** ***The Dominion of Man: The Search for Ecological Responsibility.*** Edinburgh: University Press, 1970. 169 pages.

Based on an earlier series of lectures, Black's book was among the first to explore such topics as human dominion over nature, stewardship, responsibility for property, and the role of the state.

"Professor Black has examined the philosophy and worldview of Western, industrial man and has shown that the current rapid rate of environmental degradation is directly attributable to its inhabitants' beliefs and value systems. He suggests ways in which Western value systems can be changed to make them environmentally friendly."
—Steven E. Piper, editor, *Vulture News* for the Vulture Study Group Westville, Natal, South Africa

118.   **Blake, Nelson M.** *Land into Water—Water into Land: A History of Water Management in Florida.* Gainesville, FL: University Presses of Florida, 1980. 344 pages.

Blake looks at the history of the complexity and extensiveness of drainage and irrigation projects in Florida. He reviews the political and economic forces that pushed for construction of drainage ditches, flood control structures, irrigation canals, and other detrimental projects. He cites the dire impacts these activities have had on natural areas and on the flora and fauna in the state, and characterizes the role of the environmental movement in preventing or curtailing many of these projects.

119.   **Bly, Robert.** *News of the Universe: Poems of Twofold Consciousness.* San Francisco: Sierra Club, 1980. 305 pages.

Bly has selected nearly 150 poems to represent human experience with nature. The poems come from different periods of human social and intellectual development, especially with regard to nature, and represent the views of many cultures. Bly guides the reader through the poems, providing analytical commentary to help evaluate or appreciate a particular poem or group of poems.

"The most incredible collection of poetry that stirs the soul and one's ecological conscience. Keep it by your bed forever."—Gary Randorf, senior counselor, Adirondack Council

120.   **Bonta, Marcia.** *Appalachian Spring.* Pittsburgh: University of Pittsburgh Press, 1991. 187 pages.

In this personal journal, Bonta reveals not only her own special talent as a naturalist and writer, but also describes the richness and diversity of the plants and animals that live on or visit her 500-acre mountaintop farm in central Pennsylvania from March through June. On June 7, for example, while watching butterflies and moths attracted to the blossoms of a patch of dame's rocket, she recorded: "First I watched a perfect tiger swallowtail butterfly unroll its long proboscis and push it down into the middle of each blossom to collect nectar. Then came two spicebush swallowtails followed by a red admiral, an American painted lady, a sphinx moth, and a cloudy-wing skipper. But the most common butterfly, by far, was the silver-spotted skipper. At any one time I could see several clinging to the flowers" (p. 151).

121.　**Bonta, Marcia Myers. *Women in the Field: America's Pioneering Women Naturalists.*** College Station: Texas A & M University Press, 1991. 299 pages.

From Jane Colden, colonial botanist, to Rachel Carson, pioneering ecologist, Bonta documents the lives and work of twenty-five women who made important contributions to the field of natural history. This book is of interest to persons in many various disciplines, such as history, biology, and women's studies.

122.　**Bookchin, Murray. *Remaking Society.*** New York: Black Rose, 1989. 222 pages.

Through his vision of a just, humane, and ecological society, Bookchin proposes that just as humans should not dominate nature, neither should nature dominate humans. He believes that a balance, a cooperative existence, is needed instead. He also offers a proposed structure for such a society, and provides a set of blueprints to begin its construction.

Also recommended is Bookchin's *The Ecology of Freedom: The Emergence and Dissolution of Hierarchy* (Cheshire, 1982).

123.　**Borgstrom, Georg. *Too Many: A Study of Earth's Biological Limitations.*** New York: Macmillan, 1969. 368 pages.

In this sequel to *The Hungry Planet: The Modern World at the Edge of Famine* (Macmillan, 1965), Borgstrom describes both the enhancing and limiting factors that affect food production around the world.

"Borgstrom combines a deep concern and passion for the poor and hungry of the world with a broad, but very contextual understanding of the interactions of living and human systems. Before *The Limits to Growth* study [see entry 54], he sought to link all the various macrosystems and their interactions with an understanding of how various subsystems are very contextual and need to be studied in their various concepts."—Kenneth A. Dahlberg, professor of political science, Western Michigan University

124. **Botkin, Daniel B.** *Discordant Harmonies: A New Ecology for the Twenty-First Century.* New York: Oxford University Press, 1990. 241 pages.

Botkin says that "nature in the twenty-first century will be a nature that we make; the question is the degree to which this molding will be intentional or unintentional, desirable or undesirable" (p. 193). He presents several scenarios describing the nature that is possible in the future, recommending an approach in which wise management is based on adequate information, knowledge, and understanding of the biosphere. His book is an attempt to show why such an understanding is necessary, and how our current knowledge and perceptions of "natural processes" are inadequate.

125. **Boyle, Robert H., John Graves, and T. H. Watkins.** *The Water Hustlers.* San Francisco: Sierra Club, 1971. 253 pages.

Each of the three authors describes a notable case study in water hustling: a proposed large-scale transfer of water from the rivers of east Texas to the drier plains of west Texas (Graves); water imperialism and the legendary maneuverings of Los Angeles businessmen to secure the water from rivers in the Sierras and the northern part of the state (Watkins); and the wastefulness of a mammoth, leaking, inadequate infrastructure for water delivery and supply in New York City (Boyle). Not only do these projects involve actual or proposed taxpayer dollars, but they make significant alterations on the natural landscapes, both at the sites of acquisition and in the areas of use.

126. **Bramwell, Anna.** *Ecology of the Twentieth Century: A History.* New Haven, CT: Yale University Press, 1989. 292 pages.

In this political history of ecological ideas, Bramwell suggests that the emergence of the green movement was, in large part, assisted by the earlier widespread dissemination of information and ideas from scientist-activists. She draws together examples from Europe, particularly Germany and Great Britain, and America to show the role of both ideological and economic thinking in ecology and the green political movement. She provides a particularly interesting account of ecological thought in Germany under Nazi rule.

127. **Brooks, Maurice.** *The Appalachians.* Boston: Houghton Mifflin, 1965. 346 pages.

From the Gaspe peninsula in Quebec to northern Alabama, the Appalachian Mountains stretch along some 1600 miles of the mainland of North America. Brooks offers a comprehensive natural history of the mountain chain, describing its rich variety of wildlife, plants, and habitats. He also provides a chapter characterizing the people and culture of the region, as well as the unique style of Appalachian crafts.

"A warmly written ongoing history of this mountain chain, to be especially appreciated by the nature-oriented reader."—Carl Slater, president, Brooks Bird Club

128.   **Brooks, Paul.** *Speaking for Nature: How Literary Naturalists from Henry Thoreau to Rachel Carson Have Shaped America.* Boston: Houghton Mifflin, 1980. 304 pages.

In a way, Brooks provides a history of conservation in America simply by reviewing and synthesizing the works and impacts of nature writers. This digest of nature writing is very useful in that respect. He offers a unique perspective from which to assess these works, having been editor, advisor, or friend to many natural history and environmental writers. Most of the major writers he cites were born between 1800 and 1920, and a partial list of the works of these writers is provided as an appendix.

129.   **Browder, John O., ed.** *Fragile Lands of Latin America: Strategies for Sustainable Development.* Boulder, CO: Westview, 1989. 301 pages.

This collection of papers was originally presented at the Symposium on Fragile Lands of Latin America held in New Orleans in 1988. Twenty-two distinguished anthropologists, archeologists, ecologists, and geographers gathered to examine how sustainable and traditional farming practices in Latin America could be adapted for fragile lands. Initial papers in the collection provide the context for natural resource management in Latin America: the geography and classification of fragile lands; a conceptual approach to the implementation of integrated development projects; and methods for the appropriate transfer of traditional technology in the region. The remaining papers describe different resources in Latin America, and offer an overview of resource use and management in light of the varying cultural and ecological settings in the region.

See also *Lands at Risk in the Third World: Local Level Perspectives* (Westview, 1987), edited by Peter D. Little and Michael M. Horowitz; *Sustainable Resource Development in the Third World* (Westview, 1987), edited by Douglas D. Southgate and John F. Disinger, for additional looks at sustainable development issues in broader geographic contexts.

130. **Brown, Lester R.** *Building a Sustainable Society.* New York: Norton, 1981. 433 pages.

Expanding on his earlier books: *World Without Borders* (see entry 131); *By Bread Alone* (see entry 361); and *The Twenty-Ninth Day* (see entry 13); Brown warns us of the converging trends which threaten to destroy the underpinnings of our civilization. He urges us to begin immediately on the path to a sustainable society, one in which population size is stable, energy is used more efficiently and comes largely from renewable sources, materials are recycled, agricultural lands are protected and maintained, and humans enjoy a simpler, more frugal life-style in which well-being is not measured by material growth. Brown also offers some initial steps that we can take to get started on that path. For example, he tells us that we can begin by introducing widespread family planning services, with the maintenance of population stabilization as a social goal. We can undertake widespread voluntary materials recycling efforts, eventually adopting mandatory programs. Brown uses examples where such changes are occurring and discusses the role that businesses, educational institutions, the media, and religious organizations can play in making the public more aware of the need for a transition to a sustainable society, as well as their role in helping to make that transition less difficult.

"This is an appealing statement of the need, as well as the step, for putting society on a sustainable path for the future."—Stephen R. Gliessman, director, Agroecology program, University of California–Santa Cruz

131. **Brown, Lester R.** *World Without Borders.* New York: Random House, 1972. 395 pages.

An insightful analysis of how interdependent the different human societies really are, and how we must reorganize our institutional and economic structures to be able to deal effectively with environmental and human welfare concerns. This is an early model for the "new world order."

"Gave me my first significant appreciation and understanding of the global interconnectedness of things and of the need for integrated analysis of the forces at work on the planet."—Russell W. Peterson, president emeritus, National Audubon Society

132. **Bullard, Robert D.** *Dumping in Dixie: Race, Class and Environmental Quality.* Boulder, CO: Westview, 1990. 165 pages.

In studying the location of hazardous waste facilities and other polluting industries in the American South, Bullard convincingly demonstrates that they are disproportionately sited in or near poor, politically powerless, black neighborhoods. His book has played an important role in the awareness and debate about "environmental racism" in the United States and has contributed to minority group efforts to organize against the contamination of their communities.

133.   **Buzzworm Magazine.** *1992 Earth Journal: Environmental Almanac and Resource Directory.* Boulder, CO: Buzzworm Books, 1991, 447 pages.

This is a comprehensive guide to the "ecoculture of the '90s" by the editors of the award-winning environmental journal, *Buzzworm.* The almanac contains an "Earth Diary," a review of important daily environmental events that occurred around the world during the past year; a two-part "Earth Pulse," which looks at nineteen mega-trends and issues that dominate the environmental agenda and which also discusses and rates the environmental conditions of regions around the world; and "Ecoculture," which reviews environmental movies, books, software, and products, environmental education programs, ecotravel outfitters, and environmental organizations. Also included is a green ranking of cities.

134.   **Caldwell, Lynton Keith.** *Environment: A Challenge to Modern Society.* Garden City, NY: Natural History, 1970. 292 pages.

Written for the general public, this book suggests that it is the duty of governments to engage in active "environmental administration" if environmental problems are to be effectively resolved. There are several key chapters in which the author elaborates on the concept of environmental management as applied science, as a public function, and as an ethical system.

"The earliest exposition of the institutionalization of environmental protection policy by a premier political scientist."—Clarence A. Schoenfeld, professor emeritus of journalism, wildlife ecology, and environmental studies, University of Wisconsin–Madison

135.   **Capra, Fritjof.** *The Turning Point: Science, Society and the Rising Culture.* New York: Simon & Schuster, 1982. 464 pages.

Capra offers a new look at the world that stresses a holistic approach to knowledge, rather than one that segregates the world into discrete, seemingly unrelated, specialties. He proposes that we move beyond the mechanistic, Cartesian perception of the world—which he suggests is the origin of our contemporary social and ecological crisis—to a new paradigm which integrates Eastern philosophy, feminism, alternative medicine, and appropriate technology. Capra believes that we need this New Age vision to solve the problems of cancer, crime, pollution, inflation, and spiritual crisis, as well as to foster our psychological health.

"This book clarified for me how deeply the thoughtways of science influence the way we think, the way we define problems, the way we lay out alternatives, and the character of our discourse. The thoughtways of science are themselves changing but our societal discourse is still stuck in the old dysfunctional mode. Our environmental problems stem in large part from that dysfunction in our thinking. Our society is in desperate need of a new, more realistic, more controlling perspective on our relationship to science and technology."—Lester W. Milbrath, director, Research Program in Environment and Society, State University of New York at Buffalo

Also recommended is Capra's *The Tao of Physics: An Exploration of the Parallels Between Modern Physics and Eastern Mysticism* (Random House, 1984).

136.   **Carr, Archie.** *The Windward Road: Adventures of a Naturalist on Remote Caribbean Shores.* New York: Knopf, 1955. 258 pages.

Carr, a biologist and conservationist noted particularly for his work in the Caribbean region, reflects on his years of "nosing around the tropics," studying and collecting information on sea turtles (green, loggerhead, ridley, hawksbill, and trunkback).

137.   **Carrighar, Sally.** *One Day on Beetle Rock.* New York: Knopf, 1944. 196 pages.

The first readers of Carrighar's book probably found the descriptions of Beetle Rock to be wonderful and peaceful, in contrast to the tensions of the war that gripped the world then. This is a highly readable book, in which Carrighar describes a small area in the Sierra Nevada mountains. She reveals the inhabitants of Beetle Rock in a series of nine essays, each focussing on a different animal: weasel, grouse, chickaree (squirrel), black bear, lizard, coyote, deer mouse, Stellar's jay, and mule deer. Carrighar's sequel is *One Day at Teton Marsh* (Knopf, 1947).

138. **Carson, Rachel.** *The Edge of the Sea.* Illustrations by Bob Hines. Boston: Houghton Mifflin, 1955. 276 pages.

Carson is very adept at describing the intricate balance of life on the beaches and in tidal pools. She is to the Atlantic Ocean what Eddie Ricketts is to the Pacific (see entry 297). Her text, combined with the more than 150 line drawings by Bob Hines, a coworker at the U.S. Fish and Wildlife Service, makes this a fascinating outing for the whole family.

"Holistic approach to understanding where land meets sea. Covers geology, biology, human interaction, and physical sciences, as well as philosophy of conflicting uses in the coastal zone."—Kristie Seaman, education director, Sanibel-Captiva Conservation Foundation

Also recommended are two additional books that Carson wrote about the ocean: *Under the Sea-Wind: A Naturalist's Picture of Ocean Life* (Simon & Schuster, 1941), her first book; and *The Sea Around Us* (Oxford University Press, 1951), winner of the National Book Award.

139. **Carter, Vernon G., and Tom Dale.** *Topsoil and Civilization.* Norman: University of Oklahoma Press, 1974 (orig. pub. 1955 as *Topsoil and Civilization*). 292 pages.

The authors document the role of soil fertility and soil stability in sustaining past civilizations, particularly those of the Mediterranean Basin. They cite the relationship between the decline or collapse of the civilizations and the loss of topsoils on which the societies depended. Their conclusions are then projected onto the situation in the United States, as an attempt to forecast the long-term viability of agricultural productivity for this country.

"The basic bible of conservation. It gives the long view of neglect of soil and water resources as doom."—Charles McLaughlin, chair, board of trustees, Iowa Natural Heritage Foundation

140. **Castner, James L.** *Rainforests: A Guide to Research and Tourist Facilities at Selected Tropical Forest Sites in Central and South America.* Gainesville, FL: Feline, 1990. 380 pages.

Anyone thinking of heading into the tropical forests in Latin America should read this guide first! It lists research and tourist facilities in Peru (10 sites), Ecuador (9), French Guiana (5), Venezuela (8), Trinidad (3), Costa Rica (8), and Panama (6). Even if you are not planning to visit one of the sites mentioned in the guide, the overall descriptions are still probably useful. Castner reviews each site and packs his reviews with information on: locations, contact persons, addresses, logistics, forest types, seasonalities, facilities, trail systems, costs, and relevant travel group or agency information. He also includes lists of books, maps, tourist information sources, conservation organizations, and scientific organizations of interest to those traveling in Latin America.

141. **Catton, William R. *Overshoot: The Ecological Basis for Revolutionary Change*.** Urbana: University of Illinois Press, 1980. 298 pages.

A testimony to the bleak predicament of human society in which, as Catton suggests, we are stealing from the future. The book considers the negative long-term effects of global human population growth that, in the author's assessment, already extends beyond the natural carrying capacity of the earth. Catton shows how ecological limits have been ignored in many areas due to expansionist passions, unsound development policies, faith in technology, and the tendency to exploit the natural resources that should be reserved for future generations.

142. **Caufield, Catherine. *In the Rainforest: Report from a Strange, Beautiful, Imperiled World*.** Chicago: University of Chicago Press, 1986 (orig. pub. 1984, Knopf). 304 pages.

Caufield documents how the wondrous tropical rainforests from Brazil to Borneo are being destroyed by unrelenting human activities: an immense new reservoir and a hydroelectric power project in the Amazon; agriculture and cattle ranching in Central America; and gold mining in New Guinea are just a few of these activities. Caufield, a science and environmental journalist, writes with a clear and concerned style, showing us why we should be alarmed about the loss of rainforests. Her book was an early messenger of what was happening in the rainforests, and helped popularize the concerns many scientists and environmentalists had felt for years.

143. **CEIP Fund. *The Complete Guide to Environmental Careers*.** Covelo, CA: Island, 1989. 328 pages.

Since 1972, the CEIP Fund (formerly the Center for Environmental Intern Programs) has helped place thousands of students in environmental internships and jobs. Based on this experience, the CEIP Fund staff has produced a guide that no student wanting a career in conservation or environmental management can do without. The guide is also useful for teachers, faculty, counselors, and administrators who advise students on career opportunities. It contains several chapters on the nuts and bolts of environmental jobs (for example, the types available, expectable salary levels, entry requirements, and how to find and apply for jobs). The guide then devotes separate chapters to detailed descriptions of different types of jobs in ten areas: planning; environmental education and communications; solid waste management; hazardous waste management; air quality; water quality; land and water conservation; fishery and wildlife management; parks and outdoor recreation; and forestry. It also gives numerous profiles of individuals working in those areas. Additional related references include *The Environmental Career Guide: Job Opportunities with the Earth in Mind* (Wiley, 1991), by Nicholas Basta; *Environmental Careers: A Practical Guide to Opportunities in the 90s* (Lewis, 1992), by David J. Warner; *Fixing the Environment: A Guide to Science/Engineering Careers in Environmental Conservation* (Wiley, 1992), by Nicholas Basta; *Careers for Nature Lovers and Other Outdoor Types* (VGM Career Horizons, 1992), by Louise Miller; *Opportunities in Environmental Careers* (VGM Career Horizons, 1991), by Odum Fanning; and *Careers in Conservation* (Kogan Page, 1989, 4th ed.), by John McCormick.

144.   **Chase, Alston.** *Playing God in Yellowstone: The Destruction of America's First National Park.* New York: Atlantic Monthly, 1986. 446 pages.

A frank assessment of how we as a society, through the agency of our government, manage (or mismanage) our vast wilderness and natural areas. Chase reveals to us that our ideals of "naturalness" are often unnatural, and shows how these misshapen and mistaken images conflict with reality.

"I hesitate to get involved in books that deal with government bureaucracy, but this book is an exception. Far from watering down the facts, it details with copious footnotes 'the destruction of America's first national park' and how it still continues. I found this to be a fascinating, though depressing, story, but one so well-written and thoroughly documented, that I read it from cover to cover."—James A. Fowler, former chair, Michigan Natural Areas Council

145.   **Clark, William C., and R. E. Munn, eds.** *Sustainable Development of the Biosphere.* New York: Cambridge University Press, 1987. 491 pages.

This book is a comprehensive collection of essays and studies prepared by collaborators at the International Institute for Applied Systems Analysis, an East-West think tank located just outside Vienna in Austria. The introductory chapter by Clark is particularly useful in summarizing, from both historical and contemporary perspectives, the concepts of sustainable development and related research themes pursued by the group. The remaining chapters serve as commentaries on a range of issues related to sustainability. The chapter bibliographies contain citations of a number of works, particularly reports and scientific studies, which are not widely publicized.

146. Clark, William S. *A Field Guide to Hawks.* Illus. Brian K. Wheeler. Boston: Houghton Mifflin, 1987. 198 pages.

A Field Guide to Hawks expands upon the "field marks" technique of identifying birds that was previously developed by Roger Tory Peterson (see entry 72). The author, William Clark, was director of the Raptor Information Center for the National Wildlife Federation. Illustrator Brian Wheeler is noted for his paintings of hawks. The more advanced birder will find useful the detailed information on the thirty-nine species of North American diurnal raptors. A 480-entry bibliography directs the interested user to a variety of related books, reports, and scientific papers.

"Recommended for in-depth study of variations in plumages and color, emphasizing shape, pattern, and special field marks."— Myriam Moore, secretary, Hawk Migration Association of North America

147. Collard, Andree, with Joyce Contrucci. *Rape of the Wild: Man's Violence Against Animals and the Earth.* London: Women's Press, 1988. 187 pages.

This is a stinging indictment of the male-dominated scientific enterprise that has exploited animals and nature. The authors call for an end to these practices and a restructuring of our social attitudes in general, toward each other and toward the planet and propose a shift to a feminist value structure that appreciates and respects all life.

148. Commoner, Barry. *The Poverty of Power: Energy and the Economic Crisis.* New York: Knopf, 1976. 314 pages.

Published shortly after the "energy crisis" of the early 1970s, Commoner's book analyzes the debates about energy use and its availability, through a discussion of theories about the relationships between technology, society, and the environment.

"Good exposition of thermodynamics and ecological principles in re-lation to energy issues."—Walter Westman, former senior researcher, Lawrence Berkeley Laboratory and the National Aeronautics and Space Administration Ames Research Center

149.   Comstock, Anna Botsford. *Handbook of Nature Study for Teachers and Parents.* Ithaca, NY: Comstock, 1911. 927 pages.

Comstock, an entomologist by training, was keenly interested in helping educate people about nature. Her handbook was one of the most popular nature guides during the first half of this century. It contains a substantial amount of explanatory text that describes in great detail hundreds of species of animals and plants, as well as the components of the earth and sky. She suggests how teachers and par-ents can best engage in nature instruction, and offers guidelines on how to keep a field notebook and conduct field trips. She also shows how nature study is correlated with other fields of study, such as lan-guage, drawing, geography, history, and arithmetic. Marcia Myers Bonta, author of *Women in the Field* (see entry 121), writes in that book that schoolteachers across America called Comstock's book the "Na-ture Bible," and that "a generation of schoolchildren were introduced to nature by teachers who had been educated and inspired by Anna's book" (p. 154).

150.   Conant, Francis, Peter Rogers, Marion Baumgardner, Cyrus Mc-Kell, Raymond Dasmann, and Priscilla Reining, eds. *Resource In-ventory and Baseline Study Methods for Developing Countries.* Wash-ington, DC: American Association for the Advancement of Science, 1983. 539 pages.

Designed to help meet the need for more effective management of natural resources, this book reviews a variety of qualitative and quan-titative methods of determining resource inventories, and of provid-ing baseline studies of renewable resources in developing countries. The book is divided into four resource types: aquatic ecosystems, soil, plants, and wildlife. For each resource type, a variety of methods for inventory and monitoring are presented.

"Comprehensive, definitive review of the information requirements for environmental management."—John McLaughlin, professor of surveying engineering, University of New Brunswick, Fredericton, Canada

The reader might be interested in several related books: *Land Infor-mation Management: An Introduction with Special Reference to Cadastral*

Problems in Third World Countries (Oxford University press, 1988), by Peter F. Dale and John McLaughlin, which emphasizes methods of recording and maintaining information on land tenure and land use in Third World countries; *The Shrinking Planet: U.S. Information Technology and Sustainable Development* (World Resources Institute, 1988), by John Elkington and Jonathan Shopley, which looks at the role of satellite remote sensing and geographic information systems in monitoring environmental changes, with particular emphasis on the problems of cost and access for researchers in developing countries; and *Remote Sensing and Tropical Land Management* (Wiley, 1986), edited by Michael J. Eden and John T. Parry, which describes the application of satellite imagery and aerial photography to the management of different resources in tropical countries. Another book of interest is *Monitoring Ecological Change* (Cambridge University Press, 1991), by Ian F. Spellerberg, which reviews a variety of methods and techniques for measuring and analyzing ecological change.

151.   **Connor, Jack.** *Season at the Point: The Birds and Birders of Cape May.* New York: Atlantic Monthly, 1991. 230 pages.

Connor describes the men and women who work at and enjoy Cape May, New Jersey, which is one of the most popular birding spots in North America. He characterizes the unique qualities of this area and its importance for numerous migrating bird species. His vast experience and knowledge of birding—he is also author of *The Complete Birder: A Guide to Better Birding* (Houghton Mifflin, 1988)—and a flowing literary style make this book engaging and very easy to read.

152.   **Conservation Foundation.** *State of the Environment: A View Toward the Nineties.* Washington, DC: Conservation Foundation, 1987. 614 pages.

This is the third report in a continuing series from The Conservation Foundation on progress concerning long-term environmental threats to the United States. This book is similar to the *Environmental Quality* reports published by the Council on Environmental Quality during the 1970s (see entry 24). It addresses contaminants, toxic and hazardous pollutants, land, water, energy resources, protected lands, critical areas, and wildlife. The book also includes several chapters on policy issues in agriculture, waste management, airborne toxics, and biological diversity.

153.   **Cotgrove, Stephen F.** *Catastrophe or Cornucopia: The Environment, Politics, and the Future.* New York: Wiley, 1982. 154 pages.

Cotgrove looks at the new environmentalism that began in the early 1980s, and its influence on society and the political system. He contrasts the differences within the environmental movement and shows how ideological variations affect perceptions and expectations of environmental policymaking. Throughout the book, Cotgrove weaves in the results and analyses of a questionnaire survey he administered to some 2400 citizens, scientists, and members of environmental groups, in which he assessed levels of concern for various environmental issues.

"A scholarly examination of the many perspectives in environmental disputes."—Alan Miller, professor of psychology, University of New Brunswick, Fredericton, Canada

154.   **Cousteau Society.** *The Cousteau Almanac: An Inventory of Life on Our Water Planet.* New York: Doubleday, 1981. 838 pages.

This 800-page, fact-filled encyclopedia was one of the earliest works to provide an inventory of the planet's environmental condition. Several hundred short articles describe, in detail, the status and prospects of numerous aspects of the biosphere, highlighting the role of humans in affecting local and global changes.

"Full of interest. Way ahead of its time. Useful at all levels of environmental interest."—Philip Neal, general secretary, National Association for Environmental Education, Walsall, England

155.   **Cox, George W., and Michael D. Atkins.** *Agricultural Ecology: An Analysis of World Food Production Systems.* San Francisco: Freeman, 1979. 721 pages.

Cox and Atkins promote an ecological approach to agriculture, with an emphasis on developing sustainable systems. In addition to discussing the climatic, soil, nutrient, and biological aspects of agriculture, the authors analyze farming methods and outline major constraints to increased food production in both developed and developing nations. The book's final section discusses prospects and pitfalls of existing farming systems and suggests better management techniques.

"This is a pioneer book in the field of agroecology, and served to help begin uniting agronomists and ecologists in solving problems focusing on agriculture."—Stephen R. Gliessman, director, Agroecology program, University of California–Santa Cruz

Additional related books on the topic include: *Agricultural Sustainability in a Changing World Order* (Westview, 1984), edited by Gordon K. Douglass; *To Feed the Earth: Agro-Ecology for Sustainable Development* (World Resources Institute, 1987), by Michael J. Dover and Lee M. Talbot; and *Agricultural Ecosystems: Unifying Concepts* (Wiley, 1984), edited by Richard Lowrance, Benjamin R. Stinner, and Garfield J. House. All three books extend the discussion initiated by Cox and Atkins concerning the interconnections of agricultural production and environmental quality.

156. **Cronon, William. *Nature's Metropolis: Chicago and the Great West.*** New York: Norton, 1991. 530 pages.

By analyzing the economic relationships between urban Chicago and the rural Midwest region during the late nineteenth century, Cronon, an environmental historian and author of *Changes in the Land* (see entry 25), creates a framework with which to evaluate the significant environmental changes that have occurred in the region.

157. **Dahlberg, Kenneth A. *Beyond the Green Revolution: The Ecology and Politics of Global Agricultural Development.*** New York: Plenum, 1979. 256 pages.

Focusing on the spread of the Green Revolution, this book explores the environmental and cross-cultural dimensions of agriculture. The author, a political scientist at Western Michigan University, describes what he considers to be inadequacies of traditional Western agriculture and its application in many parts of the world, including the employment of conventional disciplinary approaches in agriculture. Dahlberg offers new ways to deal with future problems of agricultural and rural development through the use of appropriate technology.

158. **Dankelman, Irene, and Joan Davidson. *Women and the Environment in the Third World: Alliance for the Future.*** London: Earthscan, 1988. 210 pages.

This book shows the importance of women as resources of aid with regard to several issues—land, water, forests, energy, and housing—in the Third World. It also shows how women are the changemakers in their communities, who promote environmental conservation and the use of appropriate technologies. A related book is *Women and the Environment* (Zed, 1991), prepared by Annabel Rodda for the *Women and World Development Series* under the auspices of the United Nations Nongovernmental Liaison Service.

159.   **Darling, F. Fraser.** *A Herd of Red Deer: A Study in Animal Behavior.*
London: Oxford University Press, 1956. 215 pages.

————. *Wilderness and Plenty.* Introduction by Paul Brooks. Boston:
Houghton Mifflin, 1970. 84 pages.

————, **and J. Morton Boyd.** *The Highlands and Islands.* London:
Collins, 1964 (orig. pub. 1947). 336 pages.

Originally from Scotland, Fraser was director of research and vice
president of The Conservation Foundation in Washington, D.C. from
1959 to 1972. These are three of his more notable books.

160.   **Darwin, Charles.** *The Voyage of the Beagle.* Introduction by H. Graham Cannon. London: Dent, 1959 (orig. pub. 1839). 496 pages.

This is Darwin's day-to-day chronicle of his three-year journey, in
which he encountered a rich and varied world of flora and fauna.
There are passages which indicate how his thoughts were beginning
to formulate the ideas later expanded upon in *The Origin of Species*
(see entry 28). Of his visit to the Galapagos Island, he wrote of the
different types of finches and the variations in beaks that he had observed: "Seeing this gradation and diversity of structure in one small,
intimately related group of birds, one might really fancy that from an
original paucity of birds in the archipelago, one species had been
taken and modified for different ends."(p. 365)

"I don't know whether Darwin would be an environmentalist were he
alive today, but environmentalists would do well to have minds as
open to fact and experience as was his, and to have equal courage and
honesty in drawing lessons from fact and experience. Besides, evolution is a concept critical to understanding the natural world."—James
R. Conner, chair, Montana chapter of the Sierra Club

"The first great ecotourist!"—George Schaller, Wildlife Conservation
International, New York Zoological Society

A useful, illustrated and interpretive companion book is *Darwin and
the Beagle* (Harper, 1969) by Alan Moorhead.

161.   **Dasmann, Raymond F.** *Environmental Conservation.* 6th ed. New
York: Wiley, 1986 (orig. pub. 1959). 486 pages.

In this textbook, widely used for more than three decades, Dasmann
provides a history of human attitudes and behavior toward the envi-

ronment, and gives a background of basic ecological terminology, major biomes of the earth, and environmental concerns such as global population, energy use, forest management, agriculture, and protection of wildlife areas. The concluding section of the book looks at basic human needs with regard to future generations, and presents the concept of ecodevelopment. Dasmann defines ecodevelopment as a means of managing the environment with a view to future generations, with an emphasis on the provision of basic human needs and local self-reliance.

"The first book to bridge the old conservation and the new environmentalism."—Clarence A. Schoenfeld, professor emeritus of journalism, wildlife ecology, and environmental studies, University of Wisconsin–Madison

Also recommended: *Ecological Principles for Economic Development* (Wiley, 1973), by Raymond F. Dasmann, John P. Milton, and Peter H. Freeman.

162.　**Davies, J. Clarence, III, and Barbara S. Davies. *The Politics of Pollution.*** 2d ed. Racine, WI: Western, 1975 (orig. pub. 1970). 254 pages.

An analytical look at American legislative, administrative, and judicial processes, and the real behind-the-scenes operations of individuals and groups that affect environmental legislation, policy, and rulings. The activities discussed occurred in the 1970s.

"Shows how laws regarding pollution and environmental protection are frequently violated and ineffective. Sobering analysis for those who think legislation is the answer to problems."—Marion Clawson, senior fellow emeritus, Resources for the Future

163.　**De Bell, Garrett, ed. *The New Environmental Handbook.*** rev. ed. San Francisco: Friends of the Earth, 1980 (orig. pub. 1970, Ballantine). 351 pages.

In conjunction with Earth Day in 1970, schools and colleges across the country sponsored environmental "teach-ins," in which lectures and classroom discussions were devoted entirely to environmental concerns. This proved to be very effective in helping to bring an environmental consciousness to millions of students. In preparation for these activities, the environmental group Friends of the Earth sponsored the publication of this guide. It contains nearly fifty short articles and book excerpts that provide background (at least from the perspective of the late 1960s and 1970s) on a range of environmental issues. Also included in the handbook is an extensive presentation of "ecotactics" intended to help citizens and groups become involved and more effective in working for environmental protection.

"Coming out of the Earth Day movement of 1970, this placed environmental issues in a broad context that personally inspired me in a deep way."—Jay Walljaspar, editor, the *Utne Reader*

164. **Denslow, Julie Sloan, and Christine Padoch, eds.** *People of the Tropical Rain Forest.* Berkeley: University of California Press in association with Smithsonian Institution Traveling Exhibition Service, 1988. 231 pages.

This collection of articles, illustrated with colorful photographs, describes the character and diversity of rain forest environments and the people whose livelihood depends on them. Each chapter explores the ways in which people use the forest and how they are influenced by the outside world. The notion of sustainability is inherent throughout the book and is explicitly discussed in several chapters.

165. **Deudney, Daniel, and Christopher Flavin.** *Renewable Energy: The Power to Choose.* New York: Norton, 1985. 448 pages.

Deudney and Flavin provide an overview of renewable energy technologies and the application of each in world development efforts. The technologies discussed are solar, photovoltaics, wood, biomass energy from crops and waste, hydrothermal, wind, and geothermal. The authors suggest a strategy for a transition to renewable energy use and evaluate its potential impact on different parts of the world.

166. **Diamond, A. W., and F. L. Filion, eds.** *The Value of Birds.* Cambridge, England: International Council for Bird Preservation, 1987. 267 pages.

The twenty-five technical papers in this publication consider birds as a socioeconomic "resource" to be valued, managed, and protected. This line of reasoning may be anathema to some environmentalists, but the papers do offer some concrete advice concerning the intangible concept of bird preservation.

"A compendium of over twenty papers on the uses to which birds can be put (e.g. sport, birdwatching, bio-indicators) and their direct economic value to societies in all parts of the world, from richest to poorest. A must for those who underrate birds as a reason for environmental protection."—Steven E. Piper, editor, *Vulture News* for the Vulture Study Group, Westville, Natal, South Africa

167. **Dobson, Andrew, ed.** *The Green Reader: Essays Toward a Sustainable Society.* New York: Mercury, 1991. 280 pages.

Dobson has collected some of the best writings on bioregionalism, ecofeminism, ecophilosophy, and sustainable agriculture and development. The readings help to define the "green" philosophy and act as a complement to an earlier book, *Green Parties: An International Guide* by Sara Parkin (see entry 279), which describes the influence of many of the same writings on the development of green parties worldwide.

168. **Dorst, Jean.** *Before Nature Dies.* Translated by Constance D. Sherman. New York: Houghton Mifflin, 1970 (orig. pub. 1965 as *Avant que Nature Meure*). 352 pages.

Some environmentalists have said this book was the French counterpart to Rachel Carson's *Silent Spring* (see entry 19). Dorst, curator of mammals and birds at the National Museum of Natural History in Paris, documents human impacts on the natural world, and offers cogent arguments for preserving nature.

"This is a comprehensive analysis of the dangers threatening man and nature. It presents plausible solutions for reconciling these dangers for the sake of preservation of life."—Giselda Castro, vice president, Ação Democrática Feminina Gaúcha—Amigos da Terra, Porto Alegre, Brazil

"Further evidence of the relationship between man and nature. Another broad approach to world problems demanding an international policy of restraint and a programme of rational and management action."—Roger J. Wheater, director, the Royal Zoological Society of Scotland, Edinburgh

169. **Douglas, Mary.** *Risk Acceptability According to the Social Sciences.* New York: Russell Sage Foundation, 1985. 115 pages.

A review of such topics as public concern about risk, the psychology of human emotions and their influence on risk perception, theories of risk aversion and risk taking, and the role of culture and social values in allocating blame.

"Provides the most compelling solution to the question of why we worry about some risks but not others of comparable magnitude and probability. A scintillating critique of the dominant models of national choice theory, psychology, and economics, arguing that divergent moral principles shape perceptions of nature and technology."—Steve Rayner, deputy director, Global Environmental Studies Center, Oak Ridge National Laboratory

170.   **Dubos, Rene. *The Wooing of Earth*.** New York: Scribner's, 1980. 183 pages.

Dubos, the humanist, shares in this book his passion for landscapes, both natural and human-made. His view of the world, however, is human-centered; he believes that the earth offers its greatest potential when manipulated by human creativity and labor. This idea of an earth-to-be-nurtured, Dubos feels, should logically lead one to feel a sense of responsibility. That is to say that humankind, in its expression of achievement, should have the responsibility of managing the earth both with care and with an aesthetic purpose. Yet he sees that responsibility too often overpowered by unattractive human characteristics, resulting in a planet that often is plundered or neglected. Dubos hopes for the beauty of environmentally responsible human design in the world, yet sees also the ugliness of human greed and indifference.

171.   **Dunne, Peter, David Sibley, and Clay Sutton. *Hawks in Flight*.** Illustrated by David Sibley. Boston: Houghton Mifflin, 1988. 254 pages.

This "guide" presents a new way to see twenty-three species of raptors (buteos, accipiters, falcons, kites, eagles, vultures, northern harrier, and osprey). It goes beyond the traditional system of recognition that uses "field marks," and instead emphasizes other characteristics related to the bird and its context. This is an excellent book to supplement the traditional field guides, and should be of interest to both novice and advanced birders. (See also entry 224 for a related book on hawk migration.)

"The new approach to identifying birds seen flying hundreds of yards away against the sky, by flight style, general body shape, place, and season in which their species are most likely to be seen . . . a matter of overall impression. The first holistic bird guide."—Myriam Moore, secretary, Hawk Migration Association of North America

172.   **Durrell, Lee. *State of the Ark*.** Foreword by Gerald Durrell. Garden City, NY: Doubleday, 1986. 224 pages.

Richly illustrated, this book thoroughly reviews the status of wildlife around the world. It discusses human impacts on the biosphere, considers the diversity of ecosystems and the wildlife within them, examines threats to the survival of various species, and assesses the growth and impact of conservation organizations and activities. The book contains an abundance of colorful maps, illustrations, and photographs, with scores of case study capsules that illustrate major concepts.

173. **Eckholm, Erik P.** *Losing Ground: Environmental Stress and World Food Prospects.* Elmsford, New York: Pergamon, 1978. 223 pages.

To draw attention to the global threat of ecosystem destruction and its capacity to undermine food production is the intent of this book. Eckholm describes ecological degradation from forest destruction, soil erosion and siltation, and excessive exploitation of land and aquatic resources, to show that the number of options for providing food for humanity is declining. His book was one of the earliest to highlight the problem of desertification in many parts of the world. He cites historic and contemporary cases to illustrate the incompatibility of most conventional agricultural methods with viable ecological systems, and recommends ways to make them more compatible.

Also recommended is Eckholm's *Down to Earth: Environment and Human Needs* (Norton, 1982). This book was commissioned by the United Nations Environment Programme to give a popularized overview of the condition of the world's environment ten years after the 1972 U.N. Conference on the Human Environment in Stockholm, Sweden.

174. **Ehrenfeld, David.** *The Arrogance of Humanism.* New York: Oxford University Press, 1978. 286 pages.

Ehrenfeld critiques the humanistic viewpoint, showing how its perspective has dominated for centuries the relationship between humans and the rest of the biosphere. He questions the notion of conservation of natural resources as merely an extension of selfish, human-centered consumption. In discussing such preservation, he suggests that "the humanistic world accepts the conservation of Nature only piecemeal and at a price: there must be a logical, practical reason for saving each and every part of the natural world that we wish to preserve" (p. 177).

175. **Ehrlich, Paul R., and Anne H. Ehrlich.** *The Population Explosion.* New York: Simon & Schuster, 1990. 320 pages.

This book brings us up-to-date on the devastating impacts of unchecked human population growth forecasted in Paul Ehrlich's *The Population Bomb* (see entry 32). These impacts on the environment have been significant and their consequences seem difficult to avoid.

"The dynamic duo are back again with a thoroughly documented and cogently argued demonstration that human numbers do count. They show that the population time bomb is ticking faster and why it is the most serious threat to the future of humans and nonhumans alike. For too long, the one-dimensional arguments about the (very real) evils of maldistribution have been allowed to disguise the fact that no matter how we cut the cake, human society is now so big that its numbers threaten to destroy the very oven in which it is baked."—Sandy Irvine, associate editor, *The Ecologist,* Newcastle Upon Tyne, England

176. **Ehrlich, Paul R., David S. Dobkin, and Darryl Wheye.** *The Birder's Handbook: A Field Guide to the Natural History of North American Birds.* New York: Simon & Schuster, 1988. 785 pages.

This is a comprehensive reference book on birds of North America, which was designed to be used with identification guides. For each species, there is a half page of detail on breeding habitat, courtship display, nest and egg characteristics, diet, and other useful information. The user is encouraged to supplement these facts with data from personal field observations and contribute to the knowledge of bird biology. In addition to the data entries, there are hundreds of "essays" that explore a variety of topics on birds and birders. A substantial bibliography of references is provided. See also the authors' more recent book, *Birds in Jeopardy: The Imperiled and Extinct Birds of the United States and Canada, including Hawaii and Puerto Rico* (Stanford University Press, 1992).

"Not since *The Birds of America* [Macmillan, 1937; by John James Audubon] has a book more perfectly blended identification and essay copy, and in such an updated way."—Carl Slater, president, Brooks Bird Club

177. **Eiseley, Loren C.** *The Invisible Pyramid.* Woodcuts by Walter Ferro. New York: Scribner's, 1970. 173 pages.

A reflection by Eiseley on his life and on the human species, its consciousness of self and of the universe, and its destiny on earth and beyond.

"My top choice for an environmental book. This is the Eiseley of mature years, reflecting on society, its environment, and the sweep of evolution that brought us here. The invisible pyramid of the title is the scientific-rationalist society in which we find ourselves. He has hope, but is not optimistic. Near the end of the book he says, 'By those destined to create the future, my voice may not, perhaps, be trusted. I know only that I speak from the timeless country revisited, from the cold of vast tundras and the original dispersals, not from the indrawings of men.' "—John Steinhart, professor of geophysics and of environmental studies, University of Wisconsin–Madison

178. **Eiseley, Loren C. *The Night Country*.** Illustrations by Leonard Everett Fisher. New York: Scribner's, 1971. 240 pages.

Another inspiring book by Eiseley, the scientist and philospher, in which he ponders numerous occurrences in his past and how they shaped his attitudes and actions later in life.

"This is one of those books which takes you back to your own childhood when you were wordlessly aware of the natural world around you, if you were that kind of child (and I was). Then brings you up through the thinking of the adult about natural things. If I had read this twenty years before I did it would have had as much effect on me as Thoreau. Eiseley's use of English is magical."—Mary P. Sherwood, chair, Walden Forever Wild

Also recommended are Eiseley's *The Firmament of Time* (Atheneum, 1960) and *Notes of an Alchemist* (Scribner's, 1972).

179. **Elkington, John, Julia Hailes, and Joel Makower. *The Green Consumer*.** New York: Penguin, 1990. 342 pages.

The slogan on the cover of this book says, "Be a Green Consumer Today and Help Save the Earth for Tomorrow." Given that citizens in the industrialized countries are consuming a disproportionate (some would say exorbitant) amount of the world's energy and resources, the guide is a small attempt to show concerned citizens how they can curtail their wasteful and harmful consumption patterns. Specifically, it shows how individuals can take beginning steps to deal with seven major environmental problems: acid rain, global warming and the greenhouse effect, ozone depletion, air pollution, loss of rain forests and biodiversity, garbage, and water pollution. The authors urge the reader to select products without a lot of packaging, recycle as much as possible, stop the delivery of junk mail, reduce fuel consumption, and select and use nontoxic products. A chapter on "how to get involved" highlights steps that more activist persons might want to use to affect political or economic changes, beyond simply altering personal consumption patterns. A bibliography of readings and a listing of environmental organizations is also provided. A related book is *Going Green: A Kid's Handbook to Saving the Planet* (Puffin, 1990), by John Elkington, Julia Hailes, Douglas Hill, and Joel Makower.

180.   **Elton, Charles. S. *The Ecology of Invasions by Animals and Plants.*** London: Methuen, 1958. 181 pages.

A well-illustrated and well-documented book with maps showing the points of invasion and distribution patterns of invading animals and plants introduced into new environments of continents, remote islands, and marine areas. The examples Elton chooses to illustrate these ecological invasions are: the bubonic plague in the United States; the African malaria mosquito in Brazil; the Asiatic chestnut blight in the United States; the European starling in the United States; and Chinese mitten cats in Europe. He combines notions of history, ecology and conservation to show the impacts of invaders on their new ecosystems. An interesting look at Elton's life and work from 1932 to 1967 can be found in *Elton's Ecologists: A History of the Bureau of Animal Population* (University of Chicago Press, 1991), by Peter Crowcroft.

"This first impressed me with the significance of ecological diversity. It is one of the best environmental books ever written and was most impressive when published."—John L. Cloudsley-Thompson, professor emeritus of zoology at University College, London

181.   **Emerson, Ralph Waldo. *Nature.*** A Facsimile of the First Edition with an Introduction by Jaroslav Pelikan. Boston: Beacon, 1985 (orig. pub. 1836). 95 pages.

Nature is an inherent experience of human existence, yet, as Emerson states, "few adult persons can see nature" (p. 11). Emerson's outline of the experiential process between humans and nature has been the foundation for the work of successive generations of naturalists and nature writers.

"Emerson's seminal essay outlines the thesis that nature is the American religion. Thoreau, Bryant, and the transcendentalists follow where he led. No one speaks with more original force on what we should learn from nature."—J. William Futrell, president, Environmental Law Institute

182. **Evernden, Neil.** *The Natural Alien: Humankind and Environment.* Toronto: University of Toronto Press, 1985. 160 pages.

This is an interesting discussion about the conceptions humans have had of the environment and of their position in the environment. Evernden suggests that "there are grounds for regarding humans as exotics of a sort, since technological innovation may effectively cast its creator out of context" (p. 122).

"Phenomenology brought to life. Insightful, deep, penetrating."— Bill Devall, author/teacher, Humboldt State University

183. **Farb, Peter.** *Face of North America: The Natural History of a Continent.* New York: Harper, 1963. 316 pages.

With the art of a travel writer and the knowledge of a scholar versed in geology, biology, and history, Farb takes the reader on a tour of the best natural wonders all over North America. He skillfully describes the natural features encountered in different landscapes across the continent and gives an understandable and thorough explanation of the processes that have created these environments.

"Although a number of books have dealt with the subject of the natural history of a continent, this is one of my favorites, in part because the author is outstanding, but also because the subject is covered so completely and the text is so readable."—James A. Fowler, former chair, Michigan Natural Areas Council

Also recommended is Farb's *Living Earth* (Harper, 1959).

184. **Farvar, M. Taghi, and John P. Milton, eds.** *The Careless Technology: Ecology and International Development.* Garden City, NY: Natural History, 1972. 1030 pages.

Commissioned by The Conservation Foundation, this collection of fifty papers was one of the earliest to examine in detail the ecological implications of international development. Too often, such development projects are planned and implemented without consideration of the long-term environmental implications. And tragically, the negative impacts of these projects happen in countries that are the most vulnerable and can least afford environmental mistakes. This book calls for a review of development goals so that a harmony can exist between technological advances, the biosphere, and the biological potential of humans.

"Dramatized through case studies the negative environmental consequences of development schemes."—C. Dart Thalman, former director, Quebec-Labrador Foundation/Atlantic Center for the Environment

185.   Fisk, Erma J. *The Peacocks of Baboquivari.* Illustrated by Louise Russell. New York: Norton, 1983. 284 pages.

From December 1978 to May 1979, Fisk, who was well past "retirement" age, became the sole human resident on a 640-acre mountain ranch located near Baboquivari Peak in southwest Arizona. At the behest of the property owner, The Nature Conservancy, she was to survey the birds of the area during the winter months. In this book she chronicles her work, life, and adventures on the mountain, and reflects on her past, including her extensive involvement in bird conservation activities in the United States and abroad. After reading this book, one gets a sense of really having known Fisk, and many readers will wonder and want to know more about her. More of Fisk is revealed in a subsequent book, *Parrot's Wood* (Norton, 1985) which describes a bird-banding expedition in Belize.

186.   Flader, Susan L. *Thinking Like a Mountain: Aldo Leopold and the Evolution of an Ecological Attitude Toward Deer, Wolves, and Forests.* Columbia: University of Missouri Press, 1974. 284 pages.

Flader examines Leopold's professional career, beginning with his stint in the U.S. Forest Service in the Gila Wilderness of Arizona, and the subsequent development and merger of his scientific and philosophical attitude toward nature. By focussing on his personal attitudes, she characterizes the evolution of his public attitudes as well. The title of this biography, *Thinking Like a Mountain,* was taken from one of the essays contained in Leopold's *A Sand County Almanac* (see entry 43), an essay Flader says was a milestone for Leopold "and the only one in which Leopold acknowledges a major change in his thinking over the years" (p. 4).

187.   Foreman, Dave. *Confessions of an Eco-Warrior.* New York: Harmony, 1991. 228 pages.

This contains the thoughts of David Foreman, the cofounder of the radical environmental group Earth First! He reflects here on the role of monkeywrenching, offers a blueprint for wilderness preservation, and laments about the "professionalization" of environmental organizations. Foreman is also the coeditor of *Ecodefense: A Field Guide to Monkeywrenching* (Ned Ludd, 1987). For an overview of monkeywrenchers and other radical environmentalists, see Rik Scarce's *Eco-Warriors: Understanding the Radical Environmental Movement* (Noble, 1990) and *The Earth First! Reader: Years of Radical Environmentalism,* edited by John Davis (Peregrine Smith, 1991).

188.   Forsyth, Adrian, and Ken Miyata. *Tropical Nature: Life and Death in Rain Forests of Central and South America.* New York: Scribner's, 1984. 248 pages.

A combination of natural history, geography, and philosophy, this book shows the beauty and wonder, as well as the treachery, to be found in the rainforests of Central and South America. The authors include a beginner's guide to tropical travel—a very useful reference.

189.   Friends of the Earth. *Progress as if Survival Mattered: A Handbook for a Conserver Society.* 2d ed. Introduction by David Brower. San Francisco: Friends of the Earth, 1981 (orig. pub. 1977). 456 pages.

A reader on a wide range of environmental issues, from one of the more visible and outspoken environmental groups.

"Along the same lines as *Small is Beautiful,* [see entry 81] but covering a wider range of topics and providing alternative perspectives on the subjects covered."—Apichai Sunchindah, project officer, Swiss Development Cooperation Regional Coordination Office, Bangkok, Thailand

190.   Frisch, Monica. *Directory for the Environment: Organisations, Campaigns and Initiatives in the British Isles.* 3d ed. London: Green Print, 1990. 263 pages.

A compilation that describes and provides addresses and telephone numbers for some 1500 environmental and conservation organizations in Great Britain. A bibliography directs the reader to important sources of information, and a topical index identifies organizations by key words. A sampling of other directories (in English) of environmental organizations around the world includes: *Directory of African Environmental and Conservation Non-Governmental Organizations* (African NGOs Environment Network, 1989); *Directory of Environmental NGOs in the Asia/Pacific Region* (Sahabat Alam Malaysia, 1988), edited by V. C. Mohan; *Environmental NGOs in India* (The Group, 1989); *The Green Pages: Directory of Non-Government Environmental Groups in Australia* (Australian Conservation Foundation, 1990), edited by George Dalton; *Directory of Non-Governmental Environmental and Development Organisations in the OECD Member Countries* (Organisation for Economic Cooperation and Development, 1992); *A Directory of European Environmental Organizations* (Blackwell, 1991), by Mireille Deziron; and *The Green List: A Guide to Canadian Environmental Organizations and Agencies* (Canadian Environmental Network, 1991). A comprehensive worldwide listing of organizations can be found in *World Environmental Directory* (Business Publishers, 1991, 6th ed.).

191. **Fritzell, Peter A.** *Nature Writing and America: Essays Upon a Cultural Type.* Ames: Iowa State University Press, 1990. 354 pages.

Fritzell, a professor of English at Lawrence University in Wisconsin, has prepared a major study and critical analysis of nature writing in America. He establishes a theory for criticizing and interpreting nature writing, both as a form of exposition and as a cultural phenomenon. He then applies his analytical framework to three works: Henry David Thoreau's *Walden* (see entry 90), Aldo Leopold's *A Sand County Almanac* (see entry 43), and Annie Dillard's *A Pilgrim at Tinker Creek* (see entry 30). His "synchronic" and "diachronic" diagrams characterizing nature writing are impressive, and can be compared with the "taxonomy of nature writing" developed by Thomas J. Lyon in *This Incomparable Lande* (see entry 238).

192. **Frome, Michael.** *Conscience of a Conservationist: Selected Essays.* Knoxville: University of Tennessee Press, 1989. 285 pages.

This is a distillation of three decades of Frome's writings into twenty-eight essays. Frome has made a lifelong commitment to conservation, crafting his books and articles primarily around issues and places in the southern Appalachian region. Many times he challenged federal and state government agencies about their wrong-headed decisions (usually road or dam projects), sometimes at a cost to his own economic security. The essays come from more than a dozen magazines, including *American Forests, Field & Stream, Smithsonian,* and *National Parks,* and from three of his more widely read books: *Whose Woods These Are—The Story of the National Forests* (Doubleday, 1962); *Strangers in High Places: The Story of The Great Smoky Mountains* (University of Tennessee Press, 1988 rev. ed.); and *Battle for the Wilderness* (Praeger, 1974).

193. **Fuertes, Louis Agassiz, and Wilfred Hudson Osgood.** *Artist and Naturalist in Ethiopia.* New York: Doubleday, 1936. 249 pages.

This is about an expedition, sponsored by the Chicago Field Museum and the *Chicago Daily News,* undertaken by Fuertes and Osgood from September 1926 through April 1927. The fascinating day-to-day accounts of their journey are complemented by the stunning watercolor illustrations by Fuertes, which portray the beauty of such birds as the malachite kingfisher, hooded vulture, Nubian vulture, white-headed vulture, lanner, black-shouldered kite, bateleur eagle, tawny eagle, black-bellied bustard, brown-hooded kingfisher, and Narina's trogon.

194. **Fukuoka, Masanobu.** *The One-Straw Revolution.* Emmaus, PA: Rodale, 1978. 181 pages.

In a village in southern Japan, Fukuoka developed his method of "natural farming," which uses no machinery, no chemicals, and minimal weeding. His ideas have taken hold thoughout Japan and many other parts of the world, altering the agricultural practices of many farmers. While he emphasizes a planned schedule of activities throughout the year, he also attempts to minimize the amount of labor involved in applying these techniques.

"A radical critique of farming, arguably man's greatest impact on the biosphere."—Peter Bane, publisher, *The Permaculture Activist*

195. **Gibbons, Felton, and Deborah Strom.** *Neighbors to the Birds: A History of Birdwatching in America.* New York: Norton, 1988. 364 pages.

This is an excellently written chronicle of bird study, bird-watching and bird preservation in the United States, beginning with the early studies by lone naturalists to the more contemporary popular movements. The analysis of the authors provides a good sense of the motivations of key individuals involved in the bird-watching movement, as well as the social and political contexts that affected them. And as Gibbons and Strom suggest, to understand the history of bird-watching in America is to understand a significant part of the overall conservation and environmental movement in this country. Whether you are a bird-watcher or not, you will find this book both entertaining and informative.

196. **Goldsmith, Edward, and Nicholas Hildyard, eds.** *The Earth Report: Monitoring the Battle for Our Environment.* London: Mitchell Beazley, 1988 (revised edition published in 1990 as *The Earth Report 2*). 240 pages.

Goldsmith has a great track record as a purveyor of insightful information on the state of the environment, both in Great Britain and globally. The first edition of *The Earth Report* contains six topical essays by James Lovelock, Lloyd Timberlake, Donald Worster, and others, followed by an encyclopedia of facts on the places, events, individuals, and other aspects related to contemporary environmental issues. The revised edition contains only an expanded version of the encyclopedia.

"A very up-to-date summary on current events and what action should be taken. Clean and precise."—John Revington, director, Rainforest Information Centre, New South Wales, Australia

Also recommended is *Blueprint for Survival* (Houghton Mifflin, 1972), prepared by Goldsmith and other staff of *The Ecologist*, which had a major impact when it was published, especially in Europe.

197.   **Goldstein, Eric, and Mark Izeman.** *The New York Environment Book.* Covelo, CA: Island, 1990. 263 pages.

Each day in New York City, approximately 7000 pounds of heavy metals are discharged into the waterways from industrial, commercial, and residential sources. Air pollutants are emitted from some 2200 incinerators around the city. Raw sewage is discharged from nearly 500 outfalls of New York's inadequate storm sewer and wastewater sanitation systems. These are a few of the facts presented in this book. Written by two environmental lawyers with the Natural Resources Defense Council, it looks at the state of New York City's environment in five areas: solid waste, waterways and the coast, air pollution, drinking water, and toxics. The authors also provide "a treasure chest of ideas" that individuals and groups can use to help eliminate many of the environmental problems described in the book.

"Takes one city and gives a very thorough account of environmental issues that face the city, including the origins and possible solutions to those problems, and presents it in a clear and comprehensive way."—Gary Benenson, associate professor of technology, City College of the City University of New York

198.   **Gore, Albert, Jr.** *Earth in the Balance: Ecology and the Human Spirit.* (Boston: Houghton Mifflin, 1992). 407 pages.

As a U.S. Senator, Gore was a leading advocate for stronger United States and global environmental policy. In this book, he presents a plea for action on issues such as global warming, ozone depletion, toxic waste, and soil erosion. He brings together an extensive review of scientific evidence with personal experience and an ethical and spiritual commitment. He also demonstrates the need for inter-generational responsibility for protecting this planet.

199. Gottlieb, Robert, and Margaret FitzSimmons. *Thirst for Growth: Water Agencies as Hidden Government in California.* Tucson: University of Arizona, 1991. 286 pages.

Written by two planning professors at the University of California–Los Angeles, this book examines the political economy of the water industry of southern California. The authors review the historical development of selected water agencies in region: the Metropolitan Water District of southern California; the City of Burbank Public Service Department; the Upper San Gabriel Valley Municipal Water District; the San Diego County Water Authority; the Kern County Water Agency; and the Imperial Irrigation District. Following is an analysis of the decision-making processes and activities of these agencies, particularly vis-à-vis their influence on the promotion of economic growth and urban expansion and in setting public policy.

200. Goudie, Andrew. *The Human Impact on the Environment.* rev. ed. Cambridge, MA: MIT Press, 1986 (orig. pub. 1981). 338 pages.

Goudie, a professor of geography at Oxford University, uses a wide range of historical examples to discuss the ways in which human activity has modified the vegetation, soil, waters, and atmosphere of the earth.

201. Gould, Stephen Jay. *The Mismeasure of Man.* New York: Norton, 1981. 352 pages.

———. *The Panda's Thumb: More Reflections in Natural History.* Norton, 1980. 343 pages.

———. *Wonderful Life: The Burgess Shale and the Nature of History.* New York: Norton, 1989. 347 pages.

Gould, professor of zoology at Harvard University and contributing writer for *Natural History* magazine, is one of the better known polymaths of our time, gaining recognition through his numerous books, magazine articles, and public lectures. His popularity seems to arise from the fact that he is such a good communicator to the public, or at least to the informed public, of what science is all about and what scientists really do. His writings convey the importance of scientific discoveries within their historical context, and show the personalities and motivations of the scientists involved in the so-called "pursuit of truth."

202.   **Graves, John.** *Goodbye to a River: A Narrative.* New York: Knopf, 1960. 306 pages.

A thoughtful chronicle of Graves's three-week canoe trip down the Brazos River in north central Texas, which was then destined to be dammed—a river where he had spent much of his youth was soon to be changed drastically.

203.   **Gray, Elizabeth Dodson.** *Green Paradise Lost.* Welesley, MA: Roundtable, 1982. 166 pages.

Expanding upon ideas about "the psycho-sexual roots of our ecological crisis," Gray addresses some key questions about our society's masculine attitudes toward nature and our need for a new consciousness of the earth, on the part of both men and women.

"A deceptively simple little book that looks at some of our attitudes towards nature and considers where they come from. Examines the ridiculousness of these attitudes in a very approachable and sensible way. Everyone I've shared this with has been captivated."—Annie Booth, doctoral candidate, Institute for Environmental Studies, University of Wisconsin–Madison

204.   **Gunn, Alastair S., and P. Aarne Vesilind.** *Environmental Ethics for Engineers.* Chelsea, MI: Lewis, 1986. 153 pages.

This book attempts to help the professional engineer see his or her actions more clearly in the context of human society as well as within the context of the natural world. Gunn and Vesilind introduce the concept of environmental ethics and document the importance it should play in professional engineering practice. They suggest that "engineering education should address not only the technical questions, but introduce the concept of values, and the methodologies for decisionmaking when values conflict" (p. 38). The authors have assembled a number of readings and case studies to emphasize certain concepts or specific instances where ethical choices had to be made. An appendix includes the Code of Ethics of the American Society of Civil Engineering, as well as a "primer" on ethical themes.

"Lays out clearly the ethical responsibilities of technologists regarding the environment, providing excerpts (by permission) from much of the best writing, and gives summary case histories of classic environmental engineering disasters."—Richard L. Perrine, professor of civil engineering, University of California–Los Angeles

205.   Hall, Bob, and Mary Lee Kerr. *Green Index: A State-by-State Guide to the Nation's Environmental Health.* Covelo, CA: Island, 1991.

Compiled by the Institute for Southern Studies in Durham, North Carolina, this guide uses a set of 256 indicators to measure and rank the environmental condition of the fifty states. One of the more exceptional tables summarizes the best and worst findings of the indicators, showing the areas in which each state excels and fails. The more motivated reader might want to follow up in his or her particular state to look more closely at what variations exist within the state, such as on a county-by-county basis, thus getting a more localized view of environmental conditions.

206.   Harrison, Paul. *The Greening of Africa: Breaking through in the Battle for Land and Food.* London: Paladin for International Institute for Environment and Development/Earthscan, 1987. 380 pages.

Harrison describes and characterizes successful, ecologically sustainable development efforts in Africa to determine if they are replicable in other locations. He provides background on environmental and food crises in Africa, and outlines specific criteria for successful development projects. The final section draws lessons from this set of projects.

Also recommended is Harrison's *Inside the Third World* (Penguin, 1982, 2d rev. ed.), an intimate look at the social and environmental stresses in developing countries.

207.   Hecht, Susanna, and Alexander Cockburn. *The Fate of the Forest: Developers, Destroyers, and Defenders of the Amazon.* New York: Verso, 1989. 266 pages.

What is happening to Brazil's environment and why? This book provides an overview of the current human use and misuse of the Brazilian Amazon, with detailed historical, environmental, political, and economic analyses of the causes and processes that have led to these contemporary conditions. Hecht, a geographer at the University of California–Los Angeles, and Cockburn, a noted political columnist, have obtained information for this book from a variety of sources: interviews, archival materials, scientific data, and personal observations. The book is illustrated with photographs, drawings, and maps, and contains several appendices, including a glossary and selected transcripts of interviews.

Three additional popular accounts of what is happening in the Amazon are: *The Decade of Destruction: The Crusade to Save the Amazon Forests* (Holt, 1990), by Adrian Cowell, which is also a Frontline television documentary; *The World is Burning: Murder in the Rainforest* (Little, Brown, 1990), by Alex Shoumatoff; and *The Burning Season: The Murder of Chico Mendes and the Fight for the Amazon Rain Forest* (Houghton Mifflin, 1990), by Andrew Revkin. Also, Suzanne Head and Robert Heinzman have edited a collection of essays in *Lessons of the Rainforest* (Sierra Club, 1990). Several academic treatments of the issues can be found in *Developing the Amazon* (University of Indiana Press, 1981), by Emilio F. Moran; *Underdeveloping the Amazon: Extraction, Unequal Exchange, and the Failure of the Modern State* (University of Illinois Press, 1981), by Stephen G. Bunker; *Human Carrying Capacity of the Brazilian Rainforest* (Columbia University Press, 1986), by Phillip M. Fearnside; and *Ecology and Land Management in Amazonia* (Belhaven, 1990), by Michael J. Eden.

208. Heilbroner, Robert L. *An Inquiry into the Human Prospect*. New York: Norton, 1974. 150 pages.

These are Heilbroner's reflections on where we are as a society and whether we can extricate ourselves from what he calls the "civilizational malaise." He suggests that there are a number of internal and external forces in society, such as population growth, wars and conflicts, and certain cultural and psychological characteristics, that simply may be too many constraints on us to overcome in order to make significant changes.

"This is a rather gloomy book, but the moderate and sane tone keeps it from being a disaster book. Heilbroner does not dwell on the details, but brings the impact on government into the environmental discussion. Most economists writing on environmental issues seem to dwell on bringing pollution costs into the marketplace. Heilbroner realizes that there is more at stake than pollution permits."—John Steinhart, professor of geophysics and of environmental studies, University of Wisconsin–Madison

209. Hoagland, Edward. *The Edward Hoagland Reader*. Edited by Geoffrey Wolff. New York: Random House, 1979. 399 pages.

More than twenty selections from the vast collection of Hoagland's books, short stories, essays and book reviews that deal with life in the wilderness and life in the city. His stories are sometimes irreverent, often with intricate details of natural landscapes and of the people and animals who live there.

210. **Holdgate, Martin W., Mohammed Kassas, and Gilbert F. White,** eds. *The World Environment 1972–82: A Report by the United Nations Environment Programme.* New York: Tycooly, 1982. 637 pages.

This book reports on progress in environmental and policy changes since the 1972 United Nations Conference on the Human Environment in Stockholm, Sweden. The authors, who are distinguished international environmental experts, review the implementation of recommendations that resulted from the Stockholm conference, and document changes in the physical environment, the human situation, and activities that modify the environment. They offer conclusions as well as their own recommendations to further the goals identified in 1972. Mostafa K. Tolba has likewise edited a related book, *Evolving Environmental Perceptions: From Stockholm to Nairobi* (Butterworth, 1988), that reports on a special session of the United Nations Environment Programme held in Nairobi, Kenya, in 1982 to evaluate changes in environmental trends since 1972. An additional comparison of progress can be made by examining the documents that resulted from the twenty-year anniversary U.N. Conference on the Human Environment, held in Rio de Janeiro, Brazil, in 1992. See also *Only One Earth* (entry 95), by Barbara Ward and Rene Dubos.

211. **Hornaday, William T.** *The American Natural History: A Foundation of Useful Knowledge of the Higher Animals of North America.* 15th ed. New York: Scribner's, 1927 (orig. pub. 1904). 449 pages.

Hornaday, as director of the New York Zoological Park, was an important figure in wildlife protection at the turn of the century. He was also very active in educating the public about nature and conservation issues. As he states in his introduction, "In these days of struggle and stress for place and power, and in these nights of insomnia and nerves, there are few side issues more restful or more pleasantly diverting to a tired brain than an active interest in some branch of natural history" (p. v). This "encyclopedia of natural history" covers mammals, birds, reptiles, amphibians, and fishes, and has more than 350 drawings and photographs to accompany the descriptions of habits and habitats of each species.

Also recommended are two other works by Hornaday: *Campfires on Desert and Lava* (Scribner's, 1908) and *Our Vanishing Wildlife: Its Extermination and Preservation* (Scribner's, 1913).

212. **Howard, Albert.** *An Agricultural Testament.* New York: Oxford University press, 1943. 253 pages.

This is one of the early classics in the literature that deals with sustainable agriculture. Howard focusses on the Indore Process, which recycles organic wastematter and is used to improve the humus content of soil. The method was developed between 1924 and 1931 at the Institute of Plant Industry in Indore, India, during Howard's tenure there as director. Howard criticizes his contemporaries in the agricultural research community and selects several examples of what he considers successful agricultural research programs.

213.   **Hughes, J. Donald.** *Ecology in Ancient Civilizations.* Albuquerque: University of New Mexico Press, 1975. 181 pages.

Hughes discusses attitudes concerning nature in ancient Greek, Roman and Judeo-Christian cultures in the Mediterranean basin. His main focus is on the role of religious and other beliefs in early environmental history. He also documents the ways in which these cultures transformed their environments through deforestation, soil erosion, pollution and hunting.

214.   **Huth, Hans.** *Nature and the American: Three Centuries of Changing Attitudes.* Lincoln: University of Nebraska Press, 1972 (orig. pub. 1957, University of California Press). 250 pages.

Huth shows how the notion of conservation developed in America, particularly during the nineteenth and early twentieth centuries. He suggests that a national conservation ethic emerged through individual efforts in art and architecture, literature, science, and through increased recreational experiences by ordinary citizens, along with other factors.

"Best exposition of the evidence in literature of the evolution of American concerns for the landscape."—Daniel B. Luten, professor emeritus of geography, University of California–Berkeley

215.   **Huxley, Anthony J.** *Green Inheritance: The World Wildlife Fund Book of Plants.* Foreword by David Attenborough. Garden City, NY: Anchor/Doubleday, 1985. 193 pages.

This is a beautifully illustrated book, containing copies of paintings and photographs that depict the variety of plant life around the world. From an anthopocentric viewpoint, Huxley documents the wide range of medicinal, agricultural, nutritional, economic, ecologic, and aesthetic uses that plants provide humans.

216.   **Independent Commission on International Development Issues.**

North-South: A Programme for Survival. Cambridge, MA: MIT Press, 1980. 304 pages.

This is the report of an international commission that was headed by Willy Brandt, the former chancellor of West Germany. The commission studied global issues and problems arising from the uneven distribution of social and economic assets. Several chapters outline the problems related to food, population, energy, and the arms buildup. Much of the report addresses the world economic situation and the strategies necessary for international economic balance. The book includes the commission's recommended reforms of the world economic order, including improvements in the monetary reserve system, balance of payments, and exchange rates. These issues were similarly studied by the World Commission on Environment and Development and reported in its book *Our Common Future* (see entry 98).

217. **International Union for the Conservation of Nature and Natural Resources.** ***The Red Data Books.*** Gland, Switzerland: IUCN.

Developed during the mid-1960s, these data books, which can be found in most large libraries, were originally loose-leaf notebooks containing lists of rare, threatened, and endangered species from around the world. There were originally five books in the series: *Mammals* (1966), by Noel Simon; *Birds* (1966), by Jack Vincent; *Amphibians and Reptiles* (1968), by Rene Honegger; *Fish* (1969), by Robert Miller; and *Flowering Plants* (1969), by Robert Melville. The series was converted to hardbound editions in the early 1980s, and a volume on *Invertebrates* (by Susan M. Wells, Robert M. Pyle, and N. Mark Collins) was added in 1983. The information for each species includes distribution (present and former), estimated numbers, number in captivity, breeding rate in the wild and in captivity, reasons for decline, and protective measures proposed or being taken. This series is certainly the authoritative international register of threatened species.

218. **International Union for the Conservation of Nature and Natural Resources, with assistance from World Wildlife Fund and United Nations Environment Programme.** ***World Conservation Strategy: Living Resource Conservation for Sustainable Development.*** Morges, Switzerland: IUCN, 1980. 55 pages.

The *World Conservation Strategy* was designed as a global guide to manage the conservation of living natural resources to meet human needs, especially in the developing countries. Its recommendations cover political and educational objectives, and include suggestions on how to improve conservation institutions and conservation planning. The guide proposes specific requirements and criteria for the management of species and ecosystems, and encompasses strategies for international cooperation and responsibility, international agencies, and nongovernmental organizations. A follow-up to *World Conservation Strategy* is presented in *Caring for Earth: A Strategy for Sustainable Living* (IUCN/UNEP/WWF, 1991).

"The WCS was intended to stimulate a more focussed approach to the management of living resources and to provide policy guidance on how this can be carried out by government policy makers, conservationists, and development practitioners."— Kevin L. Grose, librarian, United Nations Environment Programme, Nairobi, Kenya.

219. **Jackson, Wes.** *New Roots for Agriculture.* Lincoln: University of Nebraska Press, 1985 (orig. pub. 1980). 150 pages.

Wes Jackson and his wife Dana Jackson are codirectors of the Land Institute near Salina in Kansas. In this book, he offers a solution for that age-old agricultural problem: how to maintain agricultural productivity without destroying the land in the process. He urges the use of perennial crops that can be harvested annually to provide grains and seeds, yet remain firmly planted in the soil from year to year. This would eliminate the need for plowing and tilling, and would reduce soil erosion losses.

"A moving and visionary look at the need for change in agriculture, based on stewardship."—Stephen R. Gliessman, director, Agroecology program, University of California–Santa Cruz.

Also recommended is Jackson's *Altars of Unhewn Stone: Science and the Earth* (North Point, 1987).

220. **Jasanoff, Sheila.** *Risk Management and Political Culture: A Comparative Study of Science in the Policy Context.* New York: Russell Sage Foundation, 1986. 93 pages.

The author reviews how we as a society perceive the benefits and costs of technologies, and make decisions regarding them. This is especially difficult given that many of the benefits and costs are intangibles (items for which a value cannot be easily given), and that there is often scientific uncertainty concerning the risks and impacts of technologies. She discusses the ways different societies evaluate risks, and speculates on the role that "democratic values" have or should have in the decisionmaking process.

"Brilliantly illustrates the fact that information about established technologies, such as formaldehyde use, is interpreted differently by scientific advisory committees in different countries."—Steve Rayner, deputy director, Global Environmental Studies Center, Oak Ridge Laboratory.

221.　**Jorgensen, Eric P.** *The Poisoned Well: New Strategies for Groundwater Protection,* Covelo, CA: Island, 1989. 415 pages.

Prepared by the staff of the Sierra Club Legal Defense Fund, this is a comprehensive and very usable guide for citizens, government officials, and professionals concerned with groundwater protection and management. The book is divided into four parts: (1) definitions and basic concepts on groundwater occurrence, movement, and contamination; (2) advice on how individuals and groups can get the information they need and how they can become involved in the policymaking process; (3) groundwater laws, rules, and programs at the federal level; and (4) examples of state and local efforts at groundwater protection. The five appendices provide sources of further information from federal and state agencies and public interest groups.

222.　**Kash, Don E., Irwin L. White, Karl H. Bergey, Michael A. Chartock, Michael D. Devine, R. Leon Leonard, Stephen N. Salomon, and Harold W. Young.** *Energy Under the Oceans: A Technology Assessment of the Outer Continental Shelf Oil and Gas Operations.* Norman: University of Oklahoma Press, 1973. 378 pages.

This was an early and important contribution to the then-emerging field of "technology assessment," which is the process of making policy decisions based on a structured and objective review of the possible consequences of technological changes. Technology assessment considers the outcomes of alternative technologies, as well as what could be expected if the technological change or the adoption of a particular technology did not occur. Kash and his colleagues in the Science and Public Policy Program at the University of Oklahoma look at a variety of technologies used in the oil and gas operations of the outer-continental shelf, identifying possible outcomes of their implementation as well as policy options to facilitate desirable changes. This is a classic study of the interactions of science, technology, and society.

223.　**Kazis, Richard, and Richard Grossman.** *Fear at Work: Job Blackmail, Labor and the Environment.* 2d ed. New York: New Society, 1990 (orig. pub. 1982). 306 pages.

For those who need more information on the hackneyed "jobs vs. environment" debate, and for workers fearing environmental hazards in general, this new manifesto will help the reader understand what is happening and what should be happening in places of employment. It should enrage everyone into demanding safe and hazard-free working environments.

"Marshals the facts and compelling arguments against the "job blackmail" carried out by large corporations to convince workers that they can't have a clean environment, a healthy workplace, *and* employment."—Michael Belliveau, executive director, and Hannah Creighton, newsletter editor, Citizens for a Better Environment

224. **Kerlinger, Paul. *Flight Strategies of Migrating Hawks.*** Chicago: University of Chicago Press, 1989. 375 pages.

If you have ever watched a hawk "making lazy circles in the sky" and wondered how or why, this book can provide you with the answer. Written for a science-minded popular audience, it provides an interesting synthesis of research, by the author and by hundreds of other ornithologists, on hawks, their migration patterns, and the mechanics of their flight. There are numerous scientific tables and charts that supplement the text. (See also entry 146 for another useful guide to hawks.)

"Most comprehensive study yet, on migrations of birds of prey. One reviewer wrote, 'It's a wonderful synthesis of what we think we know, much of it recently acquired.' A good bit is technical, but the author in his preface gives permission for the general reader to skip the technical sections."— Myriam Moore, secretary, Hawk Migration Association of North America

225. **Kidron, Michael, and Ronald Segal. *The New State of the World Atlas.*** rev. ed. New York: Touchstone, 1991 (orig. pub. 1981). 160 pages.

With more than sixty maps, this atlas vividly portrays the political economy of the world and provides a base from which to build discussions of sustainable resource management. The maps are organized by themes, covering such topics as military expenditures, natural resources, refugee movements, exploited labor, income distribution, food production, and sources of pollution. An appendix provides notes on sources of data and comments that are relevant to each map. Kidron and Dan Smith have organized additional atlases, such as *The New State of War and Peace: An International Atlas* (Touchstone, 1991).

See also entry 310 for another atlas that deals with the problem of sustainability.

226. **King, Alexander.** *The State of the Planet.* A report prepared for the International Federation of Institutes for Advanced Study (IFIAS). Oxford: Pergamon Press, 1980. 130 pages.

This report, prepared for the International Federation of Institutes for Advanced Study (IFIAS) in Stockholm, examines the world "problematique." Its message is one of pessimism, though it provides several "pointers to survival," such as the need to spread understanding of the planet's condition. It also calls for a "world watch" program to monitor trends, world solidarity to deal with the problems, a new international economic order, alternative distributional arrangements for food and resources, disarmament, and the encouragement of scientific and technological development to be applied towards solving these problems.

227. **Kloppenburg, Jack.** *First the Seed: The Political Economy of Plant Biotechnology, 1492–2000.* New York: Cambridge University Press, 1988. 349 pages.

This is a well-written and interesting analysis about the expropriation by multinational agricultural industries of genetic resources from the natural world, primarily from what are now considered economically developing countries, in order to provide the basis for capital accumulation. This is also an excellent history of plant breeding in the United States.

228. **Krutch, Joseph Wood.** *The Great Chain of Life.* Boston: Houghton Mifflin, 1956. 227 pages.

This is Krutch's philosophical overview of nature. He touches upon such concepts as evolutionary developments (physiological and behavioral), the interconnections of species within an ecological web, and human respect and reverence for animals (as well as the not-so-reverent attitudes some humans have regarding the killing of animals for sport).

229. **Lappé, Frances Moore, and Joseph Collins, with Cary Fowler.** *Food First: Beyond the Myth of Scarcity.* rev. ed. New York: Ballantine, 1978. 619 pages.

Lappé critiques what she believes to be false notions of the causes of world hunger which tend to blame drought and overpopulation. She contends instead, that the real problems of food shortages are due to the increased dependence of once self-reliant agricultural producers on international trade and cash-crop export, which is influenced by security-minded governments and profit-minded multinational corporations.

"Probably did more than anything else to make me see that perhaps the hunger problem wasn't one of production, but rather one of distribution of land, income, and food."—Diana M. Liverman, associate professor of geography, Pennsylvania State University

Also recommended: Frances Moore Lappé's *Diet for a Small Planet* (Ballantine, 1971) and *World Hunger: Ten Myths* (Institute for Food and Development Policy, 1979).

230. **Lappe, Marc. *Chemical Deceptions: The Toxic Threat to Health.*** San Francisco: Sierra Club, 1991. 360 pages.

Lappe shows us how dependent our lives are on the products and by-products of our industrial society, and the potential health problems that exist because of that dependence.

231. **Lash, Jonathan, Katherine Gillman, and David Sheridan.** *A Season of Spoils: The Reagan Administration's Attack on the Environment.* New York: Pantheon, 1984. 385 pages.

A frank assessment of the first-term Reagan administration— which included such notables as David Stockman as head of the Office of Management and Budget, Anne Gorsuch as head of the Environmental Protection Agency, and James Watt as head of the Department of Interior—in its dealing, or not dealing, with problems concerning the environment. The book received the backing of the Environmental Policy Center, Friends of the Earth, the National Audubon Society, the National Parks & Conservation Association, the Natural Resources Defense Council, and the Wilderness Society.

232. **Lean, Geoffrey, Don Hinrichsen, and Adam Markham** *Atlas of the Environment.* New York: Prentice Hall, 1990. 192 pages.

Sponsored by the World Wide Fund for Nature (WWF), this atlas contains maps, charts, tables, and diagrams related to forty-two environmental topics. Each set of illustrations is accompanied by a brief chapter explaining the topic in more detail. Besides the usual topics one often finds in such atlases, there are explanations for such subjects as: global warming; the ozone layer; major conservation efforts (complete with a table showing which countries have ratified or signed various agreements); national parks or areas designated for protection; use of agrochemicals; trade of tropical timber; animal migration routes; and a special chapter each on environmental issues of the Arctic and of the Antarctic. There is a selected bibliography which is an especially useful guide to documents and reports published by international conservation organizations or governments.

233. **Lewis, William.** *Interpreting for Park Visitors.* Philadelphia, PA: Eastern Acorn, 1980. 158 pages.

Commissioned by the Eastern National Park and Monument Association, this small, easy-to-read guide offers tips and strategies on how to become a better interpreter. A useful checklist is provided as an aid for self-evaluation.

"An inspirational how-to book for the field naturalist. Must reading for those entering the field. The book offers numerous examples of effective interpretation drawn from the author's broad background."—Alan Leftridge, senior editor, *Legacy*

234. **Lopez, Barry.** *River Notes: The Dance of the Herons.* New York: Scribner's, 1979. 100 pages.

This is a collection of Lopez's essays, interpretations of folklore, and personal reflections interconnected by the theme of the river. It is a suitable companion to another Lopez book, *Desert Notes: Reflections in the Eye of the Raven* (Andrews & McMeel, 1976).

235. **Lowe, David W., John R. Matthews, and Charles J. Moseley, eds.** *The Official World Wildlife Fund Guide to Endangered Species of North America.* 2 vols. Washington, DC: Beacham, 1990. 1180 pages.

An important resource for information on 540 endangered and threatened species of North America. The guide is illustrated with maps, photographs, drawings, and filled with facts on each species. Volume one highlights plants and mammals; volume two covers birds, reptiles, amphibians, fishes, mussels, crustaceans, snails, insects, and arachnids.

236. **Lumholtz, Carl.** *Unknown Mexico: A Record of Five Years' Exploration among the Tribes of the Western Sierra Madre; in the Tierra Caliente of Tepic and Jalisco; and among the Tarascos of Michoacan.* 2 vols. New York: Scribner's, 1902. V. 1, 530 pages; V. 2, 483 pages.

In the early 1890s, Lumholtz led a scientific party of about thirty persons on an expedition through the western part of Mexico. The team included a physical geographer, an archaeologist, two botanists, a zoologist, and a mineralologist. Lumholtz and his party encountered an array of interesting landscapes, peoples, and biological specimens. His account of the expedition presented in these two volumes is detailed and vivid, and is an intriguing record of a land and its inhabitants nearly one hundred years ago.

"Lumholtz's immense respect for other cultures and races was well in advance of its time. The description of the natural environment in the Sierra Madre is superb!"—Exequiel Ezcurra, professor of ecology, Centro de Ecología, Universidad Nacional Autónoma de México, Mexico City

Also recommended is Lumholtz's *New Trails in Mexico: An Account of One Year's Exploration in Northwestern Sonora, Mexico, and Southwestern Arizona, 1909–1910* (Scribner's, 1912).

237.   Lynch, Kevin. *The Image of the City*. Cambridge, MA: MIT Press, 1960. 194 pages.

Lynch describes how the perceived image of the city provides important psychological and social messages to residents and visitors. He elaborates on what the different images and messages are and how city planners can design elements of the urban form to produce the desired response. In an appendix, he uses as case examples the cities of Boston, Jersey City, and Los Angeles to show how to apply the methods he presents as theory in the earlier chapters.

"From an urban planning perspective, a key work in the history of our understanding of urban environmental design and its relationship to how people function in cities."— Michael Zamm, director of environmental education, Council on the Environment of New York City

238.   Lyon, Thomas J., ed. *This Incomperable Lande: A Book of American Nature Writing*. Boston: Houghton Mifflin, 1989. Reprint. New York: Viking/Penguin, 1991. 495 pages.

This is one of the most interesting collections of nature writing available. Lyon, a professor of English at Utah State University, has carefully assembled a set of works that reflects the breadth of writers and writings on nature in America. His introductory essay, in which he outlines a "taxonomy of nature writing" and presents a brief history of the development of nature writing, is a very useful framework from which to analyze and enjoy the collected works. His annotated bibliography contains an extensive listing of nature writing, related essays, and books. See also Peter Fritzell's *Nature Writing and America* (entry 191).

239.   **MacArthur, Robert H.** *Geographical Ecology: Patterns in the Distribution of Species.* New York: Harper, 1972. 269 pages.

MacArthur characterizes the factors influencing geographical distributions of species. He examines the causes and variations of climate around the world, then looks at behavioral characteristics, such as competition, predation, and optimal foraging strategies as influences on distribution. Finally, he looks at various types of patterns, such as island patterns, and species distributions and diversity, and then makes comparisons between patterns in the tropics versus the temperate regions. Although the material is complex, he reserves the mathematical discussion for appendices at the end of each chapter.

"A somewhat technical book, but written also for lay interests. A classic in simple reasoning about the properties and functioning of natural systems."—Orie L. Loucks, professor of zoology, Miami University, Ohio

Also recommended is *The Theory of Island Biogeography* (Princeton University Press, 1967), by Robert H. MacArthur and Edward O. Wilson.

240.   **McCluhan, T. C.** *Touch the Earth: A Self-Portrait of Indian Existence.* New York: Outerbridge and Lazard, 1972. 185 pages.

A beautiful assembly of passages and quotes about Native American views of the earth, vividly enhanced by the black-and-white photographs taken by the early-twentieth-century photographer, Edward S. Curtis.

"McCluhan, through summarizing essays from Native Americans, presents a philosophical base for environmental education. This book begs the question: How different would it be if we had adopted the Native American viewpoint of the human role on earth?"—Jack Greene, National Wildlife Foundation

241.   **McHenry, Robert, and Charles Van Doren, eds.** *A Documentary History of Conservation in America.* Introduction by Lorus and Margery Milne. New York: Praeger, 1972. 422 pages.

This is an impressive assembly of poetry, articles, and selected passages from a wide range of writings about conservation, beginning with those of the earliest explorers of the New World to more contemporary leaders. Many of the more than 200 selections are not to be found in any of the other anthologies or readers on conservation.

242.   **MacLean, Norman.** *A River Runs Through It and Other Stories.* Chicago: University of Chicago Press, 1976. 217 pages.

This is a collection of three stories: "A River Runs Through It;" "Logging and Pimping and 'Your Pal, Jim';" and "USFS 1919: The Ranger, the Cook, and a Hole in the Sky." Together, they aptly capture the spirit of the West: its land, its water, and its trees. But mostly the stories capture the joy and sadness of the people who inhabit the region, who fish the waters, who cut the timber, and who are shaped, unconsciously, by its spirit.

"Beautiful story of one man's identification with his environment, his immersion in it with his family, in particular, with his brother. The environment itself is part of the fabric of his life and relationships. Not only is the story beautiful, but the prose is masterful and moving."—Joseph H. Chadbourne, president, Institute for Environmental Education

243.   **McNeely, Jeffrey A., and David Pitt, eds.** *Culture and Conservation: The Human Dimension in Environmental Planning.* London: Croom Helm, 1985. 308 pages.

This is a notable publication commissioned by International Union for the Conservation of Nature and Natural Resources (IUCN) based in Gland, Switzerland. The book advocates the organization's view that sustainable development needs to incorporate traditional knowledge about conservation in order to be successful. The editors have compiled a series of case studies that look at how different traditional cultures "practice" natural resources management. These examples come from around the world and illustrate some of the new concepts developed during the 1980s that relate to both planning and managing natural resource use. McNeely and Kenton R. Miller have edited a related book, *National Parks, Conservation, and Development: The Role of Protected Areas in Sustaining Development* (Smithsonian Institution, 1984).

Also recommended: McNeely's *Economics and Biological Diversity: Developing and Using Incentives to Conserve Biological Resources* (IUCN,

1988), which looks very closely at the economic incentives and disincentives for preserving biological diversity.

244. **McPhee, John A. *Basin and Range*.** New York: Farrar, Straus, 1981. 213 pages.

———. *In Suspect Terrain*. New York: Farrar, Straus, 1983. 210 pages.

———. *Rising from the Plains*. New York: Farrar, Straus, 1986. 213 pages.

This trilogy is essential and basic reading about the geologic processes that have shaped our continent, and about the scientists studying these processes and landforms.

245. **McPhee, John A. *Coming into the Country*.** New York: Farrar, Straus, 1977. 438 pages.

With his now familiar narrative and poetic journalistic style, McPhee takes us through the wilds of Alaska. His scenes include a canoe trip with several companions down a river above the Arctic Circle; zooming at tree-top level in a helicopter across the vast wilderness of the Alaskan interior; and settling in for a while in a village near the Canadian border. As with his other writings, McPhee transports the reader spiritually into the heart of a new environment, and it is an enchanting journey.

Also recommended is McPhee's *The Control of Nature* (Farrar, Straus, 1989).

246. **Malone, Thomas F., and John G. Roderer, eds. *Global Change*.** New York: Cambridge University Press, 1985. 512 pages.

The International Council of Scientific Unions (ICSU) held a symposium in 1984 to discuss the biogeochemical processes of the earth as a system. This book is a compilation of the thirty academic papers and commentaries that attempt to define a new paradigm for the study of the earth. The chapters discuss the new research agenda, the science of global change, new tools and technologies for monitoring and analyzing earth processes, and the role of human activity as an agent of change. A related book, *Global Change and Our Common Future* (National Academy, 1989), edited by Ruth S. DeFries and Thomas F. Malone, attempts to integrate research efforts in earth systems science with the more applied social, political and economic approaches to ecologically sustainable development.

247. **Mannion, A. M.** *Global Environmental Change: A Natural and Cultural Environmental History.* London: Longman, 1991. 404 pages.

This is a good introductory textbook on the forces of change, both natural and cultural, that have affected the global environment. Mannion looks at changes during prehistoric times, and then focuses her attention on what has happened during the past several thousand years, during the past few centuries in particular. She gives a good overview of the impacts of the pastoral, agricultural, and industrial societies. She also looks at some interesting aspects of agriculture in the developing world; forest manipulation in the developed world; the environmental impact of recreation, tourism and sport; and biotechnology as a new agent of change. A reference list of recent scientific literature on global environmental change is provided.

248. **Margalef, Ramon.** *Perspectives in Ecological Theory.* Chicago: University of Chicago Press, 1968. 111 pages.

This is based on four essays delivered by the author at the University of Chicago in 1966 on issues of ecological theory: "The Ecosystem as a Cybernetic System," "Ecological Succession and Exploitation by Man," "The Study of Pelagic Ecosystems," and "Evolution in the Frame of Ecosystem Organization."

"This book demonstrates the variations found among ecological theories that reflect the different contexts and biomes studies. Also, it is a most stimulating blend of systems theory (particularly information theory) and ecological theory."—Kenneth A. Dahlberg, professor of political science, Western Michigan University

249. **Marshall, Robert.** *Alaska Wilderness.* Berkeley: University of California Press, 1970 (orig. pub. 1956 as *Arctic Wilderness*). 173 pages.

Marshall, originally from New York City, became a forester with the U.S. Forest Service in Montana during the mid-1920s. He went on to spend two years in Alaska. This book is based on his experiences there, where he studied the physical aspects of that vast wilderness, as well as the social conditions of the people who had lived in the Arctic region for thousands of years. Though Marshall's life was brief—he died at age thirty-eight—his voice in the conservation movement had an important impact.

"Bob Marshall was the main driving force to establish the Wilderness Society and, consequently, much of the modern wilderness movement. This book describes his adventures and joys as he explored the remote Brooks Range in Alaska."— Kevin Proescholdt, executive director, Friends of the Boundary Waters Wilderness

250. **Martinez-Alier, Juan, with Klaus Schlupmann.** *Ecological Economics: Energy, Environment, and Society.* New York: Blackwell, 1987. 287 pages.

This book attempts to describe the relationship between ecological theory and economics. The authors review theories related to energy and material flows in human society and show their relevance to ecological systems analysis and the economy. They trace ecological economics back to the mid-nineteenth century and ask why the field has not found respectability or an academic home within a discipline. Martinez-Alier is a founding editor of the recently established journal *Ecological Economics.*

251. **Marx, Leo.** *The Machine in the Garden: Technology and the Pastoral Ideal in America.* New York: Oxford University Press, 1964. 392 pages.

In a way, Marx contrasts the two dependencies that epitomize the modern American. The first is on the notion of an ideal landscape, which is satisfying to the mind. The second is on the technological buffers we have fabricated between ourselves and the land. He believes that we crave the former, and could not possibly survive without the latter. Our dilemma according to Marx is that because of our joint dependency, we have inadvertently imposed destruction upon perfection.

252. **Mason, Robert J., and Mark T. Mattson.** *Atlas of United States Environmental Issues.* New York: Macmillan, 1990. 252 pages.

Mason and Mattson have assembled an astonishing array of facts on all facets of environmental issues in the United States. That information is presented in eighteen chapters focusing on such topics as rangelands and wetlands, water use and quality, energy, and environmental economics and politics. Each chapter contains extensive text that provides an overview and analysis of the particular issue, as well as numerous maps and diagrams of superior cartographic and graphic style. It is the combination of the text and illustrations that make this atlas so impressive and informative. The book also contains an extensive bibliography that lists sources of information.

253. **Matthews, Rupert O.** *The Atlas of Natural Wonders.* New York: Facts On File, 1988. 240 pages.

It seems hard to imagine the most outstanding natural features on the surface of our planet. What types of landscapes would they be? Where would they be? How would they have been formed? This atlas helps answer these questions by presenting the best examples of landscapes around the world, including the Fracassi Caves in France, the Iguacu Falls on the Brazil/Argentina border, the Urgup Cones in Turkey, Lake Baikal in Russia, and Bora Bora Island in the Pacific Ocean. In all, fifty-two locations are featured in photographs and descriptions, with brief capsules provided for another 107 places.

254. **Matthiessen, Peter.** *African Silences.* New York: Random House, 1991. 225 pages.

By one of this country's best writers and author of the classic *Wildlife in America* (see entry 53), this book presents a look at the imperiled state of wildlife and wilderness in Africa.

Also recommended are Matthiessen's *The Wind Birds* (Viking, 1973); *Far Tortuga* (Random House, 1975); and *Men's Lives: The Surfmen and Baymen of the South Fork* (Random House, 1986).

255. **Meadows, Donella H.** *The Global Citizen,* Covelo, CA: Island, 1990. 300 pages.

This collection of essays is drawn from Meadows' syndicated newspaper column, and highlights people around the country and the globe who are working for a sustainable society and environmental protection.

"Written by the coauthor of *The Limits to Growth* [see entry 54], these short essays combine science with passion, eloquently describing the complex connections and interrelationships that shape our world."— Stephen Viederman, president, Jessie Smith Noyes Foundation.

256. **Meine, Curt.** *Aldo Leopold: His Life and Work.* Madison: University of Wisconsin Press, 1988. 638 pages.

Meine's thorough and detailed biography of Leopold covers the life of this well-known and highly regarded American conservationist from childhood to his adulthood as game manager, university professor, and lyrical essayist. Meine provides an extensive bibliography of references concerning Leopold, as well a complete list of Leopold's own publications. This biography is important because it places Leopold within the broader context of events and against the backdrop of other personalities during the first half of the twentieth century. See also entries 43 and 186.

257. **Merchant, Carolyn.** *The Death of Nature: Women, Ecology and the Scientific Revolution.* San Francisco: Harper, 1980. 348 pages.

This book was a trailblazing feminist analysis of the history of science and its relationship to nature. Merchant draws many parallels between the subordination of women and the domination of nature wrought by the scientific and industrial revolutions. Encompassing as well as criticizing the work of many philosophers and scientists, the book also uses art and literature to illustrate changes in the views of nature and women. Merchant sees in the environmental and women's rights movements an opportunity to recapture more egalitarian and respectful relationships within society and towards nature.

"Merchant interprets the scientific revolutions of the seventeenth century in terms of its impacts on contemporary environmental problems. She thereby integrates both feminism and a study of science into environmental studies. Essential to read."—John H. Perkins, environmental studies faculty, Evergreen State College.

258. **Milbrath, Lester W.** *Envisioning a Sustainable Society: Learning Our Way Out.* Albany: State University of New York Press, 1989. 403 pages.

The author of *Environmentalists: Vanguard for a New Society* (State University of New York Press, 1984) continues his thoughtful analysis and elaboration of how we can transform our unsustainable society into one in which the central values are based on empathy, compassion, and a sense of justice for all, instead of on aggression and competitiveness. He suggests that only through a transformational social learning process can we begin to adopt such a value structure that could serve as the basis for a new society. And he offers a proposal to undertake such social learning. Throughout the book, his reviews and analyses of the relevant philosophical, psychological, and sociological literature are superb.

259. **Miller, Kenton, and Laura Tangley.** *Trees of Life: Saving Tropical Forests and Their Biological Wealth.* World Resources Institute Guides to the Environment, edited by Kathleen Courrier. New York: Beacon, 1991. 218 pages.

One of the "Guides to the Environment" sponsored by the World Resources Institute in Washington, D.C., this is a well- written overview of what is happening in the tropical forests, including the connections to life in the temperate zones.

260.   **Mills, Stephanie, ed.** *In Praise of Nature* Covelo, CA: Island, 1990. 258 pages.

Reviews and excerpts of notable books on nature and the environment, organized around five themes (earth, air, fire, water, spirit) for which the editor provides integrating essays.

261.   **Mollison, Bill.** *Permaculture: A Practical Guide for a Sustainable Future.* Covelo, CA: Island, 1990. 579 pages.

Mollison coined the term "permaculture," or permanent agriculture, which he defines as "the conscious design and maintenance of agriculturally productive ecosystems which have the diversity, stability, and resilience of natural ecosystems" (p. ix). Thus, permaculture involves a philosophy as well as a sense of practicality, and in a way, the author has prepared a guide to both living with and utilizing the landscape. He discusses elements of design, how to recognize natural structures and patterns in the landscape, and how to work within that structure. He reviews basic concepts of climate, water, soils, and plants, and works those concepts into the design of appropriate permaculture systems for various environments: humid tropics, drylands, humid cool to cold climates, and aquatic areas. In the final chapter, Mollison envisions the lifestyles of a society based on permaculture. The user will find the bounty of illustrations a helpful means of incorporating the concepts and strategies outlined in the text.

"Unsurpassed handbook of ecological agriculture and land restoration work."—Peter Bane, publisher, *The Permaculture Activist*

"What is really exciting about Mollison is the way he has developed design philosophies for land uses that supply human needs while retaining the self-sustaining, self-repairing, and self-regulating characteristics of unmodified ecological systems."—Sandy Irvine, associate editor, *The Ecologist,* Newcastle Upon Tyne, England

262   **Muir, John.** *The Story of My Boyhood and Youth.* Boston: Houghton Mifflin, 1913. 294 pages.

At the Wisconsin State Historical Society in Madison, there is an odd contraption on display consisting of old schoolbooks stacked around wooden gears, all atop long pointed legs that resemble drafting compasses. This device was invented by Muir as a student at the University of Wisconsin to prop open books for a specified period of time, then close the book, move the next one into place, and open it for its allotted time. Muir also had invented a mechanical device to set him upright in bed in the morning at a specified hour. He was a creative youth, and keenly aware of his world and of himself. This autobiography cover the years of his childhood in Scotland and Wisconsin, and later his years at the University of Wisconsin. What we really learn, though, is how he became (in his words) a student at the "University of the Wilderness," who embarked "on a glorious botanical and geological excursion" which lasted more than half a century (pp. 286–7).

263.   **Myers, Norman.** *The Primary Source: Tropical Forests and Our Future.* rev. ed. New York: Norton, 1992 (orig. pub., 1984). 448 pages.

This was one of the first popularized accounts, along with that of Catherine Caufield (see entry 142), of the widespread destruction of tropical forests. Through this book, Myers, who is a prolific writer on global environmental issues, helped place the issue of tropical deforestation in the mind of the public and on the agenda of international policymaking bodies. He has identified vividly the many threats that tropical forests are facing and the social, economic, and political causes of these threats.

"This is the book that has made us refocus our environmental concerns to embrace the entire earth. What happens in Peru or Kenya or Borneo does affect us here in the United States."— Marcia Bonta, naturalist/writer

264.   **Myers, Norman.** *The Sinking Ark: A New Look at the Problem of Disappearing Species.* Oxford: Pergamon, 1979. 307 pages.

Myers considers the prospects of all species on the earth, suggesting that within thirty years the earth could lose twenty to thirty percent of the planet's five to ten million species. He offers an introductory review of species abundance and diversity, the relevance of other species to humans, and political and legal dimensions of species conservation. He looks closely at the part of the world where most species are disappearing: the tropical moist forests. Finally, he considers and analyzes a number of activities aimed at halting the disappearance of species, such as the efforts of zoos, preservation of protected areas, and various economic initiatives, to name a few.

265. **Nabhan, Gary.** *The Desert Smells Like Rain: A Naturalist in Papago Indian Country.* San Francisco: North Point, 1982. 148 pages.

————. *Enduring Seeds: Native American Agriculture and World Plant Conservation.* San Francisco: North Point, 1989. 225 pages.

————. *Gathering the Desert.* Illustrations by Paul Mirocha. Tucson: University of Arizona Press, 1985. 209 pages.

Nabhan is a cofounder of Native Seeds/Southwestern Endangered Arid-Land Resource Clearing House (SEARCH) in Tucson, Arizona, a group which works to conserve traditional crop seeds and related wild seeds in Southwestern United States. He is a pioneer in the field of ethnobotany, which attempts to understand the knowledge of plants held by indigenous cultures.

266. **Nash, Roderick, ed.** *The American Environment: Readings in the History of Conservation.* 3rd ed. New York: McGraw-Hill, 1990. 398 pages.

Nash guides the reader through the history of the conservation and environmental movements with a succinct collection of the best writings on the subject. His annotations help tie the pieces together and provide a context for analysis and understanding. This seems to be one of the most popular readers used for environmental studies courses.

267. **National Research Council—National Academy of Sciences.** *Energy in Transition: 1985–2010.* San Francisco: Freeman, 1980. 677 pages.

In 1975, the National Research Council initiated a comprehensive study of the nation's energy future, with special consideration of the role of nuclear and alternative energy systems. This book details the findings of that study and illuminates the options and policy alternatives available to the United States. The committee looked at energy demand and conservation, energy supply and delivery systems, risks and impacts of energy supply and use, and models of possible future energy systems and decisionmaking.

268. **National Research Council—National Academy of Sciences.** *Resources and Man.* San Francisco: Freeman, 1969. 259 pages.

This is the final report of a two-year study by the Committee on Resources and Man of the National Academy of Sciences. The committee examined the interactions between humans and natural resources and focused on the potentials and limitations of meeting the food, mineral, and energy needs of a growing world population. The report and its recommendations, although now dated, raised important questions and stimulated discussion about these issues. Today it is a useful source of baseline information on these issues.

"The first book to impress on me the special place of this generation in using up the geochemical resources of the earth."—Dennis L. Meadows, professor of environmental studies, University of New Hampshire

269. **Nearing, Helen, and Scott Nearing.** *Living the Good Life: How to Live Sanely and Simply in a Troubled World.* New York: Schocken, 1970 (orig. pub. 1954). 213 pages.

The Nearings are legendary and were perhaps the original "back-to-the-earth" pioneers, having left New York City in the 1930s for a farm in Vermont. They wanted to become as independent as possible from the commodity and labor markets. They desired to maintain and improve their health by turning their backs on the stress of urban living for the blessings of contact with the earth and the sustenance of homegrown, organic food. And they yearned to distance themselves from a society that was engaged in exploitation of the earth and its people. They managed to prosper in their new lives and became an inspiration for several other generations of citizens who sought an alternative lifestyle. This book documents their existence on the farm: how they lived, worked, played, and flourished. It is a fascinating record of two very special people. (See also entry 319 for a book that describes an experience similar to that of the Nearings.)

270. **Oelschlaeger, Max.** *The Idea of Wilderness: From Prehistory to the Age of Ecology.* New Haven, CT: Yale University Press, 1991. 477 pages.

A comprehensive history of how human conceptions and philosophies of wilderness, including the way humans have perceived their relationship to nature, developed and change. It covers prehistoric hunter-gatherers through present-day deep ecologists, discussing ideas about nature in the Mediterranean and early Christian cultures along the way. Oelschlaeger then focuses critically on the works of Thoreau, Muir, Leopold, and others.

271. **Olson, Sigurd.** *Reflections from the North Country.* Illustrations by Leslie Kouba. New York: Knopf, 1976. 172 pages.

Olson, a renowned ecologist and naturalist who served as president of the Wilderness Society and of the National Parks Association, is as much a symbol of the "North Country" as is the common loon. In this book, Olson "reflects" on the human experience, on his own experiences in the north woods, and on the meaning of the wilderness in those experiences. This is as much a philosophical treatise as it is a naturalist's description of the world around him.

272.   **Olwig, Kenneth.** *Nature's Ideological Landscape: A Literary and Geographic Perspective on Its Development and Preservation on Denmark's Jutland Heath.* London: Unwin & Allen, 1984. 115 pages.

This is an essential contribution to the philosophical debate concerning the "management" of "natural" areas in Europe.

"This book traces the development of concerns for the 'wild' natural environment in Denmark and England. Olwig connects this growing interest in wild nature to the increasing distance between more and more urban people and 'nature in everyday life.' A secret classic."— Margaret FitzSimmons, associate professor of architecture and urban planning, University of California–Los Angeles.

273.   **Organisation for Economic Cooperation and Development.** *The State of the Environment in OECD Member Countries.* 2nd. ed. Paris: OECD, 1985 (orig. pub. 1979). 271 pages.

In recognition of the relationship between environmental status and economic growth, the Organisation for Economic Cooperation and Development (OECD) solicited regular reports from member countries on the state of their environments, and periodically published regional compilations. These reports assess both human stresses on the environment and institutional response to them. They are intended to help in the evaluation of public policy and to stimulate an improvement in the collection of environmental statistics upon which sound policies can be based.

274.   **Owen, D.F.** *Animal Ecology in Tropical Africa.* London: Oliver and Boyd, 1966. 122 pages.

This is a scientific, but nontechnical, review of a number of basic ecological principles (population dynamics; genetics; species number, abundance, and diversity; seasonal and periodical cycles) applied to the animals of tropical Africa. The book is illustrated with several line drawings and a dozen full-page black-and-white photographs.

"The first modern synthesis of this important topic."—John L. Cloudsley-Thompson, professor emeritus of zoology, University College, London

275. **Paddock, William, and Paul Paddock.** *Famine, 1975!: America's Decision, Who Will Survive?* Boston: Little Brown, 1967. 276 pages.

This was written by two brothers, one a foreign service office and the other an agronomist—who both served their careers in developing countries. Their discussion is often frank about what they see as the limits to world agricultural productivity and about the availability and distribution of food. They see an emerging "Age of Food" in which agriculture and food production activities play an increasingly important role in the global political economy. They are somewhat optimistic in their view of the United State's role in being able to aid the poor nations with starving populations.

276. **Paehlke, Robert.** *Environmentalism and the Future of Progressive Politics.* New Haven, CT: Yale University Press, 1989. 325 pages.

What is environmentalism, and what are the political positions of environmentalists? Paehlke suggests that while environmentalism can be as specific a political ideology as liberalism, conservatism, socialism, neoconservatism, or progressivism, it also can be elusive and vague. He points out that environmentalism is really not the same as any of these ideologies, but can embrace elements of all of them. He then illustrates the varying nature of environmentalism by characterizing the philosophies and positions of specific environmentalists, showing that "environmentalists occupy almost every position on the traditional right-to-left political spectrum" (p. 194). He concludes with a set of "hybrid" positions that he suggests could help describe a coherent ideology of environmentalism.

277. **Palmer, E. Laurence.** *Fieldbook of Natural History.* rev. ed. New York: McGraw-Hill, 1975 (orig. pub. 1949). 779 pages.

Palmer says he intended to write the kind of book he would have enjoyed as a youngster studying nature. He certainly endeavored to be complete in his selections, as evidenced by the inclusion of thousands of species of plants, animals, and minerals in his fieldbook. For each entry, the guide provides a short description as well as an illustration (some black-and-white photography are included, but most of the illustrations are line drawings).

278. **Palmer, Tim.** *Endangered Rivers and the Conservation Movement.* Berkeley: University of California Press, 1986. 316 pages.

A project of the River Conservation Fund of Washington, D.C., this book documents the history of river preservation in the United States and provides a better understanding of the policies and politics that can threaten or save America's "wild and scenic" rivers. The book is well-written and well-documented, and includes several useful appendices, such as an "endangered rivers list" that gives a state-by-state summary of such rivers.

Other related books by the same author include: *Rivers of Pennsylvania* (Pennsylvania State University Press, 1980); *Stanislaus: The Struggle for a River* (University of California Press, 1982); *Youghiogheny: Appalachian River* (University of Pittsburgh Press, 1984); and *The Snake River: Window to the West* (Island, 1991).

279.   Parkin, Sara. *Green Parties: An International Guide*. London: Heretic, 1989. 335 pages.

This is a fairly comprehensive guide to the origins and activities of "green parties" in about twenty countries of western Europe and in New Zealand, Australia, the United States, and Canada. It also provides information on smaller movements elsewhere, such as those in Poland, Kenya, Japan, India, Brazil, and Hungary. Parkin shows how the parties developed in their respective countries, notes differences in objectives or activities of the various national parties, indicates who are or were the influential leaders, and assesses the parties' impacts on national and international electoral politics.

280.   Pearce, David, ed. *Blueprint 2: Greening the World Economy*. London: Earthscan, 1991. 224 pages.

Written by a group of British environmental economists, this book provides creative ways of how to examine the economic issues regarding the global environment such as those related to climate change and deforestation. Pearce is also coauthor, with Anil Markandya and Edward B. Barbier, of *Blueprint for a Green Economy* (Earthscan, 1989).

281.   Pearson, Charles. *Down to Business: Multinational Corporations, the Environment and Development*. Washington, D.C.: World Resources Institute, 1985. 107 pages.

Pearson examines the role of multinational corporations in environmentally sound development. He concludes that development and environmental quality are compatible with each other. He also cites the difficulty of defining, measuring, and achieving sustainable development, and calls for new indicators and a long-term view of development by multinational corporations. Pearson then reviews current environmental conditions in developing countries, including the status of agricultural land, deforestation, pollution, and environmentally related diseases.

282. **Pepper, David.** *The Roots of Modern Environmentalism.* London: Croom Helm, 1984. 246 pages.

Pepper contrasts various philosophical and theoretical perspectives on nature such as scientific ecology, humanism, and Marxism. He is particularly concerned that students understand the origins and history of ideas about nature and the environment.

283. **Perlin, John.** *A Forest Journey: The Role of Wood in the Development of Civilization.* New York: Norton, 1989. 445 pages.

By the coauthor of *A Golden Thread* (Van Nostrand Reinhold, 1980), which is a historical look at the use of solar energy in society, this book looks at the use of wood— as fuel, for tools, for construction, and as a commodity. It begins with ancient Mesopotamia, and then covers the early societies of the Mediterranean Basin. This is followed by a look at England, the Caribbean, and Brazil, and concludes with the United States (through the nineteenth century).

"A historical perspective on the use of wood and its historical impact on global economy. Makes an extremely strong case for resource protection from historical perspective of some 6,000 years."—Paul Relis, executive director, Community Environmental Council, Inc.

284. **Peterson, Roger Tory.** *Birds Over America.* rev. ed. New York: Dodd, Mead, 1964 (orig. pub. 1948). 342 pages.

Awarded the John Burroughs medal for natural history writing, this book is an account of Peterson's travels and bird-watching expeditions across the United States. Some of his experiences include: visiting "Cranetown," of Reelfoot Lake near the Mississippi River in northwestern Tennessee; reflecting on hawkwatching at Hawk Mountain in Pennsylvania; searching for the remaining few ivory-billed woodpeckers in an 80,000-acre tract of land in Louisiana; and meeting "eagle man," a retired banker who banded eagles in Florida. His writing is polished and entertaining. And his artistry with the camera is as stunning as his drawings and paintings—as evidenced by the 105 photographs included in this book, which are the best of the more than 10,000 he had taken during the previous twenty years.

285. **Peterson, Roger Tory, ed.** *The Bird Watcher's Anthology.* New York: Harcourt, 1957. 401 pages.

A superb collection of writings by the some of the best known bird-watchers and naturalists in the country. Peterson states that he assembled eighty-five selections "that reflected the brighter light of direct observation" as well as reports of firsthand experiences. He also contributed nearly 100 of his own drawings of birds to the collection.

Also recommended is *Wild America* (Houghton Mifflin, 1955), which is the record of a 30,000-mile journey around North America by Peterson and a British colleague, James Fisher.

286. **Petulla, Joseph M.** *American Environmentalism: Values, Tactics, and Priorities.* College Station: Texas A & M University Press, 1980. 239 pages.

Petulla traces the development of environmental values in America and documents the different environmental traditions, or perspectives, that have arisen. He cites the emergence and actions of individuals from three perspectives: the biocentric, the ecologic, and the economic. He evaluates the positions each tradition has taken and some of the contradictions each contains. He concludes by assessing what effects the philosophies of these different traditions have on policy and policymaking. An earlier book by Petulla is *American Environmental History: The Exploitation and Conservation of Natural Resources* (Merrill, 1988, 2d ed.), which is an analysis of how patterns of resource exploitation throughout American history have set the stage of modern environmental problems.

287. **Pinchot, Gifford.** *Breaking New Ground.* New York: Harcourt, 1947. 522 pages.

Gifford Pinchot is known as the founder of the National Forest System. This book is Pinchot's autobiography, or as he puts it, his "personal story of how Forestry and Conservation came to America" (p. xv). Pinchot was, in fact, one of the most important forces behind the development of forestry and conservation in the United States. Originally from Connecticut, he studied forestry in Nancy, France, and began work as a forest manager in North Carolina in 1892. In 1898, he was named chief of the Division of Forestry (which became the Forest Service), of the U.S. Department of Agriculture; he served in that capacity until 1910. During his tenure in the Forest Service, lands designated as national forest areas increased from fifty million acres to 175 million acres. He established the School of Forestry at Yale University in 1900 and founded the Society of American Foresters, becoming its first president. He also served as governor of Pennsylvania from 1923 to 1927. *Breaking New Ground* is an interesting look at how American forestry began and developed during the first part of this century.

288.   **Polunin, Nicholas, ed.** *Growth Without Ecodisasters?* New York: Wiley, 1980. 675 pages.

This book contains contributed papers and transcripts of discussions from the Second International Conference on the Environmental Future, which was held in Reykjavik, Iceland, in 1977. Under the auspices of the Foundation for Environmental Conservation based in Switzerland, the conference focussed on the issue of sustainable development of the biosphere.

"The papers, superbly edited, are from a major international conference that addressed environmental problems in a global and international context. The book includes expert papers not only on the major ecological systems and problems, but also on solutions and intervening factors, such as ecodevelopment, ethics, laws, and institutions."—D. Scott Slocombe, School of urban and Regional Planning, University of Waterloo, Ontario, Canada

289.   **Porritt, Jonathan, ed.** *Save the Earth.* Foreword by HRH the Prince of Wales. Introduction by Robert Redford. Atlanta: Turner Publishing in association with Friends of the Earth International, 1991. 208 pages.

A companion to the Turner Broadcasting Network six-hour special program in anticipation of the United Nations Earth Summit, held in Brazil during June of 1992. The book contains contributions from many prominent environmentalists and is richly illustrated with color photographs.

290.   **Powell, John Wesley.** *Exploration of the Colorado River.* abr. ed. Introduction by Wallace Stegner. Chicago: University of Chicago Press, 1957 (orig. pub. 1875). 138 pages.

In 1869, the same year when John Muir was spending his first summer in the Sierra Nevada (see entry 57), John Wesley Powell and a group of scientists and adventure commenced their journey down the Green and Colorado Rivers. His log of their travels is a fascinating account of one of the final epic expeditions within the continental United States. See also *Beyond the Hundredth Meridian: John Wesley Powell and The Second Opening of the West,* by Wallace Stegner (entry 86).

291.   Pyne, Stephen J. *Burning Bush: A Fire History of Australia.* New York: Holt, 1991. 520 pages.

An intensively researched and well-written book, by a noted scholar, on the "cultural history of fire on earth." Pyne's other books include *Fire in America: A Cultural History of Wildland and Rural Fire* (Princeton University Press, 1982); *Introduction to Wildland Fire: Fire Management in the United States* (Wiley-Interscience, 1984); and *Fire on the Rim: A Fire Fighter's Season at the Grand Canyon* (Grove Weidenfeld, 1989).

292.   Rambler, Mitchell B., Lynn Margulis, and Rene Fester. *Global Ecology: Towards a Science of the Biosphere.* Boston: Academic, 1989. 204 pages.

The concept of "the biosphere" was developed in the early 1900s by the Russian biologist V.I. Vernadsky. According to the editors of this book, the biosphere is a complex interplay of inextricably linked biological, chemical, and physical processes. They argue for the formation of a "science of the biosphere," in which the walls of traditional scientific disciplines give way to new interdisciplinary exchanges on dynamics and processes of the biosphere. This is a technical book that contains six essays on such topics as gaia, geognosy, biogeochemical cycles, and photochemistry of biogenic gases. In the first chapter, there is an interesting table which lists nearly thirty publications on the gaia hypothesis (from 1965 to 1988). There is a glossary of terms and acronyms to help the reader decipher some of the scientific language.

293.   Ramsay, William. *Bioenergy and Economic Development: Planning for Biomass Energy Programs in the Third World.* Boulder, CO: Westview, 1985. 291 pages.

As Ramsay suggests, bioenergy is an alternative energy source that shows great promise for Third World countries. He provides a good overview of the various aspects of bioenergy production, distribution, and use. For instance, he offers a detailed explanation of bioenergy crop types, an assessment of the environmental impacts of bioenergy crops, a comparison of bioenergy conversion technologies, a review of the costs and financing needs of such bioenergy production, and a discussion of infrastructure, marketing and distribution. While the emphasis of his book is on small-scale bioenergy production, he also assesses large-scale commercial and nationalized operations, and other organizational and administrative arrangements.

"Illustrates the complexities and provides recommendations likely to aid future efforts to utilize bioenergy 'properly' in the economy of developing countries; illustrates a good balance between soft and hard science inputs."—Richard L. Perrine, professor of civil engineering, University of California–Los Angeles

294.   Reisner, Marc. *Game Wars: The Undercover Pursuit of Wildlife Poachers.* New York: Viking, 1991. 293 pages.

By the author of *Cadillac Desert* (see entry 74), this book gives a behind-the-scenes look at the war against the poaching of wildlife in this country, and shows the dedication, frustration, and successes of the men and women fighting in this ongoing struggle.

295.   Repetto, Robert, ed. *The Global Possible: Resources, Development, and the New Century.* New Haven, CT: Yale University Press, 1985. 538 pages.

Within the environmental community there are the "possibilists," those who firmly believe that we, as a society, can halt environmental degradation if we apply ourselves with haste and vigor to the task. This book represents the possibilist perspective, and in it the leaders of twenty countries issue an urgent call for action to reverse global environmental degradation and improve the status of the world's poor. *The Global Possible* outlines the goals of these leaders and includes recommendations on how to achieve those goals with the cooperation of governments and business, industry, the public, and nongovernmental organizations. A companion book by Repetto titled *World Enough in Time* (Yale University Press, 1986) reviews successful methods of population control, resource conservation, and sustainable agriculture, and takes a practical approach to looking at what strategies and policies should be implemented to achieve sustainable development.

"This is a broad, balanced overview of the state of the world's resources with realistic, pragmatic policy recommendations."—John McLaughlin, professor of surveying engineering, University of New Brunswick, Frederiction, Canada

296.   Richards, John F., and Richard P. Tucker, eds. *World Deforestation in the Twentieth Century.* Durham, NC: Duke University Press, 1988. 321 pages.

This is the sequel to *Global Deforestation and the Nineteenth-Century World Economy* (see entry 331). The papers presented in the current volume draw attention to the increasing pressures for food and natural resources that drive the continuing process of deforestation around the world, and discuss the role of forests as a capital resource supporting growing local and global economies. Case studies from many parts of the world illustrate the ways in which nations have converted forests, both for the timber and to expand their agricultural industries.

297.   **Ricketts, Edward F., Jack Calvin, and Joel W. Hedspeth.** *Between Pacific Tides.* 5th ed. Revised by David W. Phillips. Stanford, CA: Stanford University Press, 1985 (orig. pub. 1939). 652 pages.

The subtitle for earlier editions of this book was: An Account of the Habits and Habitats of Some Five Hundred of the Common, Conspicuous Seashore Invertebrates of the Pacific Coast between Sitka, Alaska, and Northern Mexico. As owner of a biological supply store on "cannery row" in Monterrey, California, Ricketts was an enthusiastic expert on the marine life found in the tidal pools along the Pacific coast. At the urging of his friends and companions who went with him on specimen-collecting expeditions, he began to document and describe the life histories of the creatures he had come to know so well. *Between Pacific Tides* has been a popular success, guiding and informing its delighted audience for more than fifty years.

298.   **Rifkin, Jeremy, with Ted Howard.** *Entropy: A New World View.* Afterword by Nicholas Georgescu-Roegen. New York: Viking, 1980. 305 pages.

Rifkin relates the thermodynamic concept of entropy to a philosophical discussion of social development, resource consumption, and the integrity of our planet. He suggests that we have a responsibility to future generations, because according to the second law of thermodynamics, natural processes cannot be reversed without paying a price in energy. Therefore, "the more energy each of us uses up, the less is available for all life that comes after us" (p. 259), because although energy cannot be created or destroyed, the grade of energy we leave available may not be able to support life in the future.

Also recommended: *Declaration of a Heretic* (Routledge and Kegan Paul, 1985), by Jeremy Rifkin.

299.   **Robbins, John.** *Diet for a New America.* Walpole, NH: Stillpoint, 1987. 423 pages.

This is a critical look at food consumption and food production in America. Robbins examines the agricultural industry, specifically the large-scale, mass production of crops and animals by agribusinesses. He examines the ways animals are treated and the impact this production has on the environment. He reviews the American diet, and points out that most Americans have an unhealthy diet too high in sugar, fat, and cholesterol, with not enough fiber. He says that Americans can consciously select a diet that is much healthier, while at the same time being less abusive to animals and the environment.

"Clearly, comprehensively and nonjudgmentally takes a controversial and personal subject—food and food production—and explores the environmental impacts of our food choices."—Elissa Wolfson, managing editor, and Will Nixon, associate editor, *E Magazine*

300. **Root, Terry L.** *An Atlas of North American Birds in Winter: An Analysis of Christmas Bird Count Data.* Foreword by Chandler S. Robbins. Chicago: University of Chicago Press, 1988. 312 pages.

Root provides an interesting application of the concepts of geographical distribution of species. She presents computer-generated maps showing the concentrations of bird species in various areas, based on a analysis of the annual Christmas bird count statistics gathered by bird clubs at 1282 sites in the United States and Canada during each winter during the period of 1962 to 1972. A series of transparencies can be placed over each of the species distribution maps to compare distribution pattern with a host of environmental characteristics.

301. **Sagoff, Mark.** *The Economy of Earth: Philosophy, Law, and the Environment.* New York: Cambridge University Press, 1988. 271 pages.

Sagoff analyzes the processes and products of social regulation in the United States, particularly those related to environmental protection, health and safety, and the minimization of exposure to natural and technological hazards. He looks at the tension between individual rights and the public good, especially when social regulation implies limits on choices available to individuals. And he focuses on the process of social regulation as one governed by political forces rather than ethical values alone.

"A lucid examination of the relationship of ethics to public policy in environmental issues."—Eric Katz, assistant professor of philosophy, New Jersey Institute of Technology

302. **Sarre, Phillip, ed.** *Environment, Population and Development.* London: Hodder & Stoughton for The Open University, 1991. 304 pages.

This textbook introduces and explains many of the issues of economic development and the environment, particularly about the inequities in the allocation of goods and services, as well as in the distribution of environmental impacts. The various chapters contrast the differences between the developed and developing countries and look at the short- and long-term consequences for the environment. This book is one in a series of Open University textbooks on various environmental topics.

303.   Schaller, George B. *The Year of the Gorilla.* Chicago: University of Chicago Press, 1964. 260 pages.

———. *Golden Shadows, Flying Hooves.* Chicago: University of Chicago Press, 1983. 293 pages.

In *The Year of the Gorilla,* Schaller describes his postdoctoral work studying the mountain gorillas of the Virunga volcanos region in central Africa. Written in a style as enjoyable to read as the best travel writing, this book also provides a tremendous amount of scientific information about the biology, behavior, and conservation efforts made on behalf of the mountain gorilla. Schaller also writes eloquently in this book about the culture and landscape of central Africa. *Golden Shadows, Flying Hooves* documents the years that Schaller and his family spent living in Tanzania's Serengeti National Park studying lions and their prey. He reflects on animal behavior—hunting, mating, raising young, fighting—and on the origins of the human hunter in these wild and magnificent grasslands. His scientific achievements have truly been an inspiration to a generation of biologists and conservationists.

304.   Schmookler, Andrew Bard. *The Parable of the Tribes: The Problem of Power in Social Evolution.* Berkeley: University of California Press, 1984. 400 pages.

Schmookler has written an important social commentary, in which he outlines what he calls "the destructive evolutionary process" that our species has undergone. He suggests that this process has resulted in a social system that merely serves the creation and maintenance of power, rather than the true well-being of humans and other life on the planet.

"This book clarified for me the crucial step-jump our evolution took when we began to be civilized. That step enshrined the crucial necessity for a society to seek power in order to survive. The struggle for power, which continues unabated to this day, is the central dynamic of our civilization and the principle reason why we keep destroying the planet's ecosystems. Either we will learn how to control the struggle for power or our civilization will not survive."—Lester W. Milbrath, director, Research Program in Environment and Society, State University of New York at Buffalo

305.   **Schneider, Stephen H., with Lynne E. Mesirow. *The Genesis Strategy: Climate and Global Survival.* New York: Plenum, 1976. 419 pages.**

This book was published in the mid-1970s, at a time when there were severe droughts in Africa and the United States. As a result, it received a great deal of attention and found its niche as an interesting and useful book on climate change for a popular audience.

Also recommended is *The Primordial Bond: Exploring the Connections Between Man and Nature Through the Humanities and Science* (Plenum, 1976), by Stephen Schneider and Lynne Morton; and *The Coevolution of Climate and Life* (Sierra Club, 1985), by Stephen Schneider and Randi Londer.

306.   **Schreiber, Rudolf L., Anthony W. Diamond, Roger Tory Peterson, and Walter Cronkite. *Save the Birds.* Boston: Houghton Mifflin, 1989. 384 pages.**

A project of Pro Natur, a conservation group based in Frankfurt, Germany, and the International Council for Bird Preservation in Cambridge, England, and sponsored in the United States by the ten societies of the Audubon Alliance, this book is a major effort that attempts to educate the public about birds around the world and the threats to their survival. Beautiful photographs are used to convey much of the message, along with an extensive text and other illustrations. The book provides discussions of the major ecosystems of the world, giving information on the varieties of birds and their environments in addition to the different dangers that certain species in each ecosystem encounter. Throughout the book there are case studies that highlight rare, threatened, or endangered species from around the world. And as a way to engender support for its causes, the book documents a number of "benefits" that birds provide for humans.

307.   **Schroeder, Henry A. *Trace Elements and Man: Some Positive and Negative Aspects.* Old Greenwich, CT: Devin-Adair, 1973. 171 pages.**

Two decades of scientific research in biochemistry and human physiology have certainly rendered much of Schroeder's text out-of-date (for instance, the periodic table shown contains just 103 elements). This is, however, an important summary of the general concepts of the role that trace elements play in human health, including both benefits and hazards.

"The author not only provided a lot of facts to show the importance of trace elements in the health of humans, but also explained why the trace element played such an important role, especially from the view of the theory of evolution. The book encourages readers to explore more unknown areas of the subject. It aroused my fervour to study the relationship between the structures of elements and their physiological functions."—Changsheng Li, deputy director, Research Center for Eco-Environmental Sciences, Academica Sincia, Beijing, China

308.   Schumacher, Ernst F. *Good Work.* New York: Harper, 1979. 223 pages.

Based on essays and lectures he delivered during the mid-1970s, Schumacher reiterates here his major point that both the developed and developing nations need to adopt the appropriate technologies to improve the quality of life for the poor and maintain an environmental balance.

"Correctly identifies the fundamental relationships between our attitudes toward work and our environmental problems. Classic Schumacher and even better than the more famous *Small is Beautiful* [see entry 81]."—John E. Carroll, professor of environmental conservation, University of New Hampshire

309.   Schwarz, Michiel, and Michael Thompson. *Divided We Stand: Redefining Politics, Technology and Social Choice.* London: Harvester Wheatsheaf, 1990. 176 pages.

A critical review of technological decisionmaking and why so many faulty decisions are made by individuals and groups. A particularly interesting chapter concerns the use of the juxtapositioning of ecological models and social models (in more specific terms, "myths of nature" and "the two dimensions of sociality and the four rationalities") as a means of analyzing policy debates and choices.

"Demonstrates centrality of myths of the nature of decisionmaking. Challenges fundamental assumptions about societal preferences for technology and the environment, including the simple assumptions of self-interest that are central to political science theory and economics."—Steve Rayner, deputy director, Global Environmental Studies Center, Oak Ridge National Laboratory

310. **Seager, Joni, and Ann Olson.** *Women in the World: An International Atlas.* Edited by Michael Kidron. New York: Simon & Schuster, 1986. 128 pages.

This atlas presents graphic illustrations and maps on forty topics related to women and associated issues of sustainability: work, marriage, contraception, motherhood, health, wealth, the media, the military, and government. These maps dramatically illustrate the inequitable distribution of political and economic resources between women and men around the world. The atlas is supplemented with notes on data sources, commentaries on each of the maps, and a bibliography. An additional cartographic analysis of global environmental conditions is presented in Seager's *The State of the Earth Atlas* (1990, Touchstone).

311. **Seymour, John S., and Herbert Girardet.** *Blueprint for a Green Planet: Your Practical Guide to Restoring the World's Environment.* New York: Prentice Hall, 1987. 192 pages.

What can one person do to help reduce global environmental problems? Seymour and Girardet believe that individuals can have a major impact. In fact, they propose that environmental degradation can and should be combatted by individual citizen action. Thus, the authors prepared this book as a guide to specific actions that citizens can take to help resolve the global environmental crisis. It describes the causes and consequences of some environmental problems, provides questions for analyzing household practices, and suggests actions for less damaging practices in the home. While this book was one of the first such guides, in recent years many similar books have been published that direct citizens on how to become better environmental citizens.

312. **Sharpe, Grant, ed.** *Interpreting the Environment.* New York: Wiley, 1976. 566 pages.

As Sharpe suggests, environmental interpreting is an interactive process through which a visitor develops a better awareness, appreciation, and understanding of an area. Interpretation can be an active engagement between a skilled interpreter and the visitor, or a more personal process, such as following signs along a self-guided trail. In either case, interpretation is the art through which the salient characteristics of an area can be easily and eagerly absorbed by the visitor.

Interpreting the Environment brings together the thoughts of some twenty interpretation experts to provide a framework and theoretical background for anyone who would like to become a more effective interpreter.

"The 'textbook' of interpretive methods and techniques. The book has established the groundwork for a multitude of interpretive programs worldwide."—Alan Leftridge, senior editor, *Legacy*

313. **Shelford, Victor E., ed.** *The Naturalist's Guide to the Americas.* Baltimore: Williams & Wilkins, 1926. 761 pages.

Under the auspices of the Ecological Society of America's Committee on the Preservation of Natural Conditions, this is perhaps the earliest and most comprehensive assessment of natural areas in the Americas (the most extensively detailed are within the United States, but also included are areas in Canada, Mexico, Central and South America, and the Caribbean Islands). The guide gives locations and detailed descriptions of wild areas where the original flora and fauna remain intact (although many of these areas are bound to have changed considerably since the 1920s). There are several regional maps showing general locations of the areas being described. A list of organizations, both national and local, engaged in natural areas preservation is provided as an appendix. This is an extremely interesting historical record of natural areas in the early part of this century.

314. **Shepard, Paul.** *Nature and Madness.* San Francisco: Sierra Club, 1982. 178 pages.

Shepard continues his search for an answer to the question: "Why do men persist in destroying their habitat?" (p. 1). Following the analysis he has presented in previous books, such as *Man in the Landscape: A Historic View of the Esthetics of Nature,* (Knopf, 1967); *The Tender Carnivore and the Sacred Game* (Scribner's, 1973); and *Thinking Animals: Animals and the Development of Human Intelligence* (Viking, 1978); he examines the processes of human psychological development in order to find the basis of what he calls "irrational and self-destructive" behavior toward nature and the environment.

315. **Simmons, I. G.** *Changing the Face of the Earth: Culture, Environment, History.* New York: Blackwell, 1989. 487 pages.

Simmons admits that in 1956, as an undergraduate in college, he was tremendously influenced by William L. Thomas's edited collection, *Man's Role in Changing the Face of the Earth* (see entry 89). In his own book, he provides an updated and comprehensive overview of the types and levels of impacts that the earth has sustained from humans during various stages of cultural development. By looking at technological developments and changes in the use of energy and natural resources, he shows the different capacities of primitive societies, advanced hunters and gatherers, agriculturalists, industrial societies, and the nuclear age of influencing changes in the earth's biogeochemical systems. Simmons covers a lot of material, some of which is very complex, but he maintains a clear and concise style throughout. A fifty-page bibliographic essay, organized by chapter, provides a rich discussion of sources for further information.

"This relatively new book combines a historical approach with an energy flow analysis to show the delicate interweaving of people's activities and the changing character of the earth's surface. It's scholarship and lucidity are outstanding."—Ian Douglas, professor of geography, University of Manchester, England

316.   **Smith, Neil.** *Uneven Development: Nature, Capital and the Production of Space.* New York: Blackwell, 1984. 198 pages.

Smith, a professor of geography at Rutgers University, suggests that the capitalistic process of "uneven development" operates at many scales and that capitalism has transformed both humans and wild nature. Drawing from the Marxist perspective, he argues that we are now "producing" nature, and have become alienated from each other and our environment.

"The best book yet written to lay out how industrial capitalist societies must continuously destroy and create new 'natural' landscapes. Dense for those unfamiliar with Marxist theory, but absolutely worth the work."—Margaret FitzSimmons, associate professor of architecture and urban planning, University of California–Los Angeles

317.   **Sontheimer, Sally, ed.** *Women and the Environment: A Reader.* London: Earthscan, 1991. 205 pages.

This reader focuses on environment and economic development in the Third World, particularly on the role of women in balancing economic survival with sustainable use of natural resources. It shows how women are particularly vulnerable to the impacts of land degradation and pollution, but are taking actions to halt desertification, plant trees, and improve the quality of their environment and lives.

318. **Southwick, Charles H., ed.** *Global Ecology* Sunderland, MA: Sinnauer, 1985. 323 pages.

Southwick has assembled a collection of writings about the biosphere, which presents opposing views of the state of the world, the nature of biogeochemical cycles, and human effects on these cycles. The various authors analyze such issues as pollution and agricultural production problems related to acid rain, groundwater contamination, soil erosion and food production, desertification of farmland, and tropical deforestation. A number of the papers focus on the human elements of population issues, health problems, the effects of the Vietnam war, the problems of Third World countries, and the role of technology in the survival of humankind.

319. **Stanley, Joseph, and Lynn Karlin.** *Maine Farm: A Year of Country Life.* New York: Random House, 1991. 102 pages.

In 1980, Stanley was able to buy the thirty-year-old farm of two of America's most famous proponents of the nontraditional lifestyle, Helen and Scott Nearing (see entry 269). Season after season, Stanley and Karlin have managed to make their farm a sustainable operation, providing them with an abundance of nutritional and spiritual sustenance. And as evidenced by this book, the occupants of this farm near Harborside, Maine, have a lot to show and tell. We learn not only of the seasonal progress of their agricultural endeavors, but also about such activities as the building of a sauna, the crafting of dried flower arrangements, the weaving of a rag rug, and the construction of a coracle (a small boat from Ireland resembling a turtle's shell). Also included are plenty of recipes of their favorite dishes. The reader cannot help but feel as if he or she has spent a year in the country with gracious hosts and willing teachers.

320. **Stearns, Raymond Phineas.** *Science in the British Colonies of America.* Urbana: University of Illinois Press, 1970. 760 pages.

This is a scholarly and notable book that documents the development of scientific endeavors in the English-speaking New World, which was obviously influenced by the scientific traditions of Europe, yet emerged with a unique perspective in a world of "new" landscapes, peoples, and species of flora and fauna.

"A massive and thoughtful work which, in explaining the first efforts to understand the natural history of the new world, lays a basis for understanding what has gone on since."— Joseph Kastner, author

321. **Stokes, D.W.** *A Guide to Nature in Winter: Northeast and Northcentral North America.* Illustrated by Deborah Prine and D. W. Stokes. Boston: Little, Brown, 1976. 374 pages.

The first of the Stokes nature guides, this shows how being in the outdoors in winter can be as exciting as during other seasons. The guide explains how to look at weeds, trees, snow, birds and nests, mushrooms, animal tracks, and evidence of insects.

"A source of interesting vignettes about 'detective' ecology. Helps develop powers of observation in an easy and interesting way. A good means of getting interesting information to the novice." —Robert S. De Santo, chief scientist and project manager, De Leuw, Cather & Company

322. **Student Environmental Action Coalition.** *The Student Environmental Action Guide: 25 Simple Things We Can Do.* Berkeley, CA: Earth-Works, 1991. 96 pages.

One of the EarthWorks guides, this one was written by college students for college students. It is a useful reference that shows how individuals can help solve environmental problems at home, on campus, and in the community.

323. **Taylor, Paul.** *Respect for Nature: A Theory of Environmental Ethics.* Princeton, NJ: Princeton University Press, 1986. 329 pages.

Taylor dedicates his book to "the earth's wild living things." In it, he describes the three main components of a theory of environmental ethics: the moral attitude of respect itself as applied toward nature; a "biocentric" (rather than "anthropocentric") outlook on nature; and the ethical system of standards and rules that influence attitudes of respect for nature. He discusses the notion of rights (both legal and moral) and whether animals and plants have rights. In conclusion, Taylor uses several hypothetical situations to show how people can put into practice the ethics of respect for nature.

324. **Teale, Edwin Way.** *Autumn Across America.* New York: Dodd, Mead, 1956. 386 pages.

———. *Journey Into Summer.* New York: Dodd, Mead, 1960. 366 pages.

———. *North with the Spring: A Naturalist's Record of a 17,000 Mile*

Journey with the North American Spring. New York: Dodd, Mead, 1951. 366 pages.

————. *Wandering Through Winter.* New York: Dodd, Mead, 1965. 370 pages.

In these four books Teale has presented, perhaps better than anyone else, the enchantment and excitement of nature changing through the seasons. He was a prolific naturalist writer during his time, and these books represent the best of his work. Teale certainly deserves a special place on the roster of great writers. *Wandering Through Winter* won the Pulitzer prize for general nonfiction in 1966.

"I firmly believe that we must engender in people a love of nature in order to save the environment. Teale, along with Muir, Thoreau, Burroughs, and Borland, does this in his Pulitzer-prize-winning, four-book account." — Marcia Bonta, naturalist/writer

Also recommended are Teale's *A Naturalist Buys an Old Farm* (Dodd, Mead, 1974) and *The Wilderness World of John Muir* (Houghton Mifflin, 1954).

325. **Terborgh, John.** *Where Have All the Birds Gone?: Essays on the Biology and Conservation of Birds That Migrate to the American Tropics.* Princeton, NJ: Princeton University Press, 1989. 202 pages.

By a preeminent biologist at Princeton University, this book provides a rather bleak report on how human activities have greatly reduced the numbers of certain species of birds. The reasons for these declines are quite clear: the loss of habitat (forest cover, grasslands, wetlands); the introduction of exotic species and increases in the number of domestic predators (for example, cats); and the use of chemicals that pollute the environment. Terborgh suggests that the birds encounter threats both in their nesting areas and in their wintering habitats in Latin America, where environmental destruction is proceeding at an alarming rate. While his perspective is somewhat pessimistic, Terborgh does list some actions that individuals can do to better the situation, such as helping to expand the "conservation database" with field notes and observation records, taking various sorts of political actions, and making improved choices about their lifestyles.

"An environmental must for anyone concerned about the future of the world. Brings catch phrases like 'forest fragmentation' and 'tropical rainforest elimination' into real perspective." — Carl Slater, president, Brooks Bird Club

326.   **Thibodeau, Francis R., and Hermann H. Field, eds.** *Sustaining Tomorrow: A Strategy for World Conservation and Development.* Hanover, NH: University Press of New England, 1984. 186 pages.

The authors describe the political and ecological backdrop against which the World Conservation Strategy was proposed, in addition to the nature of ecological processes, the concept of sustainable yields and obstacles to achieving them, and the importance of genetic diversity in light of present agricultural practices. Needs for effective regional and international laws and improved educational outreach programs in order to instill awareness are discussed in detail.

327.   **Tilden, Freeman.** *Interpreting Our Heritage.* 3d ed. Chapel Hill: University of North Carolina Press, 1977 (orig. pub. 1957). 119 pages.

A relatively short, but significant, book that has guided the development of two generations of cultural and natural history interpreters.

"A seminal work describing six principles of interpretation. Tilden is considered the 'father' of interpretation technique, laying the groundwork for the effective methods of educating others about the biophysical and cultural worlds in informal settings."—Alan Leftridge, senior editor, *Legacy*

328.   **Tinbergen, Niko.** *Curious Naturalists.* London: Curious Life, 1950. 280 pages.

A survey of Tinbergen's studies of animal behavior, as well as his descriptions of and reflections on how these discoveries influenced himself, his naturalist colleagues, and his friends.

"Niko Tinbergen was one of the greatest naturalists and ethologists of this century. His autobiography is an inspiration to all naturalists who wish to understand the natural world around them and then wish to be able to communicate that enthusiasm to young and old."—Steven E. Piper, editor, *Vulture Study News* of the Vulture Study Group, Westville, Natal, South Africa

329.   **TreePeople, with Andy Lipkis and Katie Lipkis.** *The Simple Act of Planting a Tree.* Los Angeles: Tarcher, 1990. 237 pages.

Billed by TreePeople as "a citizen forester's guide to healing your neighborhood, your city, and your world," this book offers easy-to-follow instructions on how to organize work parties; how to publicize a tree-planting event; how to obtain, plant, and care for tree seedlings; and how to improve the "health" of the planet. The book's focus is mainly on the almost two decades of work by TreePeople in the Los Angeles area, but it offers useful advice on how to undertake projects elsewhere. A workbook at the end of the book helps the reader organize an entire activity, from planning to wrap-up.

330.   **Trimble, Stephen.** *Words from the Land: Encounters with Natural History Writing.* Salt Lake City: Peregrine Smith, 1988. 303 pages.

Trimble has assembled the writings of fifteen of the most popular contemporary naturalist writers. In his introduction, he tries to convey what nature writing means to him, to these writers, and to the readers, and describes the processes that each of the writers goes through to create their works. Each selection is prefaced by a biographical essay about the writer.

331.   **Tucker, Richard P., and John F. Richards, eds.** *Global Deforestation and the Nineteenth-Century World Economy.* Durham, NC: Duke University Press, 1983. 210 pages.

As explained in this book, deforestation is a process driven by a variety of individual and collective motives. The various papers compiled here show how the conversion and cutting of forest occurred during the nineteenth century on both a large and small scale, and describe what the different motivations were for those changes. A major conclusion of the book is that deforestation was less a response to burgeoning population growth as it was to the demands from European and Western markets for commodities and raw materials. The various regional case studies focus on the history of deforestation in North America, the Philippines, Brazil, India, Burma, China, Japan, and the Sahel in Africa. (See also entry 296 for the sequel, *World Deforestation in the Twentieth Century.*)

332.   **Turner, Tom.** *Sierra Club: 100 Years of Protecting Nature.* New York: Abrams, 1991. 288 pages.

With text by the former editor of *Not Man Apart* (the newspaper of Friends of the Earth) and stunning illustrations by noted photographers Galen Rowell, Philip Hyde, Eliot Porter, and others, this book commemorates the centennial of the Sierra Club, which is one of the oldest and largest environmental groups in the world. An additional reference on the organization is Michael P. Cohen's *The History of the Sierra Club: 1898–1980* (Sierra Club, 1988).

333.   **Tuttle, Merlin D.** *America's Neighborhood Bats: Understanding and Learning to Live in Harmony with Them.* Austin: University of Texas Press, 1988. 196 pages.

Written by the founder of Bat Conservation International, which is located in Austin, Texas, this book includes chapters on many aspects of bats: basic biology, environmental values, public health and nuisance concerns, conservation, and bat house construction. The book includes color photographs of and information about common U.S. bats; it won the Wildlife Society's 1991 Conservation Education Writing Award.

334.   **Usher, Michael B., ed.** *Wildlife Conservation Evaluation.* London: Chapman and Hall, 1986. 394 pages.

A thorough and scientific presentation on how to evaluate sites for preserving and maintaining nondomesticated species of plants and animals. In the first chapter, Usher shows how to formulate and develop the appropriate criteria to be used in assessing the attributes of an area that are relevant to a particular purpose. In additional chapters, other contributors describe some principles about wildlife conservation evaluation, discuss and compare the evaluation methods used in a variety of regions and habitats around the world, and offer practical advice on the realities of conservation evaluation and the designing of nature reserves. A 670-entry bibliography is an excellent source of information for further reading on the topic.

"The most comprehensive text on the evaluation of areas for wildlife conservation. No rational choice of new areas can be made without a working knowledge of this book's contents."— Steven E. Piper, editor, *Vulture News* for the Vulture Study Group, Westville, Natal, South Africa

335.   **Van Dyke, John C.** *The Desert: Further Studies in Natural Appearances.* Salt Lake City: Peregrine Smith, 1980 (orig. pub. 1901, Scribner's; 1918 ed. with illustrations and photographs, Smeaton Chase; 1976 ed., Arizona Historical Society). 272 pages.

Van Dyke was a prolific writer of books about art and art history. He also crafted several works about "impressions and appearances" of natural landscapes. With the trained eye of an art critic, he observed and recorded the richness of the land and life of the arid desert in this book. In one passage that describes "the make of the desert" he wrote: "The sunshafts are falling in a burning shower upon rock and dune, the winds blowing with the breath of far-off fires are withering the bushes and grasses, the sands drifting higher and higher are burying the trees and reaching up as though they would overwhelm the mountains, the cloud-bursts are rushing down the mountain's side and through the torn arroyos as though they would wash the earth into the sea" (pp. 26–27, 1918 edition). This is a superb look at an intricate and entrancing landscape.

"An *early* classic! Amazingly perceptive for its time. Sparkling writing."—David Hancocks, director, Arizona-Sonora Desert Museum

336.   Van Matre, Steve. *Acclimatization: A Sensory and Conceptual Approach to Ecological Involvement.* Martinsville, IN: American Camping Association, 1972. 138 pages.

————. *Acclimatizing: A Personal and Reflective Approach to a Natural Relationship.* Martinsville, IN: American Camping Association, 1974. 225 pages.

Van Matre's approach to learning about the environment is to get out into it and see, feel, smell, taste, and listen. In *Acclimatization,* he offers a six-day lesson plan and other suggestions that can be used to help children begin to understand and feel a part of their natural world. The sequel, *Acclimatizing,* provides additional participatory exercises for children.

"Van Matre has us out touching the Earth again—an art and way of connecting to the earth that we lost."—Mark C. Wagstaff, executive director, Wilderness Education Association

Also recommended are Van Matre's other books: *The Earth Speaks: An Acclimatization* (Institute for Earth Education, 1983); and *Earthkeepers: Four Keys for Helping Young People Live in Harmony with the Earth* (Institute for Earth Education, 1988), coauthored by Bruce Johnson.

337.   Warner, William W. *Beautiful Swimmers: Watermen, Crabs, and the Chesapeake Bay.* Drawings by Consuelo Hanks. Boston: Little, Brown, 1976. 304 pages.

Warner has captured eloquently the economic geography and natural history of a magnificent North American environment: the tidewater region of the Delmarva Peninsula. His book won a Pulitzer prize for general nonfiction in 1977.

338.   Waters, Frank. *Book of the Hopi.* Drawings and source material recorded by Oswald White Bear Fredericks. New York: Viking, 1963. 347 pages.

A fascinating description of Hopi legends and customs, and a chronicle of Hopi history in which the role of natural phenomena in Hopi culture and religion is described.

"This was the first book to tell me that a radically different view of nature is possible—a view that I could then only begin to comprehend. This is precisely the view that most professional conservationists and environmentalists seem to be lacking, as they scurry around in their new suits, shamelessly sniffing for money."—Donald Snow, director, Northern Lights Institute

339.   **Watt, Kenneth E. F.** *Understanding the Environment.* Boston: Allyn & Bacon, 1982, 431 pages.

Watt cites four major impediments that he believes prevent citizens from grasping the full nature of environmental problems: (1) few people really understand the scope of the economic-environmental interconnections; (2) the small number of environmentalist voters means that environmental policies do not have the support of a sufficient constituency; (3) individuals base their views on information rather than direct observation; and (4) human minds tend to filter out the facts and complications they don't readily understand. His text is an interdisciplinary approach on how to help overcome some of these obstacles, and he utilizes his background and experience in models and systems analysis to structure the material.

340.   **Watts, Mary T.** *Reading the Landscape of America.* rev. ed. New York: Macmillan, 1975 (orig. pub. 1967). 354 pages.

A wonderful guide on how to interpret the natural and cultural features in the landscape, and how to uncover clues that reveal history, processes, and outcomes. Watts takes us by the hand on a tour around the American landscape, while lecturing, pointing, explaining, and prodding us to think and analyze on our own. She teaches us to inquire: "What has happened here? How? And why?"

"The original edition of this book was one of the first to popularize the subject of ecology. Originally covering areas of the Midwest, the revised edition includes revisits to these areas twenty years later, as well as new areas from New England salt marshes to southwestern deserts and Pacific slope redwoods. I was particularly impressed with her use of diagrams and drawings to illustrate the ecological features she is describing."—James A. Fowler, former chair, Michigan Natural Areas Council

341.   **Western, David, and Mary C. Pearl, eds.** *Conservation for the Twenty-First Century.* New York: Oxford University Press, 1989. 365 pages.

The product of a conference held in New York in 1986 by Wildlife Conservation International of the New York Zoological Society, this collection of papers provides diverse perspectives of approaches to biological conservation around the world, and views of the prospects for wildlife and ecosystems. The authors are among the most noted international experts in the field, and represent many professional disciplines. The book considers the impacts of human activities, biological bases for conserving nature, management approaches and tools for conservation, and methods for gaining public support for conservation efforts. It concludes with an extensive discussion of an agenda for the future.

342.   **Whittaker, Robert H.** *Communities and Ecosystems.* 2d ed. New York: Macmillan, 1975 (orig. pub. 1970). 385 pages.

This is a basic textbook for beginning or intermediate courses on ecology. Whittaker's approach is to focus on communities, which are the definable and interacting systems of organisms, as the basis for presenting ecological principles and concepts. This leads to discussions of the impacts of pollution and human activities on such community characteristics as species diversity, productivity, biomass, and height and structural complexity. This is an interesting and very readable textbook—one that complements other basic biology and ecology reference works.

343.   **Wild, Peter.** *Pioneer Conservationists of Eastern America.* Missoula, MT: Mountain, 1986. 280 pages.

————. *Pioneer Conservationists of Western America.* Introduction by Edward Abbey. Missoula, MT: Mountain, 1979. 246 pages.

These two books contain biographies of thirty important conservationists, with descriptions of fifteen in each. From the West, Wild includes John Wesley Powell, John Muir, Gifford Pinchot, Stephen Mather, Enos Mills, Mary Hunter Austin, Aldo Leopold, Bernard DeVoto, Olaus Murie, Joseph Wood Krutch, William O. Douglas, David Brower, Garrett Hardin, Steward Udall, and Edward Abbey. From the East, he has chosen George Perkins Marsh, Frederick Law Olmstead, Carl Schurz, John Burroughs, George Bird Grinnell, Theodore Roosevelt, William T. Hornaday, Benton MacKaye, Robert Marshall, Franklin Delano Roosevelt, Howard Zahniser, Rachel Carson, Barry Commoner, Ralph Nader, and Amory Lovins.

344. **Wilson, Edward O.** *Biophilia.* Cambridge, MA: Harvard University Press, 1984. 197 pages.

Wilson defines biophilia as "the innate tendency to focus on life and lifelike processes" (p. 1). In this book, the reader can see how he shares the same fascination for life that has captivated so many people. He has transformed this fascination into a lifelong commitment to research the intricacies of life at varying scales; for others, it leads to such varied endeavors as artistic expressions or political activism. In the final chapter of his book, Wilson elaborates on the ethic developed by Aldo Leopold to encompass his biophilic viewpoint.

345. **World Bank.** *World Development Report.* New York: Oxford University Press. (annual).

Although the World Bank has been drawing much criticism for its inattention to environmental concerns related to development projects it funds, this annual report is a useful source of data on current economic trends and economic and social indicators for the World Bank's member countries. The topics vary each year: poverty (1990), public finance in development (1989), population (1984), and management policy (1983). Each issue contains a multitude of data tables that report on various social and economic conditions, such as population, area, gross national product (GNP), inflation, life expectancy, production growth, agriculture, energy, imports and exports, public debt, labor force, urbanization, health, education, government revenues and expenditures, and income distribution.

346. **World Resources Institute.** *The 1992 Information Please Environmental Almanac.* New York: Houghton Mifflin, 1991. 606 pages.

An extensive collection of environmental facts on food, energy conservation, water, air pollution, nature and land conservation, and recreation and ecotourism. Includes the names and addresses of the chief environmental executives in all fifty states, and gives "green" rankings of fifty major metropolitan areas.

347. **Worster, Donald.** *Dust Bowl: The Southern Plains in the 1930s.* New York: Oxford University Press, 1979. 277 pages.

Using evidence from archival sources, newspapers, and interviews, Worster pieces together a history of the causes and consequences of the Dust Bowl by focusing on Cimarron County in Oklahoma, and Haskell County in Kansas. He suggests that the capitalistic, market-driven political economy of the 1920s and 1930s led to an abuse of the land, making it more vulnerable to the ensuing drought and merciless wind. He therefore sees the farmers as having been victims of the political economic systems as much as they were victimizers of the land. See also Worster's *Under Western Skies: Nature and History in the American West* (Oxford University Press, 1992).

"I think this is Worster's best book. He meticulously traces and explains the origins of the human and environmental tragedy of the Dust Bowl. This book won the Bancroft Award for the best book in American History."—Margaret FitzSimmons, associate professor of architecture and urban planning, University of California–Los Angeles

348.   **Worster, Donald, ed. *The Ends of the Earth: Perspectives on Modern Environmental History.*** New York: Cambridge University Press, 1988. 341 pages.

This collection of essays offers a good introduction to the emerging field of environmental history. The contributors cover a range of perspectives, focusing on differing causes and impacts of environmental change such as climate variability, human population increase, colonialism, biological "invasions," inequitable political and economic structures, and varying degrees of environmental and social vulnerability. In an appendix called "Doing Environmental History," Worster reviews the models and methods used by environmental historians, and provides a listing of some 300 environmental histories.

See also *American Environmentalism: The Formative Period, 1860–1915* (Wiley, 1973), which is a collection of articles edited by Worster.

349.   **Wright, Angus. *The Death of Ramón González: The Modern Agricultural Dilemma.*** Austin: University of Texas Press, 1990. 337 pages.

This is an excellent book on pesticide use, agribusiness, and environmental policy, particularly in the developing world, and specifically in the Culiacan valley of Mexico and the Central valley of California. Wright uses the experience of one farmworker to epitomize the consequences of overuse of pesticides in the developing world. By focussing on one individual, he is able to document clearly the impacts of pesticide use and to present a more compelling and personal story.

The story of the farmworker, his life and his death, is obtained through extensive talks with members of the family and other workers. The revelations that unfold are shocking. Wright has written as stinging a critique of the misuse of pesticides as Rachel Carson did in *Silent Spring* (see entry 19), except Wright's book presents a more contemporary political and economic viewpoint.

350. **Young, John.** *Post Environmentalism.* London: Belhaven, 1990. 225 pages.

Young reviews the new environmentalism and its various philosophies, goals, and incongruities. At one point the author writes: "Deep ecology, Gaia theory and creation spirituality make an attractive but heady mixture. It may prove to be a less dangerous one than anthropocentrism mixed with advanced technology, but it is a good idea to know its political flashpoint" (p. 127). He suggests that still the best way to affect widespread change is to focus the concerns of the new environmentalism on issues with which the vast majority of voters can identify.

Part III

Other Recommended Books

351. **Alinsky, Saul.** *Rules for Radicals: A Practical Primer for Realistic Radicals.* New York: Random House, 1971. 196 pages.

A treatise, as Alinsky says, "for those who want to change the world from what it is to what they believe it should be" (p.3). Also recommended is Alinsky's *Reveille for Radicals* (Random House, 1989).

352. **Allaby, Michael.** *Dictionary of the Environment.* 3d ed. New York: New York University Press, 1989 (orig. pub. 1977). 423 pages.

A good resource for definitions and basic concepts.

353. **Andruss, Van, Christopher Plant, Judith Plant, and Eleanor Wright, eds.** *Home! A Bioregional Reader.* Philadelphia: New Society, 1990. 181 pages.

A compilation of articles by many of the most active persons in the bioregionalist movement. This reader offers a good overview of bioregional philosophies and concepts.

354. **Ashby, Eric.** *Reconciling Man with the Environment.* Leon Sloss Junior Memorial Lectures for 1977. Stanford, CA: Stanford University Press, 1978. 104 pages.

Three short essays on the process of human awareness of and responses to environmental hazards.

355. **Barnett, Harold J., and Chandler Morse.** *Scarcity and Growth: The Economics of Natural Resource Availability.* Baltimore: Johns Hopkins Press for Resources for the Future, 1969 (orig. pub. 1963). 288 pages.

"By far the best analysis of the role of human knowledge and effort in making natural resources available for human use; puts malthusian philosophy in long-run perspective. A modern classic."—Marion Clawson, senior fellow emeritus, Resources for the Future

356. **Beer, Tom.** *Environmental Oceanography: An Introduction to the Behavior of Coastal Waters.* New York: Pergamon, 1983. 262 pages.

This is an advanced textbook, by an Australian environmental consultant, which covers the physical processes of coastal waters and marine environments.

357. **Benedick, Richard Elliot.** *Ozone Diplomacy: New Directions in Safeguarding the Planet.* Cambridge: Harvard University Press, 1991. 300 pages.

As the chief negotiator for the United States, Ambassador Benedick provides a detailed history of the Montreal Protocol on Substances that Deplete the Ozone Layer, which was ratified in 1987 and revised in 1990.

358. **Berry, Wendell.** *Standing by Words.* San Francisco: North Point, 1983. 224 pages.

"Reminders of man's place on earth, shared by all beings."—Joan Eltman, executive director, St. Croix Environmental Association/Virgin Islands Conservation Society.

Also recommended is Berry's *The Long-Legged House* (Harcourt, Brace, 1969).

359. **Boyd, Doug.** *Rolling Thunder: A Personal Exploration into the Secret Healing Powers of an American Indian Medicine Man.* New York: Random House, 1974. 273 pages.

"It emphasizes the need to become more connected to ourselves, the land, and universal patterns."—Shannon Horst, director of public awareness, Center for Holistic Resource Management

360. **Bromfield, Louis.** *Malabar Farm.* New York: Harper, 1948. 405 pages.

"A poetic statement about restorative agriculture."—Dennis Meadows, professor of environmental studies, University of New Hampshire

361. **Brown, Lester R., with Erik Eckholm.** *By Bread Alone.* New York: Praeger for the Overseas Development Council, 1974. 272 pages.

"Provides a major discussion of the world food crisis."—Stephen Schneider, senior scientist, National Center for Atmospheric Research

362. **Cahn, Robert, ed.** *An Environmental Agenda for the Future.* Covelo, CA: Island 1985. 155 pages.

A collection of reports prepared by the leaders of the major environmental and conservation groups in the United States. Also recommended is Cahn's *Footprints on the Planet: A Search for an Environmental Ethic* (Universe, 1978).

363. **Caldwell, Lynton Keith.** *Science and the National Environmental Policy Act: Redirecting Policy through Procedural Reform.* University: University of Alabama Press, 1982. 178 pages.

Although several books have been written on the National Environmental Policy Act (NEPA), most are focused on the environmental impact statement or judicial interpretations of the act rather than on its policy intent. This book by one of the authors of the NEPA describes the goals of the act and the strategies to attain them.

364. **Capra, Fritjof, and Charlene Spretnak, in collaboration with Rudiger Lutz.** *Green Politics: The Global Promise.* New York: Dutton, 1984. 258 pages.

A compelling set of arguments that analyzes and supports the "green" movement in politics.

365. **Carr, Archie.** *So Excellent a Fishe: A Natural History of Sea Turtles.* Garden City, NY: Natural History Press for the American Museum of Natural History, 1967. 248 pages.

An interesting look at the ecology and life histories of sea turtles in the Caribbean Sea and around the world.

366. **Clark, Mary E.. *Ariadine's Thread: The Search for New Modes of Thinking.*** New York: St. Martin's, 1989. 584 pages.

"In a world of despair, this work of scholarship analyzes ecological concern and formulates a way forward. Great Stuff!"—Dean Graetz, principle research scientist, Division of Wildlife and Ecology at the Commonwealth Scientific and Industrial Research Organization (CSIRO), Canberra, Australia

367. **Cohen, Michael. *The Pathless Way: John Muir and the American Wilderness.*** Madison, WI: University of Wisconsin Press, 1984. 408 pages.

An insightful review of the development and maturation of Muir's philosophy of nature and how his ideas influenced the preservationist movement in this country.

368. **Constanza, Robert, ed. *Ecological Economics: The Science and Management of Sustainability.*** New York: Columbia University Press, 1991. 525 pages.

"These papers, from the first meeting of the International Society for Ecological Economics held at the World Bank in May 1990, lay out an agenda that recognizes 'oikos' as the root of both economics and ecology."—Stephen Viederman, president, Jesse Smith Noyes Foundation

369. **Cornell, Joseph. *Listening to Nature.*** Nevada City, CA: Dawn, 1987. 96 pages.

"More excellent activities and information on how to really 'listen' to nature and learn from her."—Nancy Zuschlag, president, Colorado Alliance for Environmental Education

370. **Corson, Walter, ed. *What You Can Do About the Environmental Crisis.*** Boston: Beacon, 1990. 414 pages.

Sponsored by the Global Tomorrow Coalition of Washington, D.C., this is a guide to the latest information on air, water, climate change, energy, toxic waste, tropical forests, population, and other environmental issues.

371. **Crosby, Alfred W. *Ecological Imperialism: The Biological Expansion of Europe, 900–1900.*** New York: Cambridge University Press, 1986. 368 pages.

By a noted environmental historian at the University of Texas, who is also author of *The Columbian Exchange: Biological and Cultural Consequences of 1492* (Greenwood, 1972), this book reviews some of the ecological changes undertaken during a period of 100 years of exploration and expansionism.

372. **Dasmann, Raymond.** *African Game Ranching.* New York: Macmillan, 1964. 75 pages.

"This inspired me very much at the time of its publication, stressing principles of 3-D land use by the natural fauna."—J. Cloudsley-Thompson, professor emeritus of zoology, University College, London

373. **Davis, Donald Edward. 1989.** *Ecophilosophy: A Field Guide to the Literature.* San Pedro, CA: R&E Miles, 1989. 137 pages.

A good reference to about 280 books related to environmental ethics, philosophy, and values. Also provides a list of relevant periodicals and organizations.

374. **Dawkins, Richard.** *The Blind Watchmaker.* New York: Norton, 1986. 332 pages.

"The single most important work on the biological nature of humanity and the possible interactions with the biological world."—Dean Graetz, principal research scientist, Division of Wildlife and Ecology at the Commonwealth Scientific and Industrial Research Organization (CSIRO), Canberra, Australia

375. **Dawkins, Richard.** *The Selfish Gene.* New York: Oxford University Press, 1989 (orig. pub. 1976). 352 pages.

"This book interprets the implications of the fundamental ideas proposed by Darwin for modern society. The philosophical implications of these ideas and consequences are fundamental and renders concepts of the meaning of life published before 1859 redundant."—Dean Graetz, principal research scientist, Division of Wildlife and Ecology at the Commonwealth Scientific and Industrial Research Organization, (CSIRO), Canberra, Australia

376. **Demars, Stanford E.** *The Tourists in Yosemite, 1855–1985.* Salt Lake City: University of Utah Press, 1991. 168 pages.

In this history of how Americans have viewed and used Yosemite National Park, which is an icon of the American wilderness, Demars shows how increased tourism in the area has affected changes in park management. The book is illustrated with numerous photographs that depict tourists and the landscape during this period.

377. **De Poncins, Gontran.** *Kabloona.* Alexandria, VA: Time-Life Books, 1965. (orig. pub. 1941). 322 pages.

"It shows in a sparse, crystalline fashion the integration of man's total economy and culture with natural cycles in the hyperextreme Arctic environment."—Dennis Meadows, professor of environmental studies, University of New Hampshire

378. **DeVoto, Bernard, ed.** *The Journals of Lewis and Clark.* Boston: American Heritage Library, 1973. 560 pages.

"To paraphrase, one needs to know from where we have come to know where we are going. Reading these journals one gets an honest impression of what the West was like *before* it was won. It's a good reference point for those of us who don't count themselves among the 'winners' of the West."—Meredith Taylor, chair, Wyoming chapter of the Sierra Club

Also recommended is DeVoto's *Across the Wide Missouri* (American Heritage Library, 1980).

379. **Diamond, Irene, and Gloria Orenstein, eds.** *Reweaving the World: The Emergence of Ecofeminism.* San Francisco: Sierra Club, 1989. 324 pages.

A collection of articles that outlines the emergence, significance, and alternative world view of ecofeminism.

380. **Douglas, Marjory Stoneman.** *The Everglades: River of Grass.* New York: Holt, Rinehart, 1947. 406 pages.

This is a classic environmental history of southern Florida and of the struggle to preserve the Everglades. An amazing book by an amazing person!

381. **Douglas, Mary.** *Purity and Danger: An Analysis of Concepts of Pollution and Taboo.* New York: Praeger, 1966. 188 pages.

This is an anthropological analysis of the cultural concepts and rituals related to hygiene and uncleanliness, which provides a useful construct from which to assess the human perceptions of safety and hazards in general.

382. **Dubos, Rene.** *A God Within.* New York: Scribner's, 1972. 325 pages.

"His books took the 'big picture' perspective—bigger than any discipline. I wanted to study what he had studied, but how? Where? I found my way to geography."—Eve Gruntfest, associate professor of geography, University of Colorado–Colorado Springs

Also recommended is Dubos's *So Human An Animal* (Scribner's, 1968).

383. **Dumont, Rene.** *Utopia or Else* . . . Translated by Vivienne Menkes. New York: Universe, 1975 (orig. pub. 1973). 180 pages.

"It made me (in 1975) turn into an environmentalist. The world dimension of the environmental degradation and the ways of fighting it are superbly described."—António Eloy, director, Associação Portuguesa de Ecologistas/Amigos da Terra (Friends of the Earth), Lisbon, Portugal

384. **Durrell, Gerald.** *The Amateur Naturalist.* New York: Knopf, 1983 (orig. pub. 1982). 320 pages.

"Beautiful photographs of habitats and how to ethically collect from those habitats."—Lori Colomeda, education director, Schuylkill Center for Environmental Education

385. **Durrell, Gerald.** *My Family and Other Animals.* New York: Viking, 1963. 273 pages.

"Durrel's books together with others about wildlife (e.g. Jane Goodall's) probably were the first to get me interested in nature, conservation, and environmental problems in the developing world."—Diana M. Liverman, associate professor of geography, Pennsylvania State University

386. **EarthWorks Group.** *Recycler's Handbook.* Berkeley, CA: EarthWorks Press, 1990. 132 pages.

"Excellent source of statistics and guidance to many recycling dilemmas."—Jennifer Tichenor, Environmental Action Coalition

387. **EarthWorks Group.** *50 Simple Things Kids Can Do to Save the Planet.* Berkeley, CA: EarthWorks Press, 1990. 156 pages.

A guide to easy things for children to do, complete with instructions for parents or teachers; also includes seven simple "eco-experiments."

388.   **Edborg, Rolf.** *On the Shred of a Cloud: Notes in a Travel Book.* Translated by Sven Ahman. University, AL: University of Alabama Press, 1969. 200 pages.

"Sheer poetry—the world of science and human evolution through the eyes of a poet."—John Baldwin, associate professor of urban and regional planning, University of Oregon

389.   **Epstein, Samuel S.** *The Politics of Cancer.* San Francisco: Sierra Club, 1978. 583 pages.

"A compendium of all information on the environmental sources of cancer with an analysis of the political and social causes and barriers to ending this danger."—Michael Belliveau, executive director, and Hannah Creighton, newsletter editor, Citizens for a Better Environment

390.   **Epstein, Samuel S., Lester O. Brown, and Carl Pope.** *Hazardous Wastes in America.* Foreword by Albert Gore, Jr. San Francisco: Sierra Club, 1982. 593 pages.

"This book brings to the fore the institutional, political, and other special interest group perspectives on a major environmental problem facing us today."—R. Rajagopal, professor of geography and of civil and environmental engineering, University of Iowa

391.   **Estes, Richard Despard.** *Behavior Guide to African Mammals.* Drawings by Daniel Otte. Berkeley: University of California Press, 1991. 611 pages.

This is an impressive compilation of information about the behavior of hoofed mammals, carnivores, and primates of Africa, richly illustrated with line drawings. This is an important resource for naturalists and travelers.

392.   **Ferguson, Nancy, and Denzel Ferguson.** *Sacred Cows at the Public Trough.* Maverick, 1983. 260 pages.

"The Fergusons have a vendetta and share it with the American public well enough to be very convincing and to develop allies."—Meredith Taylor, chair, Wyoming chapter of the Sierra Club

393. **Finch, Robert, and John Elder, eds.** *The Norton Book of Nature Writing.* New York: Norton, 1990. 928 pages.

More than 125 selections from the best of American nature writing; an excellent resource.

394. **Ford, Daniel.** *Three Mile Island, Thirty Minutes to Meltdown: The Untold Story—Why It Happened and How It Can Happen Again.* New York: Viking, 1982. 271 pages.

"In reporting the results of cost-cutting measures at Three Mile Island, Ford prompts us to try to avoid the next accident, as confidence increases and cost-cutting again becomes policy."—Jane Sharp, former president, Conservation Council of North Carolina

395. **Freudenberg, Nicholas.** *Not In Our Backyards!: Community Action for Health and the Environment.* New York: Monthly Review, 1984. 320 pages.

"Hazardous waste from the citizen's view of meeting the problems head-on—as opposed to cover-ups of chemical companies and of slow-downs of governments."—Jane Sharp, former president, Conservation Council of North Carolina

396. **Frost, Robert.** *The Poetry of Robert Frost.* Edward C. Lathem, ed. New York: Holt, 1969. 607 pages.

"There's a lasting quality in poetry not found in most prose writing. Frost's poetry is both ecological and understandable."—John Gustafson, treasurer, American Nature Study Society

397. **Garreau, Joel.** *The Nine Nations of North America.* Boston: Houghton, Mifflin, 1981. 427 pages.

Through descriptions of cultural and physical features, Garreau characterizes nine regions in North America: New England, the Foundry, Dixie, the Islands, MexAmerica, Ecotopia, the Empty Quarter, the Breadbasket, and Quebec.

398. **Geisler, Charles C., and Frank J. Popper, eds.** *Land Reform, American Style.* Totowa, NJ: Rowan and Allanheld, 1984. 353 pages.

"Excellent introduction to the institutional dimensions of resource management."—John McLaughlin, professor of surveying engineering, University of New Brunswick, Fredericton, Canada

399.   Georgescu-Roegen, Nicholas. *The Entropy Law and Economic Process.* Cambridge, MA: Harvard University Press, 1971. 457 pages.

"Many books have claimed to be revolutionary; this one really is. It demolishes the edifice upon which rest schools of economics ranging from monetarism to Marxism. It develops the critique with an unrelenting rigour which makes me think that perhaps it should be passed in a brown paper envelope from one consenting adult to another."— Sandy Irvine, associate editor, *The Ecologist,* Surrey, England

400.   Giono, Jean. *Joy of Man's Desiring.* Translated by Katherine A. Clarke. San Francisco: North Point, 1980. 472 pages.

"Beautiful writing, good translation. Allegorical/historical novel carrying values of sustainability, permaculture, and deep awareness of nature/farm values in prewar France."—Ianto Evans, cofounder and manager, Aprovecho Institute

Also recommended is Giono's *The Man Who Planted Trees* (Chelsea Green, 1985).

401.   Gofman, John. *Radiation and Human Health: A Comprehensive Investigation of the Evidence Relating Low-Level Radiation to Cancer and Other Diseases.* San Francisco: Sierra Club, 1981. 928 pages.

"Basic source book for information, explanation, and reliable data on radiation exposures and dangers by one of the best qualified people in the USA. Brilliant!"—Jane Sharp, former president, Conservation Council of North Carolina

402.   Goldsmith, Edward. *The Great U-Turn: De-Industrializing Society.* Bideford, United Kingdom: Green Books, 1988. 217 pages.

"His book is a collection of brilliant essays on what we must do to turn around the environmental degradation wrought by our over-industrialized society."—Eugene Bazan, member services director, National Association for Science, Technology, and Society

403.   Goodman, Percival, and Paul Goodman. *Communities: Means of Livelihood and Ways of Life.* Chicago: University of Chicago Press, 1947. 141 pages.

"The most perceptive and prescient examination of urban environments."—Frank J. Popper, chair, urban studies department, Rutgers, the State University of New Jersey

404. **Gorz, Andre.** *Critique of Economic Reason.* Translated by Gillian Hardyside and Chris Turner. London: Routledge, 1989. 300 pages.

"Gorz, a reformed Marxist, takes as his model Immanuel Kant's *Critique of Pure Reason,* (Dulton, 1969) and weaves a tightly reasoned yet lucid and penetrating analysis of the limits of economic reason, without which we will not be able to escape the ever greater clutch of economics. Without such a break, we cannot expect to save the environment."—Eugene Bazan, member services director, National Association for Science, Technology, and Society

405. **Government Institutes, Inc.** *Directory of Environmental Information Sources* Rockville, MD: Government Institutes, 1990. 299 pages.

A thorough guide on how to get environmental information, with an emphasis on "maximizing your use" of federal and state government resources; it lists professional, scientific, and trade organizations, as well as newsletters, periodicals and magazines. Another useful resource is *The Nature Catalog* (Tilden, 1991), by Joel Makower.

406. **Graber, Linda H.** *Wilderness as Sacred Space.* Washington, DC: Association of American Geographers, 1976. 124 pages.

"Exceptionally well-written, presenting a view of geopiety which goes unrecognized unless one reads this book. It helps one differentiate between preservation, conversation, and stewardship."—Robert De Santo, chief scientist and project manager, De Leuw, Cather & Company

407. **Graham, Frank.** *The Dragon Hunters.* New York: Dutton, 1984. 334 pages.

By looking at a variety of projects that use alternatives to pesticides, Graham gives a good overview of the potential of an integrated pest-management system and biological pest control.

408. **Graham, Frank.** *Since Silent Spring.* Boston: Houghton Mifflin, 1970. 333 pages.

"An interesting review of the predictions made by Rachel Carson and the action, or lack of it, since the publication of her book."—Roger Wheater, director, Royal Zoological Society of Scotland, Edinburgh

409. **Gramfors, Bo, and Siv Eklund.** *Concise Earthfacts.* Denver, CO: Earthbooks, 1990. 184 pages.

A pocket-sized encyclopedia of geography and history.

410. **Grinder, Alison, and E. Sue McCoy.** *The Good Guide: A Sourcebook for Interpreters, Docents and Tour Guides.* Ironwood, 1985. 146 pages.

"Targets effective docent presentation techniques in museums, but is applicable to all interpreter situations. The book offers insight into educational psychology, group dynamics, and program development without being technical. An excellent resource for those starting a new program."—Alan Leftridge, senior editor, *Legacy*

411. **Halle, Louis J., Jr.** *Spring in Washington.* New York: Sloane, 1947. 227 pages.

A birder's journal of springtime, and the changes it brings in and around Washington, D.C. Halle's other popular book was *Birds Against Men* (Viking, 1938).

412. **Hardin, Garrett.** *Promethean Ethics: Living with Death, Competition, and Triage.* Seattle: University of Washington Press, 1980. 92 pages.

"The most inspiring and compelling book on ethics and morality I have ever read."—Dean Graetz, principal research scientist, Division of Wildlife and Ecology at the Commonwealth Scientific and Industrial Research Organization (CSIRO) Canberra, Australia

413. **Hawken, Paul.** *The Next Economy.* New York: Holt, Rinehart 1983. 215 pages.

Hawken, whose garden implement business has flourished, suggests that the next economy for this country should be an "informative economy," in which products are built better, last longer, and use less material than those in the current economy.

414. **Henderson, Hazel.** *The Politics of the Solar Age: Alternatives to Economics.* Garden City, NY: Doubleday, 1981. 433 pages.

"Brings the conflict between economics and ecology into real numbers."—William Ellis, editor, *TRANET*

415. **Hesse, Hermann.** *Siddhartha.* Translated by Hilda Rosner. New York: New Directions, 1951. 122 pages.

"I think the environmentalist's bookshelf should have some element that describes the quite different attitudes of the world's major civilizations and religions to the interrelationship between man and the rest of creation. The Western perception of man as being a quite unique phenomenon is in very sharp contrast to the Indian perception of the oneness of the universe. *Siddhartha* is highly readable, short, and relatively easy to grasp by some from our culture."—William Drayton, president, Ashoka: Innovators for the Public

416.   **Holling, C. S., ed.** *Adaptive Environmental Assessment and Management.* New York: Wiley, 1978. 377 pages.

"The best book, still, on a realistic approach to environmental management through application of models and analysis."—William Clark, professor, John F. Kennedy School of Government, Harvard University

417.   **Holling, Holling C.** *Paddle-to-the-Sea.* Boston: Houghton Mifflin, 1941. 63 pages.

"This is a children's book. However, its art and story-telling capture the awe of the Great Lakes and their watershed. It reminds me of my Buffalo, New York, and Indiana childhood. It also keeps me reminded of the need to work to preserve and bring back this marvelous natural resource."—John Rowen, books editor, *Albany Report* of the Environmental Planning Lobby

418.   **Horton, Tom.** *Bay Country.* Illustrations by Charles R. Hazard. Baltimore: Johns Hopkins University Press, 1987. 223 pages.

Horton, an award-winning journalist with the *Baltimore Sun*, writes about the natural and cultural features of the Chesapeake Bay region.

419.   **Hudson, W. H.** *Far Away and Long Ago: A Childhood in Argentina.* New York: Hippocrene, 1984. 332 pages.

"The description of the nineteenth-century pampas (now lost to modern agriculture) is excellent."—Exequiel Ezcurra, professor of ecology, Centro de Ecología at the Universidad Nacional Autónoma de México, Mexico City

420.   **Jacobs, Jane.** *The Death and Life of Great American Cities.* New York: Vintage, 1961. 458 pages.

"Another brilliant look at how urban environments work and don't work."—Frank J. Popper, chair, urban studies department, Rutgers, the State University of New Jersey

421.   **Jeffries, Richard.** *The Gamekeeper at Home.* London: Oxford University Press, 1948 (orig. pub. 1878). 352 pages.

"A personal (and early) favorite: the smell of damp bracken between two covers."—Thomas Urquhart, executive director, Maine Audubon Society

422.   **Jones, Stephen.** *Backwaters.* New York: Norton, 1979. 256 pages.

"Marvelous stories about the estuary, or coastal zone; should be made into a PBS special."—John Rowen, books editor, *Albany Report* for the Environmental Planning Lobby

423.   **Kaplan, Fred.** *The Wizards of Armageddon.* New York: Simon & Schuster, 1983. 452 pages.

"Literally a detailed, almost incident-by-incident, account of the rise and decline of nuclear nationalists."—Stephen Schneider, senior scientist, Advanced Study Program, National Center for Atmospheric Research

424.   **Kaufman, Wallace, and Orrin Pilkey.** *The Beaches are Moving: The Drowning of America's Shoreline.* Garden City, NY: Anchor/Doubleday, 1979. 326 pages.

"So much of the predicted disaster in this book has already occurred, we really ought to read it and see if we can protect the future."—Jane Sharp, former president, Conservation Council of North Carolina

425.   **Kelly, Katie.** *Garbage: The History and Future of Garbage in America.* New York: Saturday Review, 1973. 232 pages.

"Simple, easy-to-understand introduction to the problem of solid wastes."—Robert Lewis, science teacher

426.   **King, F. H.** *Farmers of Forty Centuries; or, Permanent Agriculture in China, Korea and Japan.* Emmaus, PA: Rodale, 1948 (orig. pub. 1911). 379 pages.

An important early book on sustainable agriculture, written by a professor of agricultural physics at the University of Wisconsin.

427. **Kozlovsky, Daniel G.** *An Ecological and Evolutionary Ethic.* Englewood Cliffs, NJ: Prentice-Hall, 1974. 116 pages.

"This book has unfortunately been long out-of-print. It is unique, consisting of a series of short essays and contemplations. I was astonished to find, on the Everglades Park nature trail, a quotation from this book cast in bronze."—John Steinhart, professor of geophysics and environmental studies and chair of the Energy Analysis and Policy curriculum, University of Wisconsin–Madison

428. **Krieps, Robert, ed.** *Environment and Health: A Holistic Approach.* Brookfield, VT: Avebury, 1989. 237 pages.

"Environment and health are irretrievably linked in fact but often separated in administration and education. This book tries to bring the two together."—M. Pugh Thomas, director, Environmental Resources Unit, University of Salford, Salford, England

429. **Krimsky, Sheldon, and Alonzo Plough.** *Environmental Hazards: Communicating Risks as a Sound Process.* Dover, MA: Auburn House, 1989. 333 pages.

The authors look at five case studies of different environmental risks and examine the communication process by which the public became aware of the hazards. They critique the role of technical experts and the impacts of cultural, psychological, and political forces in affecting the messages presented and received.

430. **Krupnik, Igor I.** *Artic Ethnoecology.* Moscow, Russia: Nauka, 1989. 270 pages.

"A new aspect of the Arctic history (the historic evolution of the indigenous Arctic population) is revealed instead of a textbook view of 'equilibrium societies' development."—Olga Bykova, faculty, Institute of Geography, Russian Academy of Sciences, Moscow

431. **Krutch, Joseph Wood.** *The Desert Year.* New York: Sloane, 1952. 270 pages.

A colorful description of the American Southwest, based on several visits Krutch made to New Mexico, Arizona, and southern Utah.

Also recommended are Krutch's *Grand Canyon: Today and All Its Yesterdays* (Sloane, 1958); and *The Forgotten Peninsula: A Naturalist in Baja California* (Sloane, 1961).

432. **Kuhn, Thomas S.** *The Structure of Scientific Revolutions.* 2d ed. Chicago: University of Chicago Press, 1970 (orig. pub. 1962). 210 pages.

"Kuhn analyzes how changes in basic scientific concepts may take place in an evolutionary manner—adapting to changed environment and at the same time creating a new environment. I find this a hopeful model since science should provide the tools for sound environmental decisions."—Elissa Landre, secretary, Association of Field Ornithologists

433. **LaBastille, Anne.** *Woodswoman.* New York: Dutton, 1976. 277 pages.

An inspirational work about the author's life in a log cabin, which she built herself, in the Adirondack Park of New York.

434. **Levine, Steven.** *Planet Steward: Journal of a Wildlife Sanctuary.* Illustrated by Armando Busick. Santa Cruz, CA: Unity, 1974. 229 pages.

"A beautiful, poet's approach to land stewardship. Makes it clear why we should care about land—from one piece of it to the entire globe."—Amory Lovins and L. Hunter Lovins, codirectors, Rocky Mountain Institute

435. **Livingston, John A.** *The Fallacy of Wildlife Conservation.* Toronto: McClelland and Stewart, 1981. 117 pages.

"Takes deep ecology's major premise, that conventional or 'shallow' environmentalism fails to work, and works it through regarding one major aspect, wildlife conservation. Without labeling itself deep ecology and without getting lost in academic philosophy jargon/constructs, it reaches similar conclusions—that relationships with beings and with nature must be established that recognize that each participant in the relationship must be seen as different yet equally valued parts of a whole. This is the book that got me lost in asking questions about human/nature relationships and why I'm in the Ph.D. process today."—Annie Booth, doctoral candidate, Institute for Environmental Studies, University of Wisconsin–Madison

436. **London, Jack.** *The Call of the Wild.* New York: Macmillan, 1903. 231 pages.

One of London's most famous adventure tales, this story takes place in turn-of-the-century Alaska, where the line between civilization and wilderness—tameness and wildness—becomes blurred.

437.   **Lovins, Amory, and L. Hunter Lovins.** *Brittle Power: Energy Strategy for National Security.* Andover, MA: Brick House, 1983. 486 pages.

The authors argue that the United States has become increasingly reliant on an energy system that is "prone to sudden, massive failures." They present an alternative energy strategy for the country.

438.   **Luten, Daniel B.** *Progress Against Growth: Daniel B. Luten on the American Landscape.* Edited by Thomas R. Vale. Introduction by Garrett Hardin. New York: Guilford, 1986. 366 pages.

A collection of writings over three decades by a foremost natural resources geographer at the University of California, which covers population, food and agriculture, energy, water, wild nature, and conservation.

439.   **Lutzenberger, Jose A.** *Fim do Futuro? Manifesto Ecologico Brasileiro.* Porto Alegre, Brazil: Editora Movimento, 1976. 96 pages.

"A somber, comprehensive analysis of the whole problem, which brought the issue to the public's consciousness in Brazil."—Giselda Castro, vice president, Ação Democrática Feminina Gaúcha/Amigos da Terra (Friends of the Earth), Porto Alegre, Brazil

440.   **McCloy, John, Nathan Pearson, and Beverly Matthews.** *The Great Oil Spill, The Inside Report: Gulf Oil's Bribery and Political Chicanery.* New York: Chelsea House, 1976. 340 pages.

"While this book is 16 years old, it is documented, and many of the same illegal actions, once thought barred, have occurred again in the 80s and 90s under Reagan and Bush—great background."—Jane Sharp, former president, Conservation Council of North Carolina

441.   **McIntosh, Robert P.** *The Background of Ecology: Concept and Theory.* New York: Cambridge University Press, 1985. 385 pages.

An excellent and captivating presentation on the emergence and development of ecological ideas, and on the scientists who contributed those ideas.

442.   **McNeill, William H.** *Plagues and Peoples.* Garden City, NY: Anchor, 1976. 368 pages.

An intriguing look by a distinguished historian at how diseases and parasites have affected human societies, as well as the impacts that humans have in turn had on the environment.

443.   **Malthus, Thomas R.** *First Essay on Population.* Notes by James Bonar. New York: Kelley, 1965 (orig. pub. 1798 as *Essay on the Principle of Population as it Affects the Future Improvement of Society*). 396 pages.

"Malthus articulated two principles central to environmental concern: populations growth as detrimental to human progress and environment as a constraint on human activities. The left-wing critics of Malthus agree with the right-wing critics of environmental concern: both see nature as infinite and human power as unlimited; both sorts of critics are anti-environmentalist!"—Thomas R. Vale, professor of geography, University of Wisconsin–Madison

444.   **Mander, Jerry.** *Four Arguments for the Elimination of Television.* New York: Morrow, 1978. 371 pages.

"Three people I have respect for have told me this book changed their whole life. Me too. It's about not just TV, but the whole way our culture and psychology responds to the media."—Ianto Evans, cofounder and manager, the Aprovecho Institute

445.   **Mander, Jerry.** *In the Absence of the Sacred: The Failure of Technology and the Survival of the Indian Nations.* San Francisco: Sierra Club, 1991. 400 pages.

"A new book on native peoples and technology, which raises important issues at the same time as it critiques the social systems and philosophical views behind the ecological crisis."—Jay Walljaspar, editor, the *Utne Reader*

446.   **Margulis, Lynn, and Karlene V. Schwartz.** *Five Kingdoms: An Illustrated Guide to the Phyla of Life on Earth.* 2d ed. New York: Freeman, 1988 (orig. pub. 1982). 376 pages.

For those who want a comprehensive introduction to the various life forms found on the earth, this is a well-illustrated and very organized text that describes the various phyla of plants, animals, fungi, protoctists (certain types of water-dwellers), and bacteria.

447.   **Mathews, Jessica Tuchman, ed.** *Preserving the Global Environment:*

The Challenge of Shared Leadership. New York: Norton, 1991. 362 pages.

This collection of papers, sponsored by the American Assembly and the World Resources Institute, looks at the potential threats to peace and security posed by declining environmental conditions around the world, and stresses the role that governments should be playing in order to work toward solutions.

448. **Matthiessen, Peter.** *Sand Rivers.* Photographs by Hugo van Larrick. New York: Viking, 1981. 210 pages.

A personal reflection on the natural history of the Selous Game Reserve in Tanzania, and on the human role in its peril and preservation.

449. **Matthiessen, Peter.** *The Snow Leopard.* New York: Viking, 1978. 338 pages.

Based on a scientific expedition that Matthiessen took with biologist George Schaller in Himalaya, which was to become a spiritual journey as well.

450. **Merchant, Carolyn.** *Ecological Revolutions: Nature, Gender, and Science in New England.* Chapel Hill: University of North Carolina Press, 1989. 379 pages.

Merchant develops a theory for the study of environmental history that considers the cultural and intellectual changes that occurred simultaneously, and in a sense interactively, with the physical ecological changes of the New England landscape during the colonial to pre-Civil War period.

451. **Mowat, Farley.** *Sea of Slaughter.* Toronto: McClelland and Stewart, 1984. 438 pages.

This book documents the legacy of overexploitation of fish, birds, whales, and other animals in the waters around Newfoundland and the Maritime provinces of Canada.

Also recommended are Mowat's *A Whale for the Killing* (McClelland and Stewart, 1972) and *People of the Deer* (Souvenir, 1989).

452. **Mumford, Lewis.** *The City in History: Its Origins, Its Transformations, and Its Prospects.* New York: Harcourt, 1961. 657 pages.

By one of this century's greatest scholars, this is a comprehensive overview of the development of the urban form of social interaction. Includes an extensive annotated bibliography.

Also recommended is Mumford's *Technics and Civilization* (Harcourt, 1934).

453. **Nance, John J.** *What Goes Up: The Global Assault on Our Atmosphere.* New York: Morrow, 1991. 324 pages.

Nance offers a close look at the interaction and conflict between the science and the politics of regulating atmospheric pollutants.

454. **Nash, Roderick F.** *The Rights of Nature: A History of Environmental Ethics.* Madison: University of Wisconsin Press, 1989. 290 pages.

Nash, who has contributed significantly to the development of environmental history as a scholarly craft, reviews here the emergence of different philosophies and attitudes of respect for nature.

455. **Newton, David.** *Taking a Stand Against Environmental Pollution.* New York: Watts, 1990. 157 pages.

"A book for teenagers about environmental action by youth and others—refreshing and needed."—Michael Zamm, director of environmental education, Council on the Environment of New York City

456. **Nicholson, Max.** *The Environmental Revolution: A Guide for the New Masters of the World.* New York: McGraw-Hill, 1970. 366 pages.

An excellent presentation on the physical geography of the planet and the impact of human society on the earth. By the author of *The New Environmental Age* (Cambridge University Press, 1987).

457. **Nollman, Jim.** *Dolphin Dreamtime: The Art and Science of Interspecies Communication.* New York: Bantam, 1987. 176 pages.

"Doesn't impose human viewpoints on other species—Nollman tries to learn from them as separate but equal beings—an important attitude for humans to incorporate into our lives."—Elissa Wolfson, managing editor, and Will Nixon, associate editor, *E Magazine*

458. **Norwood, Vera, and Janice Monk.** *The Desert is No Lady: Southwestern Landscapes in Women's Writing and Art.* New Haven, CT: Yale University Press, 1987. 281 pages.

"Beautifully demonstrates how we respond to our environment differently at various times in our life cycles and gives excellent examples of how perceptions of landscape are portrayed in art, including pottery, quilts, photographs, as well as more traditional art forms."—Eve Gruntfest, associate professor of geography, University of Colorado–Colorado Springs

459.   **Odum, Eugene.** *Ecology and Our Endangered Life Support Systems.* Sunderland, MA: Sinauer, 1989. 283 pages.

A popularized version of Odum's classic textbook, *Fundamentals of Ecology* (see entry 65).

"The best citizen's guide to ecology and systems thinking. Nontechnical, but accurate. Well-illustrated with helpful diagrams, charts and photographs."—Dennis W. Cheek, coordinator of curriculum development, Science, Technology, and Society Education Project of the New York State Education Department

460.   **Ornstein, Robert, and Paul Ehrlich.** *New World—New Mind: Moving Toward Conscious Evolution.* New York: Doubleday, 1989. 302 pages.

"This is a book that proposes new ways to think and act in order to respond better to the long-term problems created by our short-term minds. A fascinating book."—Isabelle De Geofroy, information coordinator, TreePeople

461   **Owen, Mark, and Delia Owen.** *Cry of the Kalahari.* Boston: Houghton Mifflin, 1984. 341 pages.

A remarkable book about two young graduate students who sell all their worldly possessions, travel to Botswana, and set up a field camp to study lions and other mammals of the Kalahari.

462   **Peattie, Donald C.** *Flowering Earth.* Wood engravings by Paul Landacre. New York: Putnam, 1939. Reprint. Bloomington: Indiana University Press, 1991. 260 pages.

"A poetic and gentle treatise on botany, how plants work, and why they are exciting. I've read it four or five times over forty years and it refreshes me each time. This is Peattie's autobiography in a way."—Ianto Evans, cofounder and manager, Aprovecho Institute

463.   **Pittman, Nancy, ed.** *From "The Land."* Covelo, CA: Island, 1988.
478 pages.

Part of the Island Press *Conservation Classics* series, this book contains
some eighty essays and poems from the magazine, *The Land*, published by Friends of the Land during the 1940s and 1950s. The anthology was initiated at the urging of Wes Jackson, codirector of the
Land Institute in Salina, Kansas, who had managed to acquire the
entire collection of the "green-covered" magazine.

464.   **Rifkin, Jeremy.** *Biosphere Politics: A New Consciousness for a New
Century.* New York: Crown, 1991. 388 pages.

Rifkin offers yet another thought-provoking message to the human
community: we need to adopt a new paradigm for viewing the world,
in which we see ourselves not as the center of everything, but rather as
merely one of many components of the earth.

465.   **Roberts, Elizabeth, and Elias Amidon, eds.** *Earth Prayers from
Around the World.* San Francisco: Harper, 1991.

A valuable and useful collection of praises for the earth, for all seasons
and all occasions, divided into sections, such as "The Ecological Self,"
"The Elements," "The Passion of the Earth," and "Cycles of Life." A
similar book is *The Precious and Wild: A Book of Nature Quotes* (Fulcrum, 1991), compiled by John K. Terres and containing quotes from
154 authors.

466.   **Robinson, John G., and Kent H. Redford, eds.** *Neotropical Wildlife
Use and Conservation.* Chicago: University of Chicago Press, 1991.
520 pages.

Nearly fifty experts in the emerging field of conservation biology discuss in this book the varying ways to manage wildlife and maintain
biological diversity in the Americas.

467.   **Rousseau, Jean-Jacques.** *The First and Second Discourses.* Edited,
with introduction and notes, by Roger D. Masters. Translated by
Roger D. Masters and Judith R. Masters. New York: St. Martin's,
1964 (orig. pub. 1750). 248 pages.

————. *The Reveries of a Solitary.* Translated with an introduction by
John Gould Fletcher. New York: Bert Franklin, 1971 (orig. pub.
1762). 196 pages.

"Rousseau presents all the themes of romantic environmentalism in their first incarnation. *The Discourses* set up the anti-civilization themes, the self in society and nature. *The Reveries* are the source of mystic nature writing."—Peter Timmerman, researcher, Institute for Environmental Studies, University of Toronto, Ontario, Canada

468.   **Sampson, R. Neil.** *Farmland or Wasteland: A Time to Choose, Overcoming the Threat to America's Farm and Food Future.* Emmaus, PA: Rodale, 1981. 422 pages.

"The emphasis is on agricultural practices. Some of the data becomes obsolete as volatile situations change, but the thesis is challenging."—Charles McLaughlin, chair, Board of Trustees, Iowa Natural Heritage Foundation.

469.   **Sauer, Carl O.** *Land and Life: A Selection of Writings of Carl Ortwin Sauer.* Edited by John Leighly. Berkeley: University of California Press, 1963. 435 pages.

"This book is another classic on the interaction of human population and environmental quality—the role of human populations in modifying environmental conditions."—Charles H. Southwick, professor of biology, University of Colorado–Boulder

Also recommended is Sauer's *Agricultural Origins and Dispersals* (American Geographical Society, 1952).

470.   **Sax, Joesph L.** *Defending the Environment: A Strategy for Citizen Action.* Introduction by George McGovern. New York: Knopf, 1971. 252 pages.

"Sax's book inspired and taught thousands of attorneys to become environmental lawyers."—J. William Futrell, president, Environmental Law Institute

471.   **Schoemaker, Joyce M., and Charity Y. Vitale.** *Healthy Homes, Healthy Kids: Protecting Your Children from Everyday Environmental Hazards.* Covelo, CA: Island, 1991. 180 pages.

A useful guide for parents on how to reduce or eliminate the exposure of children to environmental hazards around the home.

472.   **Schwartzman, Steven.** *Bankrolling Disasters: International Development Banks and the Global Environment; A Citizen's Guide to the*

World Bank and the Regional Multilateral Development Banks. San Francisco: Sierra Club, 1986. 32 pages.

"Excellent monograph detailing the negative environmental impacts of multilateral development projects. Uses a case-study approach to highlight specific World Bank projects throughout the world."— Richard Hellman, environmental attorney and president, United States Committee for the United Nations Environment Programme

473. **Schweitzer, Albert.** *Out of My Life and Thought.* Translated by C. T. Campin. New York: Holt, 1933. 288 pages.

"Schweitzer's autobiography relates his work in the African wilderness which led to his realization of reverence for life as a basis for contemporary ethics. His formulation provides a Christian and humanitarian basis for environmental work."—J. William Futrell, president, Environmental Institute

474. **Seed, John, Joanna Macy, and Arne Naess.** *Thinking Like a Mountain: Towards a Council of All Beings.* Philadelphia: New Society, 1988. 128 pages.

A strong package of ideas about the human awareness of self, and of all other life.

"Inspiring, empowering, and encouraging, it enforces the fact that human beings are not the crown of creation."—John Revington, director and editor, Rainforest Information Centre, Lismore, New South Wales, Australia

475. **Seredich, John, ed.** *Your Resource Guide to Environmental Organizations.* Irvine, CA: Smiling Dolphins, 1991. 514 pages.

A guide to some 150 public interest environmental groups, with a listing of more than 300 federal and state offices in the United States that deal with conservation and environmental issues. An additional resource is *The Nature Directory: A Guide to Environmental Organizations* (Walker, 1991), by Sandra D. Lamzier-Graham.

476. **Shepard, Paul.** *The Tender Carnivore and the Sacred Game.* New York: Scribner's, 1973. 302 pages.

"A new-romantic celebration of the primitive human being and way of life that provides a radical benchmark for the critique of modernism."—J. Baird Callicott, professor of philosophy and of natural resources, University of Wisconsin–Stevens Point

477. **Simon, Julian.** *The Ultimate Resource.* Princeton, NJ: Princeton University Press, 1981. 415 pages.

"This book is a strong challenge to the pessimism of much environmental literature. It is generally condemned in environmental circles, and I think Simon's argument has flaws. Nevertheless, I frequently have students read it and an environmentalist who does not understand this book (both its strengths and weaknesses) is in bad shape. Simon has an excellent critique of population control efforts."—John H. Perkins, environmental studies faculty, Evergreen State College

478. **Sinclair, Patti, ed.** *E for Environment: An Annotated Bibliography of Children's Books with Environment Themes.* New York: Bowker, 1992. 292 pages.

This is an exhaustive record of children's books on nature and the environment, and is an essential reference for parents, teachers, and librarians.

479. **Singer, Peter.** *Animal Liberation.* London: Jonathan Cape, 1990. 320 pages.

The manifesto for the animal rights movement; a thought-provoking and sometimes-shocking book.

480. **Smith, Frank E.** *The Politics of Conservation.* New York: Pantheon, 1966. 338 pages.

"An excellent inside look at the conservation roots of the environmental movement."—Clay Schoenfeld, dean emeritus of Inter-College Programs and professor emeritus of journalism, wildlife ecology, and environmental studies, University of Wisconsin–Madison

481. **Smith, Henry Nash.** *Virgin Land: The American West as Symbol and Myth.* New York: Vintage, 1950. 305 pages.

Smith looks at the influence of the American wilderness on the nation's cultural and social development during the nineteenth century, giving a brief account of its origins in the eighteenth century.

482. **Snyder, Gary.** *Turtle Island.* New York: New Directions, 1974. 114 pages.

"Celebrates spirit in the animal world."—Joan Eltman, executive director, St. Croix Environmental Association/Virgin Islands Conservation Society

Also recommended are Snyder's *Earth Household* (New Directions, 1969); and *The Practice of the Wild* (North Point, 1990).

483.   **Stegner, Wallace.** *The Sound of Mountain Water.* Lincoln: University of Nebraska Press, 1985 (orig. pub. 1969 Doubleday). 286 pages.

A collection of essays, most of which are personal reflections on the American West, which Stegner wrote during the previous two decades.

Also recommended is Stegner's *The American West as Living Space* (University of Michigan Press, 1987).

484.   **Storer, John H.** *The Web of Life: A First Book of Ecology.* New York: Devin-Adair, 1953. 142 pages.

One of the earliest popular presentations of the concept of "ecology" which shows the many interconnections humans have within the delicate "web of life."

485.   **Sullivan, Walter.** *Continents in Motion: The New Earth Debate.* 2d ed. New York: American Institute of Physics, 1991 (orig. pub. 1974, McGraw-Hill). 430 pages.

A popularized account of plate tectonics, by an esteemed science writer for the *New York Times*.

486.   **Suzuki, Daigetz T.** *Zen and Japanese Culture.* Princeton, NJ: Princeton University Press, 1970 (orig. pub. 1938 as *Zen Buddhism and Its Influence on Japanese Culture*). 478 pages.

"The most accessible and influential exploration of Japanese views of nature and the interdependence of nature and culture in ceremony attitudes."—Peter Timmerman, researcher, Institute for Environmental Studies, University of Toronto, Ontario, Canada

487.   **Thomas, Keith.** *Man and the Natural World: A History of the Modern Sensibility.* New York: Pantheon, 1983. 426 pages.

A book that tries "to reunite the studies of history and literature" by focusing on the changing and sometimes radically different social attitudes toward nature, from cultivationist to preservationist perspectives.

488. **Thresh, John C., John F. Beale, and Ernest V. Suckling.** *The Examination of Waters and Water Supplies.* 4th ed. Philadelphia: Blakiston's, 1933 (orig. pub. 1904). 824 pages.

"First published in 1904. Standard work on the pollution of water, examination of water and how to combat and prevent water pollution."—R. Maitland Earl, chair, International Society for the Prevention of Water Pollution, Hampshire, England

489. **Tuan, Yi-Fu.** *Topophilia: A Study of Environmental Perception, Attitudes and Values.* Englewood Cliffs, NJ: Prentice Hall, 1974. 260 pages.

"Provides a cross-cultural perspective on seeing the world and forces the reader to evaluate many preconceived notions."—Eve Gruntfest, associate professor of geography, University of Colorado—Colorado Springs

490. **Tzu, Chuang.** *Chuang Tzu: Basic Writings.* Translated by Burton Watson. New York: Columbia University Press, 1964. 148 pages.

"Chuang Tzu, an ancient Chinese philosopher, eloquently describes the meaning of 'nature.' Perhaps our scientists will approach the knowledge he has shared . . . if they keep up their quest for a few thousand years."—Jonathan Stoke, chair, Sawtooth Group of the Sierra Club

491. **von Frisch, Karl.** *Bees: Their Vision, Chemical Senses, and Language.* rev. ed. (orig. pub. 1950). Ithaca, NY: Cornell University Press, 1971. 157 pages.

"The classic story of the honey bee communication system—simple and dramatic—that shows how elegantly simple experiments can be. A model of science and science writing."—Charles Walcott, executive director, Cornell University Laboratory of Ornithology

492. **von Hagen, Victor Wolfgang.** *South America: The Green World of the Naturalists, Five Centuries of Natural History in South America.* London: Eyre and Spottiswoode, 1948. 392 pages.

An anthology of writings by early explorers, scientists, and naturalists who visited and lived in South America.

493.   **Wathern, Peter, ed.** *Environmental Impact Assessment: Theory and Practice.* New York: Allen & Unwin, 1988. 332 pages.

"A clear presentation on EIA, well-written and interesting and adding detail to the standard textbooks."—M. Pugh Thomas, director, Environmental Resources Unit, University of Salford, Salford, England

494.   **Webb, Walter Prescott.** *The Great Plains.* Lincoln: University of Nebraska Press, 1959 (orig. pub. 1931, Ginn). 525 pages.

"This 1931 book is still the best study of the most fateful piece of America."—Frank J. Popper, chair, urban studies department, Rutgers, the State University of New Jersey

Also recommended is Webb's *The Great Frontier* (Houghton Mifflin, 1952).

495.   **Welty, Joel C.** *The Life of Birds.* 2d ed. Philadelphia, PA: Saunders, 1975 (orig. pub. 1962). 623 pages.

"Excellent foundation about birds written in an expressive and very readable style."—Stephen W. Kress, staff biologist, National Audubon Society field office

496.   **Westman, Walter E.** *Ecology, Impact Assessment, and Environmental Planning.* New York: Wiley, 1985. 532 pages.

An essential test that assists biologists, geographers, planners, engineers, and others who need to measure, interpret, or forecast changes brought about by human activities.

497.   **White, Gilbert F., ed.** *Natural Hazards: Local, National, Global.* New York: Oxford University Press, 1974. 288 pages.

White, a professor emeritus of geography at the University of Colorado, is perhaps the world's most recognized expert on natural hazards. This collection of papers provides a thorough overview of theories and concepts, as well as case studies, concerning natural hazards of all types and at all scales.

498.   **Wild, Russell, ed.** *The Earth Care Annual.* Emmaus, PA: Rodale, 1992 (annual). 237 pages.

Under the auspices of the National Wildlife Federation, this book analyzes a number of environmental issues by presenting case studies and by focusing on ordinary citizens, as well as environmental professionals, who are making a difference. The book also contains a useful "citizen's guide to personal action."

499. **Willers, Bill, ed.** *Learning to Listen to the Land.* Covelo, CA: Island, 1991. 250 pages.

A collection of literary writing which helps illuminate the relationship between people and the land. Includes important, but perhaps lesser-known, works by such writers as Edward Abbey, Barry Commoner, David Ehrenfeld, Anne and Paul Ehrlich, James Lovelock, Norman Myers, Wallace Stegner, and E. O. Wilson.

500. **Wilson, Edward O.** *Sociobiology: The New Synthesis.* Cambridge, MA: Belknap/Harvard University Press, 1975. 697 pages.

A major work which synthesizes the systematic study of the biological basis for social behavior.

Part IV

Respondents to the Questionnaire

The following are the survey respondents who provided recommendations and comments for books included in *The Environmentalist's Bookshelf.* The responses given are those of the individuals listed, and are not necessarily official statements from the organizations with which they are associated. Addresses and telephone numbers are provided only for those respondents affiliated with conservation or environmental organizations.

Lisa J. Allen is editor of *Tuebor Terra,* a publication of the Michigan United Conservation Clubs, the nation's largest statewide nonprofit conservation organization. The Michigan United Conservation Clubs believes the key to conservation is education. It has 450 affiliate clubs and 140,000 members, and serves as a National Wildlife Federation affiliate. Address: Michigan United Conservation Clubs, 2101 Wood St., P.O. Box 30235, Lansing, MI 48909, Tel. (517) 371–1041.

Anne Marie B. Amantia is librarian/information manager for the Population Crisis Committee, which works to educate policymakers around the world about population issues and about the impacts of population growth on environmental conditions and economic development. Address: Population Crisis Committee, 1120 19th St., NW, Suite 550, Washington, DC 20036, Tel. (202) 659–1833.

Mary A. Angle-Franzini is assistant secretary for the Save-the-Redwoods League, established in 1918 by Stephen Mather, William Kent, John C. Merriam, Madison Grant and Henry Fairfield Osborn. The league has been the most successful in the drive to preserve the Coast Redwoods and Giant Sequoias. Through members' donations, redwood lands are purchased and given to national, state and local parks to be preserved forever for the enjoyment of the public. Address: Save-the-Redwoods League, 114 Sansome St., Room 605, San Francisco, CA 94104, Tel. (415) 362–2352.

Paul J. Baicich is with the American Birding Association (ABA), which promotes recreational birding, educates the public in the appreciation of birds and their contribution to the environment, and contributes to the study of birds in their natural habitats. ABA supports and encourages efforts to protect wild bird populations and their habitats. Address: American Birding Association, P.O. Box 6599, Colorado Springs, CO 80934, Tel. (800) 634–7736.

Marvin W. Baker, Jr. is an associate professor of geography at the University of Oklahoma in Norman, and has served both as regional vice president for the Sierra Club and as chair of the club's publications committee. He was named Oklahoma's Conservation Educator of the Year in 1975 by the National and Oklahoma Wildlife Federations.

John Baldwin is an associate professor of urban and regional planning at the University of Oregon in Eugene, and is secretary of the International Society for Environmental Education. He is author of *Environmental Planning and Management* (Westview, 1985).

Peter Bane is publisher of *The Permaculture Activist,* the quarterly journal for North American permaculture, based in Kailua-Kona, Hawaii. Permaculture describes designed ecosystems which are food- and energy- producing, and which attain diversity, stability, and resilience of natural systems. Address: *The Permaculture Activist,* P.O. Box 3630, Kailua-Kona, HI 96745.

Kirsten Barrere is bookstore manager for the San Francisco Bay chapter of the Sierra Club in Oakland, California. Address: Sierra Club Bookstore, San Francisco Bay chapter, 6014 College Ave., Oakland, CA 94618. (For organizational information, see listing for Jon Beckmann.)

Eugene Bazan is member services director for National Association for Science, Technology and Society, which is dedicated to empowering citizens to question, understand, and guide the technology that surrounds and extends us. Bazan himself grapples with the question: How can men, women, and children together create communities rooted in place and soil? His consulting has taken him into entrepreneurial and nonprofit startups, and the realm of the indeterminate problem. Address: National Association for Science, Technology and Society, 133 Willard Bldg., University Park, PA 16802, Tel. (814) 865–9951.

Jon Beckmann is publisher of Sierra Club Books in San Francisco, California. The Sierra Club is a nonprofit member-supported, public interest organization that promotes conservation of the natural environment by influencing public policy decisions—legislative, administrative, legal, and electoral. The purpose of the organization is to explore, enjoy, and protect the wild places of the earth, to practice and promote the responsible use of the earth's ecosystems and resources, to educate and enlist humanity to protect and restore the quality of the natural and human environment, and to use all lawful means to carry out these objectives. Address: Sierra Club, 730 Polk St., San Francisco, CA 94109, Tel. (415) 776–2211.

William Befort is an assistant professor of forestry and environmental conservation at the University of New Hampshire, in Durham.

Michael Belliveau is executive director of Citizens for a Better Environment (CBE), which combines scientific research, legal action, policy advocacy and public education to bring about environmental reform in California. CBE focuses on hazards to human health in air, water, and on the land. Address: Citizens for a Better Environment, 501 Second St., #305, San Francisco, CA 94107, Tel. (415) 243–8373.

Gary Benenson is an associate professor of technology at City College of the City University of New York and is president of United Community Centers in Brooklyn. He is interested in using the urban environment as a practical means of teaching students about science and technology.

William G. Berberet has served as dean of the College of Liberal Arts at Willamette University in Salem, Oregon, as president of the North American Association for Environmental Education, as treasurer of the International Society for Environmental Education, and as chair of the Oregon Committee for the Humanities.

Kathleen Blanchard is director of research and education for the Quebec-Labrador Foundation (QLF)/Atlantic Center for the Environment, a nonprofit organization incorporated in the United States and Canada. Atlantic Center for the Environment is an umbrella name for QLF environmental programs. Through a variety of projects, QLF works to build support for conservation of natural resources within cultural contexts. Broadly defined, the primary program areas of QLF are rivers and watersheds, wildlife and habitats, rural landscapes, and community development in northern New England, Quebec, and the Atlantic Provinces of Canada. Address: Quebec-Labrador Foundation/Atlantic Center for the Environment, 39 South Main St., Ipswich, MA 01938, Tel. (508) 356–0038.

David E. Blockstein is executive director of the Committee for the National Institutes for the Environment, based in Washington, D.C. He has taught zoology at Connecticut College and teaches ornithology at the University of Minnesota's field biology station. He conducts research on endangered birds in Grenada, West Indies. Address: Committee for the National Institutes for the Environment, 730 11th St., NW, Washington, DC 20001, Tel. (202) 628–4303.

Jon Blyth is with the Charles Stewart Mott Foundation in Flint, Michigan. Address: Charles Stewart Mott Foundation, 1200 Mott Foundation Bldg., Flint, MI 48502, Tel. (313) 238–5651.

Marcia Bonta is a naturalist/writer living with her family on a 500-acre mountain reserve near Tyrone, Pennsylvania. She is author of four books, including *Appalachian Spring* (see entry 120) and *Women in the Field: America's Pioneering Women Naturalists* (see entry 121), as well as more than 130 magazine articles on nature and the environment.

Annie Booth is a doctoral candidate at the Institute for Environmental Studies of the University of Wisconsin–Madison. Her research looks at a synthesis of ideas among deep ecology, bioregionalism, ecological feminism, and Native American world views.

Mary Borchardt is development director for the Institute for Food Development and Policy (Food First), which works for greater democracy and equity as a means not only of ending hunger, but also of saving the environment. The belief is that Third World ecological devastation results not from a conflict between people and the environment, but rather from a contradiction between unequal social structures and the environment. Address: Institute for Food Development, 145 Ninth Street, San Francisco, CA 94103, Tel. (415) 864–8555.

Peter Borrelli is former editor of *The Amicus Journal,* a publication of the Natural Resources Defense Council. He currently serves as vice president of the Open Space Institute, and on the board of directors of the Adirondack Council and Island Press.

Diane Bowen is chair of the Loma Prita chapter of the Sierra Club in Portola Valley, California. Address: Sierra Club, Loma Prita Chapter, 135 Deer Meadow Lane, Portola Valley, CA 94025. (For more organizational information, see listing for Jon Beckmann.)

Charles C. Bradley and **Nina Leopold Bradley** are curators of the Aldo Leopold Memorial Reserve in Baraboo, Wisconsin. Address: Aldo Leopold Memorial Reserve, E12919 Levee Rd., Baraboo, WI 53913, Tel. (608) 356–8956.

Don DeHart Bronkema is senior publications review officer for the U.S. Environmental Protection Agency, the nation's principal environmental regulatory agency. Address: U.S. Environmental Protection Agency, 401 M St., NW, Washington, DC 20460, Tel. (202) 382–4700.

Lila Brooks is director of the California Wildlife Defenders (CWD). The organization has developed an ordinance, enacted in several cities and counties in southern California, which prohibits the feeding of wildlife in urban areas. CWD has obtained wildlife drinking ponds in the hills of southern California to keep wild creatures that are destined for extinction out of urban communities. The organization also publishes educational materials for hillside residents to help make coexistence with urban wildlife a reality. Address: California Wildlife Defenders, P.O. Box 2025, Hollywood, CA 90078, Tel. (213) 663–1856.

Lester R. Brown is president of the Worldwatch Institute in Washington, D.C., a major environmental think tank. Brown is author of a dozen books, is a MacArthur Foundation fellow, and in 1989 won a prize in the category of environment that is awarded by the United Nations. He is editor of *World Watch* magazine, director and coauthor of the annual *State of the World* series (see entry 14) and *By Bread Alone* (see entry 361), and is author of *The Twenty-Ninth Day: Accommodating Human Needs and Numbers to the Earth's Resources* (see entry 13); *Building a Sustainable Society* (see entry 130); and *World Without Borders* (see entry 131). Address: Worldwatch Institute, 1776 Massachusetts Ave, NW, Washington, DC 20036, Tel. (202) 452–1999.

John Burke is head of communications for the International Union for the Conservation of Nature and Natural Resources (IUCN)-The World Conservation Union. (For organizational information and address, see listing under Martin W. Holdgate.)

Olga Bykova is part of the faculty of the Institute of Geography of the Russian Academy of Sciences in Moscow. She works on the assessment and mapping of ecological areas, and is involved in developing a world map of critical ecological areas.

Ellen Byrne is with the public affairs office of the Sierra Club, San Francisco, California. (For organizational information and address, see listing for Jon Beckmann.)

John Cairns, Jr. is university distinguished professor of zoology and director of the University Center for Environmental and Hazardous Materials Studies at Virginia Polytechnic Institute and State University, in Blacksburg. He has conducted extensive research and published hundreds of articles on ecosystem damage and restoration. He is coeditor of *Rehabilitating Damaged Ecosystems* (CRC Press, 1988); *Managing Water Resources* (Greenwood, 1986); and *Biological Methods for the Assessment of Water Quality* (American Society for Testing Materials, 1972).

Lynton Keith Caldwell is Arthur F. Bentley professor emeritus of political science at Indiana University in Bloomington. He has been active in public affairs relating to the environment, and was one of the drafters of the National Environmental Policy Act of 1969. He is author of numerous books, including *International Environmental Policy: Emergence and Dimensions* (see entry 16); *Environment: A Challenge to Modern Society* (see entry 134); and *Science and the National Environmental Policy Act: Redirecting Policy Through Procedural Reform* (see entry 363).

Brant Calkin is executive director of the Southern Utah Wilderness Alliance, which is dedicated to the wise management of public lands on the Colorado River Plateau, and advocates wilderness preservation for qualifying federal lands in Utah's priceless canyon country. Address: Southern Utah Wilderness Alliance, P.O. Box 518, 15 South 300 West, Cedar City, UT, Tel. (801) 586–8242.

Ernest Callenbach, a writer and lecturer living in Berkeley, California, is author of *Ecotopia: The Notebooks and Reports of William Weston* (see entry 17), *Ecotopia Emerging* (Banyan Tree, 1981); and is text author of the poster titled "Earth's Ten Commandments," with art by David Lance Goines.

J. Baird Callicott is a professor of philosophy and of natural resources at the University of Wisconsin–Stevens Point. His numerous articles and six books have been at the center of the new field of environmental philosophy, and include *In Defense of the Land Ethic: Essays in Environmental Philosophy* (State University of New York Press, 1988); *Nature in Asian Traditions: Essays in Environmental Philosophy* (State University of New York Press, 1989), edited with Roger T. Ames; and *The River of the Mother of God and other Essays* (University of Wisconsin Press, 1991) by Aldo Leopold, edited by Callicott and Susan F. Flader. He speaks regularly to diverse audiences on topics ranging from moral philosophy to agroecology.

David Carr is executive director of the Caribbean Conservation Corporation, which is dedicated to protecting marine life, and marine turtles in particular, in the Caribbean and throughout the world. Address: Caribbean Conservation Corporation, P.O. Box 2866, Gainesville, FL 32602, Tel. (904) 373–6441.

John E. Carroll is a professor of environmental conservation at the University of New Hampshire in Durham, and has served as director of programs for the Coolidge Center for Environmental Leadership. He is an expert in transnational environmental disputes and is author of *Environmental Diplomacy: An Examination of Prospective Canadian-U.S. Transboundary Environmental Relations* (University of Michigan Press, 1983), and editor of *International Environmental Diplomacy: The Management and Resolution of Transfrontier Environmental Problems* (Cambridge University Press, 1988).

Giselda Castro is vice president of the Ação Democrática Feminina Gaúcha/Amigos da Terra (Friends of the Earth), which works for the promotion of active citizenship, objectively leading and advocating the participation of citizens in the social and political process at the national and international level. Address: Ação Democrática Feminina Gaúcha/Amigos da Terra, Rua Miguel Tostes, 694, CEP 90420, Porto Alegre/RS, Brazil, Tel. (0512) 32–8884.

Joseph H. Chadbourne is president of the Institute for Environmental Education, a nonprofit educational foundation chartered in Ohio in 1971. It was organized to improve the environmental quality of life through education and training. The goal of the institute is to develop environmental education programs which serve civic and educational groups, and business and industry. Historically, its education programs have used actual problems in the community as their focus, to give those involved the benefits of cooperative, practical, and hands-on learning, growth, and problem-solving techniques. Address: Institute for Environmental Education, 32000 Chagrin Blvd., Cleveland, OH 44124, Tel. (216) 464–1775.

Dennis W. Cheek is coordinator of curriculum development for the Science, Technology, and Society Education Project of the Department of Education in Albany, New York. He is a certified science and social science teacher and is author of *Thinking Constructively about Science, Technology and Society Education* (State University of New York Press, 1992).

William C. Clark is a professor at the John F. Kennedy School of Government at Harvard University in Cambridge, Massachusetts. He was coordinator of the Sustainable Development of the Biosphere Project at the International Institute for Applied Systems Analysis in Vienna, Austria. In 1983, he was named a MacArthur Foundation fellow. He is editor of *Carbon Dioxide Review, 1982* (Oxford University Press, 1982); and is coeditor of *Sustainable Development of the Biosphere* (see entry 145); and *The Earth Transformed by Human Action: Global and Regional Changes in the Biosphere Over the Past 300 Years* (see entry 92).

Marion Clawson is senior fellow emeritus for Resources for the Future, a nonprofit, private research and educational institution in Washington, D.C. He has held a number of posts in government and is author of approximately thirty books and monographs on land use, land economics, and natural resources management, including *The Federal Lands: Their Use and Management* (Johns Hopkins University Press, 1957); *Land Use Information: A Critical Survey of U.S. Statistics* (Johns Hopkins University Press, 1966); and *From Sagebrush to Sage: The Making of a Natural Resource Economist* (Ana Publications, 1987). Address: Resources for the Future, 1616 P St., NW, Washington, DC 20036, Tel. (202) 328–5000.

John L. Cloudsley-Thompson is professor emeritus of zoology at University College in London, England. He is founding editor of the *Journal of Arid Environments* and author of thirty books, including *The Zoology of Tropical Africa* (Weidenfeld & Nicolson, 1969); *Terrestrial Environments* (Wiley, 1975); and *Man and the Biology of Arid Zones* (E. Arnold, 1975).

Lori Colomeda is education director for the Schuylkill Center for Environmental Education, an urban environmental education center with a staff of fourteen on a nature park of 500 acres. The center operates in cooperation with Temple University, Pennsylvania State University, and Benner College, and hosts about 80,000 students per year. Address: Schuylkill Center for Environmental Education, 8480 Hagy's Mill Rd., Philadelphia, PA 19128, Tel. (215) 482–7300.

James R. Conner is an editor and photographer in Kalispell, Montana, and serves as chair of the Montana chapter of the Sierra Club. Address: Sierra Club, Montana Chapter, 78 Konley Dr., Kalispell, MT 59901. (For more organizational information, see listing for Jon Beckmann.)

Matthew B. Connolly, Jr. is executive vice president of Ducks Unlimited (DU), the world's leader in wetlands and waterfowl conservation for over half a century. Since its founding in 1937, DU has enhanced, restored, and conserved over 5.5 million acres of prime wildlife habitat on the North American continent. The Ducks Unlimited Foundation's Wetlands America program works with other organizations to preserve major wetland ecology and waterfowl biology in living laboratories throughout North America. Overall, 600 species of wildlife depend on DU's conservation work. Supported by over half a million members, Ducks Unlimited works with state, provincial, and federal governments and many others in the private sector to ensure a healthy environment for generations to come. Address: Ducks Unlimited, One Waterfowl Way, Long Grove, IL 60047, Tel. (708) 438–4300.

Michael F. Corcoran is executive vice president of the North Carolina Wildlife Federation, the largest private conservation group in North Carolina, dedicated to the wise use and sound management of wildlife and other natural resources of the state. Address: North Carolina Wildlife Federation, P.O. Box 10626, Raleigh, NC 27605, Tel. (919) 833–1923.

Kathleen Courrier is publications director for the World Resources Institute in Washington, DC and a book columnist for *Sierra* magazine. Address: World Resources Institute, 1709 New York Ave., NW, Suite 700, Washington, DC 20006, Tel. (202) 638–6300.

Hannah Creighton is newsletter editor for Citizens for a Better Environment, San Francisco, California. (For organizational information and address, see listing for Michael Belliveau.)

Kenneth C. Cross is assistant attorney general for the state of Texas, specializing in environmental litigation. He is an expert on beach preservation and has successfully defended challenges against the Texas Open Beach law.

Kenneth A. Dahlberg is a professor of political science at Western Michigan University in Kalamazoo, Michigan. His research areas include natural resource systems, biological and genetic diversity, and global environmental issues. He is author of *Beyond the Green Revolution: The Ecology and Politics of Global Agricultural Development* (see entry 157), and coeditor with John W. Bennett of *Natural Resources and People: Conceptual Issues in Interdisciplinary Research* (Westview, 1986).

Raymond F. Dasmann is professor emeritus of environmental studies at the University of California–Santa Cruz. He has served in senior positions of The Conservation Foundation and the International Union for the Conservation of Nature and Natural Resources (IUCN). He is author of a dozen books on conservation, and wildlife biology and management, including *Environmental Conservation* (see entry 161); *African Game Ranching* (Pergamon, 1964); and *A Different Kind of Country* (Macmillan, 1968).

Ian Dawson is librarian for the Royal Society for the Protection of Birds, a conservation organization of about 450,000 members in Great Britain and around the world. Address: Royal Society for the Protection of Birds, The Lodge, Sandy, Bedfordshire SG19 2DL, England, Tel. 0767–680551.

Isabelle de Geofroy is information coordinator for TreePeople, a nonprofit environmental organization that moves people from awareness to action by providing information, training, and support. Programs include citizen forest training, community outreach, school education, youth projects, and a nursery. Address: TreePeople, 12601 Mulholland Drive, Beverly Hills, CA 90210, Tel. (818) 753–4600.

H. Grant Dehart is director of the Maryland Environmental Trust, a statewide land trust devoted to the conservation of farmland, Chesapeake Bay shorelands, historic sites, and natural areas. It holds 35,000 acres of donated easements, and encourages the formation of local land trusts. Address: Maryland Environmental Trust, 275 West St., Ste. 322, Annapolis, MD 21401, Tel. (301) 974–5350.

William M. Denevan is a professor of geography at the University of Wisconsin–Madison, who specializes in cultural ecology, prehistoric agriculture, the Andes, and the Amazon. He is coeditor with Christine Padoch of *Swidden-fallow Agroforestry in the Peruvian Amazon* (New York Botanical Garden, 1987); editor of *The Native Population of the Americas in 1492* (University of Wisconsin Press, 1976); and author of

The Aboriginal Cultural Geography of the Llanos de Mojos of Bolivia (University of California Press, 1966).

Robert S. De Santo is chief scientist and project manager for De Leuw, Cather & Company in East Lyme, Connecticut. He was founding editor of the journal *Environmental Management* and is author of *Concepts of Applied Ecology* (Springer-Verlag, 1978) and coauthor of *Elements of Marine Ecology* (Springer-Verlag, 1974).

Bill Devall is a teacher at Humboldt State University in Arcata, California. He is coauthor, with George Sessions, of *Deep Ecology: Living as if Nature Mattered* (see entry 29), and author of *Simple in Means, Rich in Ends: Practicing Deep Ecology* (Peregrine Smith, 1990).

John F. Disinger is a professor of environmental science and management, and educational theory and practice at Ohio State University in Columbus. He is also associate director of the Educational Resources Information Center (ERIC) Clearinghouse for Science, Mathematics, and Environmental Education there. Disinger is also coeditor with Douglas D. Southgate of *Sustainable Resource Development in the Third World* (Westview, 1987).

Diana Donlon is a program officer with the Goldman Environmental Foundation. (For organizational information and address, see listing for Duane Silverstein.)

Ian Douglas is a professor of geography at the University of Manchester in Manchester, England. He is author of *The Urban Environment* (E. Arnold, 1983).

William Drayton is president of Ashoka: Innovators for the Public (formerly the Ashoka Society) in Washington, DC and codirector of Environmental Safety, a public-interest watchdog of federal environmental agency programs. He was named a MacArthur Foundation fellow in 1986. Through its fellows program, Ashoka seeks to provide assistance to changemakers and public-interest entrepreneurs in economically and socially disadvantaged countries around the world. Address: Ashoka: Innovators for the Public, 1200 Nash St., Ste. 1156, Arlington, VA 22209, Tel. (202) 628–0370.

R. Maitland Earl is chair of the International Society for the Prevention of Water Pollution, which exists to prevent the pollution of water worldwide by ascertaining causes of pollution, suggesting cures, and bringing pressure to bear on all concerned to carry out curative measures. Address: International Society for the Prevention of Water Pollution, "Little Orchard," Bentworth, Alton, Hampshire GU34 5RB, England.

Paul Ehrlich is Bing Professor of Biological Sciences and director of the Conservation Biology Program at Stanford University and author and coauthor of many important environmental books, including *The Population Bomb* (see entry 32) and *The Population Explosion* (see entry 175); *Ecoscience: Population, Resources, Environment* (see entry 34); *Extinction: The Causes and Consequences of the Disappearance of Species* (see entry 33); and *The Birder's Handbook: A Field Guide to the Natural History of North American Birds* (see entry 176). Winner of many honors, he is also a recipient of a MacArthur Prize Fellowship.

Herb Eleuterio is active in the National Association for Science, Technology and Society and has served on advisory panels to the National Science Foundation, the National Research Council, and several universities. He is director of special studies for the Dupont Company in Wilmington, Delaware, and is interested in the role and responsibility of industry in environmental protection. (For organizational information and address, see listing for Eugene Bazan.)

William Ellis is editor of *TRANET*, a bimonthly newsletter directory that abstracts the most important events, publications, and people involved in the Alternative and Transformational (A & T) movements. Its goal is to bring environmentalists, feminists, and human rights, peace, and other activists into a universal movement. Address: *TRANET*, P.O. Box 567, Rangeley, ME 04970, Tel. (207) 864–2252.

António Eloy is director of the Associação Portuguesa de Ecologistas/Amigos da Terra (Friends of the Earth) based in Lisbon, Portugal. Address: Associação Portuguesa da Ecologistas/Amigos da Terra, Travessa da Laranjeira, 1-A, 1200 Lisbon, Portugal, Tel. (01) 347–0788.

Joan Eltman is executive director of the St. Croix Environmental Association/Virgin Islands Conservation Society, a nonprofit, membership-supported, volunteer, conservation, and activist organization. Address: St. Croix Environmental Association/Virgin Islands Conservation Society, P.O. Box 3839, Christiansted, St. Croix, VI 00822.

Ianto Evans is cofounder and manager of the Aprovecho Institute. The institute helps people worldwide take better charge of their own lives, through technologies that are ecologically and culturally sustainable. It is a collective of a few dozen professionals scattered all over the world, and maintains a research center and headquarters in

Oregon. Address: Aprovecho Institute, 80574 Hazelton Rd., Cottage Grove, OR 97424, Tel. (503) 942–9434.

Exequiel Ezcurra is a professor of ecology at the Centro de Ecología at the Universidad Nacional Autónoma de México in Mexico City. His research interests include desert ecology and environmental history.

Philip M. Fearnside is a professor of ecology at the National Institute for Research in the Amazon (INPA) in Manaus, Amazonas, Brazil. He is author of *Human Carrying Capacity of the Brazilian Rainforest* (Columbia University Press, 1986). Address: INPA, C. 478, 69.000 Manaus, Amazonas, Brazil.

John Firor served as director of the National Center for Atmospheric Research in Boulder, Colorado. He is a fellow of the American Meteorological Society and the American Association for the Advancement of Science, and serves on the board of trustees of the Environmental Defense Fund and the World Resources Institute. He is author of *The Changing Atmosphere: A Global Challenge* (Yale University Press, 1990).

Margaret FitzSimmons is an associate professor of architecture and urban planning at the University of California–Los Angeles. She is coauthor with Robert Gottlieb of *Thirst for Growth: Water Agencies as Hidden Government in California* (see entry 199), and author of a forthcoming book on the political economy of agriculture in the United States and its impact on environmental quality.

Dave Foreman is cofounder of the radical environmental group Earth First! and author of *Confessions of an Eco-Warrior* (see entry 187), coauthor with Howie Wolke of *The Big Outside* (Ned Ludd, 1989), and coeditor with Bill Hapwood of *Ecodefense: A Field Guide to Monkeywrenching* (Ned Ludd, 1987). He publishes *The Big Outside Catalog* which includes selected favorite books of his on nature and the environment.

Michael S. Foster is secretary of the Western Society of Naturalists, the oldest west coast scientific society devoted to natural history and ecology. Address: Western Society of Naturalists, P.O. Box 450, Moss Landing Marine Labs, Moss Landing, CA 93950, Tel. (408) 755–8650.

James A. Fowler is former chair of the Michigan Natural Areas Council, which has as its goal the preservation of areas of outstanding scenic beauty or scientific value which are representative of the full variety of Michigan's natural habitat. Address: Michigan Natural Areas Council, University of Michigan Botanical Gardens, 1800 N. Dixboro Rd., Ann Arbor, MI 48105.

John Francis is project manager for environmental impact assessment with the U.S. Coast Guard in Washington, D.C., and is also a United Nations Environmental Programme Goodwill Ambassador to the World.

Sharon F. Francis served as assistant to Lady Bird Johnson for beautification and conservation and is coordinator of the New Hampshire Natural Resources Forum, which forms coalitions to address environmental problems in New Hampshire, and stimulates public discussions. Address: New Hampshire Natural Resources Forum, P.O. Box 341, Charlestown, NH 03603.

Alice L. Fuller is a nature writer in State College, Pennsylvania, and a member of the board of directors of the State College Bird Club in State College, Pennsylvania, which celebrated its fiftieth anniversary in 1991. Members of the organization participate in the Pennsylvania Breeding Bird Atlas survey, the annual Audubon Christmas Bird Count, and many other programs.

J. William Futrell is president of the Environmental Law Institute, a national interdisciplinary nonprofit organization which seeks to advance environmental protection by improving environmental law, policy and management. The institute forges effective solutions through research, education, training, and convening all sectors. Address: Environmental Law Institute, 1616 P St., NW, Washington, DC 20036, Tel. (202) 328–5150.

Warren Gartner is president of the Environmental Education Association of Indiana in Indianapolis.

Stephen R. Gliessman is a professor of environmental studies, serves as director of the Agroecology program and holds the Alfred E. Heller Endowed Chair of Agroecology at the University of California–Santa Cruz. He has worked extensively in Mexico and Central America as a tropical biologist and ecologist. He is editor of *Agroecology: Researching the Ecological Basis for Sustainable Agriculture* (Springer-Verlag, 1989).

Rob Goldberg is a science writer for Environmental Associates of the Academy of Natural Sciences, which was established in 1972 to sponsor research needed to provide a sound basis for environmental decisions, to disseminate objective information to the public, and to provide guidance to industry on water pollution research and water quality maintenance programs. The Academy of Natural Sciences, founded in 1812, communicates and interprets the wonder and excitement of the natural world, and seeks to stimulate concern and responsibility toward the earth and its many life forms. Address: Environmental Associates, Academy of Natural Sciences, 19th and the Parkway, Philadelphia, PA 19103, Tel. (215) 299–1108.

Edward Goldsmith is editor of *The Ecologist* and coauthor of several books, including *Blueprint for Survival* (Penguin, 1972); *The Earth Report: Monitoring the Battle for Our Environment* (see entry 196); and *The Great U-Turn: De-Industrializing Society* (see entry 402). Address: *The Ecologist*, 9 Montague Rd., Richmond, Surrey TW10 6QW England, Tel. (081) 948–1418.

Dean Graetz is principal research scientist for the Division of Wildlife and Ecology at the Commonwealth Scientific and Industrial Research Organization (CSIRO) in Canberra, Australia. He takes a long view of life, which he tries to share with all who will listen. While fundamentally concerned about the global situation, he tries not to use the language of despair and holds the view that humanity can yet reject its present death wish.

Jack Greene is with the National Wildlife Federation in Washington, D.C. Address: National Wildlife Federation, 1400 Sixteenth St., NW, Washington, DC, 20036, Tel. (202) 797–6800.

Kevin L. Grose is librarian for the United Nations Environmental Programme (UNEP), which is based in Nairobi, Kenya, and was created after the United Nations Conference on the Human Environment in 1972 to assist nations in dealing with global environmental issues. Address: UNEP, P.O. Box 30552, Nairobi, Kenya.

Eve Gruntfest is an associate professor of geography at the University of Colorado–Colorado Springs, and is an internationally known expert on flood hazards. She also teaches courses on land use planning, analysis of environmental systems, women's roles in changing the face of the earth, natural hazards, and public policy. She is author of *What Have We Learned from the Big Thompson Flood?* (Natural Hazards Research and Applications Center, 1987).

John A. Gustafson is treasurer of the American Nature Study Society, which was founded in 1908 and is the oldest environmental education organization in North America. It is dedicated to bringing about environmental sensitivity and literacy through its publications, workshops, and field excursions. Address: American Nature Study Society, 5881 Cold Brook Rd., Homer, NY 13077, Tel. (607) 749–3655.

David Haenke is director of the Ecological Society Project of the Tides Foundation, which develops and implements solutions to the major problems of humanity based on ecology, and works to bring humanity and the natural world into a cooperative alliance in the context of ecological communities and societies. Address: Ecological Society Project/The Tides Foundation, Rt. 1, Box 20, Newburg, MO 65550, Tel. (314) 762–3423.

David Hancocks is director of the Arizona-Sonora Desert Museum, a natural history museum specializing in display and interpretation of the Sonoran desert region. Address: Arizona-Sonora Desert Museum, Tucson Mt. Park, Rt. 9, Box 900, Tucson, AZ 85743, Tel. (602) 883–1380.

F. Kenneth Hare is provost emeritus of Trinity College at the University of Toronto in Ontario, Canada, and is professor emeritus of geography. He is a specialist in climate change, and is author of *Climate Variations, Drought and Desertification* (World Meteorological Organization, 1985), and *The Experiment of Life: Science and Religion* (University of Toronto Press, 1983).

Herbert S. Harris, Jr. is president of the Natural History Society of Maryland, which is dedicated to the conservation of all living things and the environment. Address: Natural History Society of Maryland, 2643 North Charles St., Baltimore, MD 21218, Tel. (301) 235–6116.

Randy Harrison, an environmental activist involved with several central Pennsylvania organizations, serves on the executive committees of the Moshannon Group of the Sierra Club, the State College Bird Club, and the League of Conservation Voters of Pennsylvania.

Randy Hayes is director of the Rainforest Action Network, a non-profit activist organization that works to save the world's rainforests. Founded in 1985, the Rainforest Action Network works internationally in cooperation with other environmental and human rights organizations on major campaigns to protect rainforests. Address: Rainforest Action Network, 301 Broadway, Ste. A, San Francisco, CA 94133, Tel. (415) 398–4404.

Julie Hellerud is former assistant editor of *Buzzworm,* an environmental magazine that reports on the condition of worldwide environmental conservation. Address: *Buzzworm*, 2305 Canyon Dr., Suite 206, Boulder, CO 80302, Tel. (303) 442–1969.

Richard A. Hellman is an environmental attorney and president of the United States Committee for the United Nations Environment Programme. Address: USC/UNEP, 2013 Q St., NW, Washington, DC 20009, Tel. (202) 234–3600.

Martin W. Holdgate is director general of the International Union for the Conservation of Nature and Natural Resources (IUCN)-The World Conservation Union, which is based in Gland, Switzerland. He is coeditor of *The World Environment 1972–82: A Report by the United Nations Environment Programme* (see entry 210). The IUCN is a preeminent forum for the world's governments and conservation organizations, through which they can meet on equal footing. The union provides information that serves as basis for policies on sustainable use of the world's natural resources. Its work is designed to yield practical tools for conservation policy and action. Address: IUCN-The World Conservation Union, Avenue du Mont-Blanc, CH-1196, Gland, Switzerland.

Shannon A. Horst is director of public awareness for the Center for Holistic Resource Management, an organization and movement that is restoring the vitality of communities and the natural resources on which they depend by promoting a holistic approach to resource management. The organization has produced the book, *Holistic Resource Management,* written by Allan Savory (Island Press, 1988). Address: Center for Holistic Resource Management, 5820 Fourth St. NW, Albuquerque, NM 87107, Tel. (505) 344–3445.

Louis A. Iozzi is interim dean of academic and student affairs at Cook College of Rutgers, the State University of New Jersey, in New Brunswick. He served as president of the North American Association for Environmental Education in 1989 and chaired the North American Commission for Environmental Education from 1981 to 1988.

Sandy Irvine is associate editor of *The Ecologist* in Newcastle Upon Tyne, England. She is a green activist in England and supporter of deep ecology approaches. She is author of *Beyond Green Consumerism* (Friends of the Earth, 1989), and coauthor of *A Green Manifesto* (Optima, 1988). (For organization address, see listing for Edward Goldsmith.)

Wes Jackson and **Dana Jackson** are codirectors of The Land Institute in Salina, Kansas. Wes Jackson is author of *Altars of the Unhewn Stone: Science and the Earth* (North Point, 1987) and *New Roots for Agriculture* (see entry 219), and is coeditor of *Meeting the Expectations of the Land* (see entry 41). He was named a MacArthur Foundation fellow in 1992. Dana Jackson is editor of the institute's publication, *The Land Report.* The Land Institute is a private, nonprofit, educational-research organization established in 1976 along the bank of the Smoky Hill River southeast of Salina, Kansas. Its student curriculum and public programs examine the technology that could sustain the long-term ability of the earth to support a variety of life and culture. Research in this idea of sustainable agriculture focuses on the development of perennial grain crops in prairie-like mixtures to replace annual crops on erodible land. Address: The Land Institute, Rt. 3, Salina, KS 67401, Tel. (913) 823–5376.

James D. Jensen is executive director of the Montana Environmental Information Center, an activist organization that works to keep Montana the "Last Best Place" in the United States. Address: Montana Environmental Information Center, P.O. Box 1184, Helena, MT 59624, Tel. (406) 443–2520.

Huey D. Johnson is president of the New Renaissance Foundation in Sausalito, California. He is former director of The Nature Conservancy, former chair of the Council of Economic Priorities, and former secretary for California's Resources Agency. Address: The New Renaissance Foundation, 1055 Ft. Cronkite, Sausalito, CA 94965, Tel. (415) 332–8082.

Joseph Kastner was the first nature editor of *Life* magazine. He is author of *A Species of Eternity* (Knopf, 1977), which was nominated for a National Book award, *A World of Watchers* (Knopf, 1986, dist. by Random House), and *The Bird Illustrated, 1550–1900: From the Collections of the New York Public Library* (Abrams, 1988). He writes about nature for the *New York Times* editorial page, and resides in Grandview, New York.

Robert W. Kates is director of the Allan Shaw Feinstein Center for World Hunger at Brown University in Providence, Rhode Island. He is author of *Risk Assessment of Environmental Hazard* (Wiley, 1978), and coeditor of *Climate Impact Assessment: Studies of the Interaction of Climate and Society* (Wiley, 1985).

Daniel Katz is president of the Rainforest Alliance, which works for the conservation of the world's tropical forests. Address: Rainforest

Alliance, 270 Lafayette St., Suite 512, New York, NY 10012, Tel. (212) 941–1900.

Eric Katz is an assistant professor of philosophy and of the science, technology, and society program at the New Jersey Institute of Technology in Newark.

Dennis R. Keeney is director of the Aldo Leopold Center for Sustainable Agriculture at Iowa State University in Ames.

J. Padgett Kelly is director of conservation education for the Department of Education in Nashville, Tennessee.

Katie Kenney is office manager for the Michigan Nature Association (MNA), a nonprofit group of citizen volunteers dedicated to saving the habitat for native Michigan wildlife. Its unique land preservation program has established 127 nature sanctuaries in forty-seven counties of Michigan without using any government money. MNA owns more than 6300 acres of natural areas, which protect examples of forty percent of wildlife species that are endangered, threatened or of special concern in Michigan. The organization has published *Walking Paths in Keweenaw* (1989). Address: Michigan Nature Association, 7981 Beard Rd., Box 102, Avoca, MI 48006, Tel. (313) 324–2626.

Charles Kidd is director of the Population, Resources and Development Program of the American Association for the Advancement of Science in Washington, DC.

V. Klemas is a professor of marine studies and director of the Center for Remote Sensing at the University of Delaware in Newark. He serves on the editorial board for the journal *Environmental Management.*

Ilana Kotin is associate editor of *Buzzworm,* an environmental magazine, (For organizational information and address, see listing for Julie Hellerud.)

Stephen W. Kress is staff biologist with the National Audubon Society field office in Ithaca, New York and is director of the society's Puffin Project. He is author of *The Audubon Society Handbook for Birders* (Scribner's, 1981) and *The Audubon Society Guide to Attracting Birds* (Scribner's, 1985). Address: National Audubon Society Field Office, 159 Sapsucker Woods Rd., Ithaca, NY 14850, Tel. (607) 257–7308.

Elissa Landre is secretary for the Association of Field Ornithologists (AFO). The association publishes the *Manual of Field Ornithology,* which includes papers on life histories, neotropical birds, field research, and other aspects of ornithology. AFO also awards student research grants and actively promotes cooperation with Latin American ornithologists. Address: Association of Field Ornithologists, 278 Eliot St., South Natick, MA 10760, Tel. (617) 655–2296.

Janet M. Lavin is executive assistant to the president of the International Wildlife Coalition. The coalition has the three directives: to prevent cruelty to wildlife; to prevent killing of wildlife; and to prevent destruction of wildlife habitat. Address: International Wildlife Coalition, 634 N. Falmouth Hwy., P.O. Box 388, N. Falmouth, MA 02566, Tel. (508) 564–9980.

Alan Leftridge is senior editor of *Legacy,* the bimonthly magazine of the National Association for Interpretation (NAI), a professional organization devoted to furthering the goals of interpretation and to developing excellence in the delivery of interpretive service. For the purposes of NAI, an interpreter is one who practices the art of revealing meanings and relationships in the natural and cultural worlds. Address: National Association for Interpretation, P.O. Box 1892, Ft. Collins, CO 80522, Tel. (303) 491–6434.

Paul Lehman is an editor for the American Birding Association in Colorado Springs, Colorado. (For organizational information and address, see listing for Paul Baicich.)

Robert Lewis has been a science teacher for thirty years in the Brandywine School District of Wilmington, Delaware. He received the Presidential Award for Excellence in Science and Mathematics Teaching in 1985, and was named a Christa McAuliffe Fellow by the U.S. Department of Education in 1989.

Changsheng Li is deputy director of the Research Center for Eco-Environmental Science at the Academica Sinica in Beijing, China. He is an expert in biogeochemistry and has led several investigations concerning the impacts of environmental pollution on people in China.

Diana M. Liverman is an associate professor of geography at Pennsylvania State University in University Park. Her research interests include looking at the social impacts of climate change, the impacts of the greenhouse effect in Mexico, and global environmental change. She received a Mitchell Prize for Sustainable Development in 1991.

Jack Lorenz is executive director of the Izaak Walton League of America, a national organization of about 50,000 members who work to protect our streams, wetlands, and other water resources. Address: Izaak Walton League of America, 1401 Wilson Blvd., Level B, Arlington, VA 22209, Tel. (703) 528–1818.

Orie L. Loucks is a professor of zoology and Ohio Eminent Scholar of Applied Ecosystems Studies at Miami University in Oxford, Ohio. He is former director of the Holcomb Research Institute of Butler University and of the Center for Biotic Systems at the University of Wisconsin–Madison. He has served on the National Academy of Sciences Board on Water Science and Technology and is secretary of the Board of Governors of The Nature Conservancy.

Amory Lovins and **L. Hunter Lovins** are codirectors of the Rocky Mountain Institute in Snowmass, Colorado. They shared a 1982 Mitchell Prize for their essay on reallocating utility capital and a 1983 Right Livelihood Award. They are authors of several books, including *Energy Unbound: A Fable for America's Future* (Sierra Club, 1986), written with Seth Zuckerman; *Brittle Power: Energy Strategy for Natural Security* (see entry 437); and *Energy/War: Breaking the Nuclear Link* (Harper, 1982). Amory Lovins is author of *Soft Energy Paths: Toward a Durable Peace* (see entry 48). Address: Rocky Mountain Institute, P.O. Box 505, Snowmass, CO 81654, Tel. (303) 927–3128.

Diane G. Lowrie is vice president of the Global Tomorrow Coalition in Washington, D.C. Address: Global Tomorrow Coalition, 1325 G St., NW, Suite 915, Washington, DC, Tel. (202) 628–4016.

Daniel B. Luten is professor emeritus of geography at the University of California–Berkeley. A collection of his writings has been published in *Progress Against Growth: Daniel B. Luten on the American Landscape* (see entry 438), edited by Thomas R. Vale.

Sue Ellen Lyons is chair of the science department at Holy Cross High School in New Orleans, Louisiana, and president of the Louisiana Environmental Educators' Association (LEEA), an organization whose members are actively engaged in teaching environmental education at all levels and/or are otherwise involved in the promotion of environmental awareness. The purpose of LEEA is the promotion, improvement, and coordination of environmental education in the state. LEEA's goal is to foster environmental stewardship and awareness among the citizens of Louisiana. Address: Louisiana Environmental Educators' Association, 2770 Jonquil St., New Orleans, LA 70122.

Tom McKinney is an agricultural researcher at the Rocky Mountain Institute in Snowmass, Colorado. He taught biology at Warren College in North Carolina and has served on the board of the Conservation Council of North Carolina. (For address, see listing for Amory Lovins and L. Hunter Lovins.)

Charles T. McLaughlin is chair of the board of trustees of the Iowa Natural Heritage Foundation, a private, nonprofit foundation that works to preserve and enhance unique or endangered sites in Iowa, some of which are treasures of our natural heritage. Address: Iowa Natural Heritage Foundation, Insurance Exchange Bldg., Suite 1005, 505 Fifth Ave., Des Moines, IA 50309, Tel. (515) 288–1846.

John McLaughlin is a professor of surveying engineering at the University of New Brunswick in Fredericton, Canada. He has served as president of the Canadian Institute of Surveying and Mapping, the Canadian Council of Land Surveyors, and the International Land Information Assembly. He is coauthor of *Land Information Management: An Introduction with Special Reference to Cadastral Problems in Third World Countries* (Oxford University Press, 1988).

Jeffrey McNeely is chief conservation officer for the International Union for the Conservation of Nature and Natural Resources (IUCN)-The World Conservation Union, in Gland, Switzerland. He is coauthor of *Soul of the Tiger: Searching for Nature's Answers in Exotic Southeast Asia* (Doubleday, 1988); and coeditor of *Culture and Conservation: The Human Dimension in Environmental Planning* (see entry 243), and *National Parks, Conservation, and Development: The Role of Protected Areas in Sustaining Development* (Smithsonian Institution, 1984). (For address and organizational description, see entry for Martin W. Holdgate.)

John R. McNeill is a professor of history at Georgetown University in Washington, DC. He is author of environmental history articles and books on Brazil, the Mediterranean world, and the Caribbean.

Manvinder Mamak is marketing manager for the Centre for Science and Environment in India, which is a nonprofit, nongovernmental, quasi-academic research organization that has been set up to increase public awareness of the role of science and technology in national development. Address: Centre for Science and Environment, 807 Vishal Bhawan, 95 Nehru Place, New Delhi-110019, India.

Lynn Margulis is distinguished professor of biology at the University of Massachusetts in Amherst and a codeveloper of the Gaia hypothesis with James Lovelock. Her recent books include *Microcosmos: Four Billion Years of Evolution from Our Microbial Ancestors* (Summit, 1986) and *Mystery Dance: On the Evolution of Human Sexuality* (Summit, 1991), both written with Dorion Sagan. She is also coauthor of *Five Kingdoms: An Illustrated Guide to the Phyla of Life on Earth* (see entry 446); and *Global Ecology: Towards a Science of the Biosphere* (see entry 292).

Nancy Matheson is Agriculture Project coordinator for the Alternative Energy Resources Organization in Helena, Montana. Established in 1973, it is a nonprofit organization dedicated to promoting the use and development of renewable energy and conservation technology, sustainable agricultural systems, and community-based rural developmental approaches. Address: Alternative Energy Resources Organization, 44 North Last Chance Gulch, #9, Helena, MT 59601, Tel. (406) 443–7272.

Dennis L. Meadows is director of the Institute for Policy and Social Science Research at the University of New Hampshire in Durham. He is director of the Balaton Group, a consortium of institutes around the world that focuses on policies to move toward a more ecologically sustainable society. He is coauthor of the landmark study, *The Limits to Growth* (see entry 54), and of *Beyond the Limits* (Chelsea Green, 1992).

Loyal A. Mehrhoff is a botanist specializing in Hawaiian flora at the Bernice P. Bishop Museum of Natural and Cultural History in Honolulu, Hawaii. The museum is a major proponent of natural and cultural history research and educational activities throughout the Pacific.

Lester W. Milbrath is director of the Research Program in Environment and Society and professor emeritus of political science and sociology at the State University of New York at Buffalo. His research in political science has focused on lobbying, political participation, and political beliefs. He is author of *Envisioning a Sustainable Society: Learning Our Way Out* (see entry 258); and *Environmentalists: Vanguard for a New Society* (State University of New York Press, 1984).

Alan Miller is a professor of psychology at the University of New Brunswick in Fredericton, Canada.

John C. Miller is coordinator of environmental education programs for the Department of Education in St. Paul, Minnesota.

Carl Mitcham is a professor of philosophy and director of the Science, Technology and Society Program at Pennsylvania State University in University Park. He is editor of two collections of essays, *Philosophy and Technology* (Free Press, 1972) and *Theology and Technology* (University Press of America, 1984).

Myriam Moore is secretary for the Hawk Migration Association of North America, a nonprofit, continentwide organization comprised solely of volunteers, which was founded in 1974 and is dedicated to the study of hawk migrations, their habitat needs, and their conservation. Address: Hawk Migration Association of North America, P.O. Box 3482, Lynchburg, VA 24503.

Patricia A. Morton is director of education for Bat Conservation International, a nonprofit organization dedicated to educational and research activities aimed at the conservation of threatened and endangered species of bats. Address: Bat Conservation International, P.O. Box 162603, Austin, TX 78716, Tel. (512) 327–9721.

R. E. Munn is a meteorologist and former head of the Environment Program at the International Institute for Applied Systems Analysis in Vienna, Austria. He is editor in chief of the *International Journal of Boundary-Layer Meteorology* and is editor in chief of environmental monographs for the International Council of Scientific Unions-Scientific Committee on Problems of the Environment (ICSU–SCOPE). He is also author of *Biometeorological Methods* (Academic Press, 1970), and *Descriptive Micrometeorology* (Academic Press, 1966); and is coeditor of *Sustainable Development of the Biosphere* (see entry 145).

Norman Myers is an internationally renowned independent scientist and self-employed consultant in Oxford, England, who specializes in the areas of environment and development. He is author and editor of many books on global environmental issues, including *Gaia: An Atlas of Planet Management* (see entry 61); *The Primary Source: Tropical Forests and Our Future* (see entry 263); and *The Sinking Ark: A New Look at the Problem of Disappearing Species* (see entry 264).

Bud Nagelvoort is acting executive director for Trout Unlimited, the largest nonprofit membership organization that works to protect cold-water fisheries. Address: Trout Unlimited, 501 Church Street, NE, Vienna, VA 22180, Tel. (703) 281–1100.

Roderick Nash is a professor of history and environmental studies at the University of California–Santa Barbara, where he has taught for twenty-five years. He is a pioneer in environmental education and environmental history, and is author of *Wilderness and the American Mind* (see entry 63), and *The Rights of Nature: A History of Environmental Ethics* (see entry 454); he is also editor of *The American Environment: Readings in the History of Conservation* (see entry 266).

Philip Neal is general secretary of the National Association for Environmental Education in England. Address: National Association for Environmental Education, Wolverhampton Polytechnic, Walsall Campus, Gorway, Walsall WS1 3BD, United Kingdom, Tel. 0922–31200.

Will Nixon is associate editor of *E Magazine* in Norwalk Connecticut. (For organizational information and address, see listing for Elissa Wolfson.)

Paul F. Nowak is a professor in the School of Natural Resources at the University of Michigan in Ann Arbor.

Timothy O'Riordan is a professor of environmental sciences at the University of East Anglia in Norwich, England. He is author of *Environmentalism* (see entry 70) and *Perspectives on Environmental Management* (Pion, 1971).

David W. Orr is a professor of environmental studies at Oberlin College in Oberlin, Ohio. He is cofounder of the Meadowcreek Project, an environmental education center in Fox, Arkansas, and he serves as education editor for the journal *Conservation Biology*. He is also coeditor of *The Global Predicament: Ecological Perspectives on World Order* (University of North Carolina Press, 1979.) and author of *Ecological Literacy: Education and the Transition to a Postmodern World* (State University of New York Press, 1992).

G. M. Oza is a reader in botany at the University of Baroda in India. He serves as general secretary of the Indian Society of Naturalists, is founding editor of *Environmental Awareness,* and serves on the editorial boards of several other journals. Address: Indian Society of Naturalists, Oza Building, Salatwada, Baroda 390001 India.

Edwin F. Paynter is membership development director for the Hoosier chapter of the Sierra Club in Indianapolis, Indiana. (For organizational information and address, see listing for Jon Beckmann.)

Dominic Perello is editor for the Santa Lucia chapter of the Sierra

Club in Santa Barbara, California. (For organizational information and address, see listing for Jon Beckmann.)

John H. Perkins is on the environmental studies faculty at Evergreen State College in Olympia, Washington. He has published books on the history of insect control and insecticides, environmental education, and the history of the green revolution, including *Insects, Experts, and the Insecticide Crisis: The Quest for New Pest Management* (Plenum, 1982), and *Pest Control: Cultural and Environmental Aspects* (Westview, 1980). He is active in professional environmental history and education societies.

Richard L. Perrine is a professor of civil engineering at the University of California–Los Angeles. He has served as editor in chief of *The Environmental Professional,* which is the journal of the National Association of Environmental Professionals, and is coeditor of *Energy—For Ourselves and Our Posterity* (Prentice-Hall, 1985).

Russell W. Peterson is president emeritus of the National Audubon Society, and has served as vice president of the International Union for the Conservation of Nature and Natural Resources (IUCN)-World Wide Fund, president of the International Council for Bird Preservation, chair of the Global Tomorrow Coalition, and president of the Better World Society. Address: National Audubon Society, 950 Third Ave., New York, NY 10022, Tel. (212) 546–9100.

Steven E. Piper is editor of *Vulture News* for the Vulture Study Group at the University of Natal in Durban, South Africa. The organization is dedicated to the continued existence of free-living populations of vultures on planet earth. Its conservation philosophy is based on the idea that a group of concerned humans can take the responsibility of caring for a group of threatened species, and implement measures necessary to ensure that those species do not become extinct. Address: Vulture Study Group, 2 Canal Drive, Westville 3630, Natal, South Africa, Tel. (011) 646–8617.

Susan E. Place is an assistant professor of geography at the California State University–Chico. She has traveled extensively in Central and South America, and her research focuses on the interaction between ecological conservation and economic development in Latin America.

Nicholas Polunin is president of the Foundation for Environmental Conservation and editor in chief of *Environmental Conservation.* He cofounded the World Campaign for the Biosphere and served as first president of the World Council for the Biosphere. He is author of over 450 research papers on botany, ecology, and conservation, and is editor of *Growth Without Ecodisasters?* (see entry 288) and *Ecosystem Theory and Application* (Wiley, 1986). Address: Foundation for Environmental Conservation, 7 Chemin Taverney, 1218 Grand-Saconnex, Geneva, Switzerland, Tel. (022) 98–2383.

Frank J. Popper is chair of the urban studies department at Rutgers, the State University of New Jersey, in New Brunswick. He is author of *The President's Commissions* (Twentieth Century Fund, 1970) and *The Politics of Land-Use Reform* (University of Wisconsin Press, 1981), and coauthor of *Urban Nongrowth: City Planning for People* (Praeger, 1976). He also serves on a number of national and international commissions dealing with planning and land use.

Yiannakis D. Potamitis is honorary secretary for the Mountaineers and Nature Friends Association of Limassol, Cyprus. Address: Mountaineers and Nature Friends Association, Riga Fereou 53, P.O. Box 34, Limassol, Cyprus, Tel. 63956.

John F. Potter is editor of *The Environmentalist* and is honorary secretary of the Institution of Environmental Sciences in London, England.

Kevin Proescholdt is executive director of Friends of the Boundary Waters Wilderness, a wilderness preservation organization that seeks to protect Minnesota's one million acre Boundary Waters Canoe Area Wilderness and the larger international Quetico-Superior ecosystem in which it lies. Address: Friends of the Boundary Waters Wilderness, 1313 5th St. SE, Ste. 329, Minneapolis, MN 55414, Tel. (612) 379–3835.

R. Rajagopal is a professor of geography and of civil and environmental engineering at the University of Iowa in Iowa City. He is a specialist in groundwater quality and management, and has published numerous articles and conducted workshops on the subject. He has served as editor of *The Environmental Professional*, the journal of the National Association of Environmental Professionals.

Gary Randorf is senior counselor for the Adirondack Council, which works to preserve forever the Adirondack Park through watchdogging, advocacy, information and interpretation, and legal action. The Adirondack Park is a unique mixture of six million acres of private and public land, which has the potential to be America's showplace of the land ethic. Address: Adirondack Council, P.O. Box D-2, Elizabeth, NY 12932.

Steve Rayner is deputy director of the Global Environmental Studies Center at Oak Ridge National Laboratories in Oak Ridge, Tennessee. He has worked in the area of the human dimensions of global environmental change, on programs concerning energy and land use policy, the industrial metabolism, societal impact and resource analysis, global risk analysis, policy implementation instruments, and transnational management of resources. He is author of *Measuring Culture: A Paradigm for the Analysis of Social Organization* (Columbia University Press, 1985).

Ann M. Regn is environmental education coordinator for the Virginia Council on the Environment in Richmond.

Bob Reiss is a contributing writer for *Outside* magazine and author of *The Road to Extrema* (Summit, 1992). He lives in Brooklyn, New York.

Paul Relis is executive director of the Community Environmental Council, Inc., which is a California-based think tank involved in the development of sustainable waste management and land use policies and programs. Address: Community Environmental Council, 930 Miramonte Dr., Santa Barbara, CA 93109, Tel. (805) 963–0583.

John Revington is editor of *World Rainforest Report* and director of the Rainforest Information Centre in Lismore, New South Wales, Australia. The Rainforest Information Centre is a voluntary, nonprofit organization that works nationally and internationally to save the world's rainforests and to assist indigenous people in the struggle against the destruction of their homeland. Address: Rainforest Information Centre, P.O. Box 368, Lismore, New South Wales 2480 Australia.

William E. Riebsame is an associate professor of geography and director of the Environmental Conservation Program at the University of Colorado in Boulder. He teaches courses on public lands, natural hazards mitigation, and global environmental management.

Walter Orr Roberts was president emeritus of the University Corporation for Atmospheric Research in Boulder, Colorado. He is since deceased.

Barbara Rodes is librarian for the World Wildlife Fund/The Conservation Foundation in Washington, DC. Address: World Wildlife

Fund, 1250 24th St. NW, Washington, DC 20037, Tel. (202) 293–4800.

John D. Rogers is librarian for the Conservation Trust Resource Bank and Study Centre in Reading, England. The trust is a charity whose primary aim is to promote environmental education to the whole community through its information services and resource center. It especially tries to reach schools, colleges, and industry who each have a vital role to play in promoting sustainability of population, resources, and environment—the welfare of spaceship earth. Address: The Conservation Trust, George Palmep Site, Northumberland Avenue, Reading RG2 7PN England.

Richard Rono is personal assistant to the executive director of the East African Wildlife Society in Nairobi, Kenya. The society is a nonprofit organization whose policy is to conserve wildlife and its habitat, in all forms, as a national and international resource. Address: East African Wildlife Society, P.O. Box 20110, Nairobi, Kenya, Tel. 748170.

Theodore Roszak is a professor of history at California State University–Hayward in Hayward, California, and author of numerous books, including *Where the Wasteland Ends: Politics and Transcendence in Post-Industrial Society* (see entry 76); *The Making of a Counterculture: Reflections on the Technocratic Society and its Youthful Opposition* (Doubleday, 1969); and *The Voice of the Earth* (Simon & Schuster, 1992).

John Rowen is books editor of the *Albany Report* for the Environmental Planning Lobby (EPL), a full-time advocacy, research, and lobbying group that represents many of New York's major environmental and conservation organizations. EPL lobbies the governor, legislature, and state agencies to ensure that environmental concerns are represented in legislative and administrative processes. EPL's newsletter, *Albany Report,* is a key document used by New York environmentalists to track crucial legislation and to learn about emerging issues. Address: Environmental Planning Lobby, RD 3, Box 179, Altamont, NY 12009.

Clayton T. Russell is program coordinator for the Sigurd Olson Environmental Institute at Northland College in Ashland, Wisconsin.

Arthur B. Sacks is senior special assistant to the dean of the graduate school of the University of Wisconsin–Madison and served as director of the university's Institute for Environmental Studies. He was president of the North American Association for Environmental Education and specializes in international environmental education.

Anne Savage is chair of the Primate Conservation Appeal in Madison, Wisconsin.

George Schaller is with Wildlife Conservation International of the New York Zoological Society in New York City. He is an ecologist who specializes in conservation-oriented studies of large, endangered mammals, such as mountain gorillas and the giant panda. He is author of numerous books, including *The Mountain Gorilla: Ecology and Behavior* (University of Chicago Press, 1963); *The Year of the Gorilla* (see entry 303); *Golden Shadows, Flying Hooves* (see entry 303); and *The Giant Pandas of Wolong* (University of Chicago Press, 1985).

Neill Schaller is associate director of the Institute for Alternative Agriculture in Greenbelt, Maryland. Address: Institute for Alternative Agriculture, 9200 Edmonston Road, Ste. 117, Greenbelt, MD 20770, Tel. (301) 441–8777.

Patricia Scharlin is an environmental consultant in New York City, who has served as director of the Sierra Club's International Office and as editor in chief of publications at the Carnegie Endowment for International Peace.

Stephen Schneider is senior scientist in the Advanced Study Program at the National Center for Atomspheric Research in Boulder, Colorado. He serves on a number of committees and councils and lectures widely on the policy implications of climate change, and global warming in particular. He is author of several books, including *Global Warming: Are We Entering the Greenhouse Century?* (see entry 80) and the *Genesis Strategy: Climate and Global Survival* (see entry 305). He was named a MacArthur Foundation Fellow in 1992.

Max Schnepf is editor of publications for the Soil and Water Conservation Society, an international scientific and educational association that advocates the conservation of soil, water, and related natural resources. Address: Soil and Water Conservation Society, 7515 NE Ankeny Rd., Ankeny, IA 50021, Tel. (515) 289–2331.

Clarence A. Schoenfeld is dean emeritus of Inter-College Programs and professor emeritus of journalism, wildlife ecology, and environmental studies at the University of Wisconsin–Madison. He was founding editor of the *Journal of Environmental Education* and is author of numerous books, including *Everybody's Ecology: A Field Guide to*

Pleasure and Perception in the Out-of-Doors (A. S. Barnes, 1971); *Wildlife Management in Wilderness* (Boxwood, 1978); and *Effective Feature Writing* (Holt, Rinehart, 1982).

Richard A. Schreiner is executive director of the Long Island Sound Taskforce, a group that strives for cleanup and restoration of the Long Island Sound through educational programs, research, and public policy and advocacy. The organization was founded in 1972 and has 1000 members from New York and Connecticut. Address: Long Island Sound Taskforce, Stanford Marine Center, Magee Ave., Stamford, CT 06902.

Kristie Seaman is education director for the Sanibel-Captiva Conservation Foundation, a nonprofit organization dedicated to the conservation and preservation of natural resources and wildlife habitat on and around the Sanibel and Captiva islands. Its four major areas of efforts are habitat management, land acquisition, research, and education. Address: Sanibel-Captiva Conservation Foundation, P.O. Box 839, 3333 Sanibel-Captiva Rd., Sanibel, FL 33957, Tel. (813) 472–2329.

Frederick Sepp is biological sciences librarian in the Life Sciences Library at Pennsylvania State University in University Park, Pennsylvania. He is active in several professional organizations, including the American Library Association, Special Libraries Association, and the American Institute of Biological Sciences. He believes that libraries should take an active role in informational and cultural issues.

George Sessions teaches in the department of humanities of Sierra College in Rocklin, California, and is coauthor, with Bill Devall, of *Deep Ecology: Living as if Nature Mattered* (see entry 29).

Jane Sharp is former president of the Conservation Council of North Carolina in Chapel Hill.

Diane Sherman is director of communications for Zero Population Growth, which is the largest national nonprofit membership organization concerned with the impacts of overpopulation. Address: Zero Population Growth, 1400 16th St., NW, Ste. 320, Washington, DC 20036, Tel. (202) 322–2200.

Mary P. Sherwood is chair of Walden Forever Wild, a grassroots organization dedicated to changing Walden from a swim-recreation park to a nature-preserve-type sanctuary, more like the natural conditions of the days of Emerson and Thoreau. Address: Walden Forever Wild, P.O. Box 275, Concord, MA 01742, Tel. (203) 429–2839.

Duane Silverstein is executive director of the Goldman Environmental Foundation, which awards the annual Goldman Environmental Prize to one environmental activist on each of the world's continents. Address: Goldman Environmental Foundation, 1160 Battery St., Ste. 400, San Francisco, CA 94111, Tel. (415) 788–1090.

Carl Slater is president of the Brooks Bird Club, a nonprofit organization set up to promote the study of ornithology and other natural sciences with special reference to West Virginia and contiguous areas; to publish the results of such studies, and to further the conservation of natural resources on a local and national basis. Address: Brooks Bird Club, 707 Werwood Ave., Wheeling, WV 26003.

D. Scott Slocombe is with the School of Urban and Regional Planning at the University of Waterloo in Ontario, Canada.

Donald Snow is director of the Northern Lights Institute, an alternative policy foundation and dispute resolution center serving the Rocky Mountain and northern Great Plains states. The institute publishes a quarterly magazine, *Northern Lights,* as well as numerous books and reports. Snow himself is editor of *Inside the Environmental Movement: Meeting the Leadership Challenges* (Island, 1992). Address: Northern Lights Institute, P.O. Box 8084, Missoula, MT 59807.

Gary Soucie is former executive editor of *Audubon,* the monthly magazine of the National Audubon Society. (For organization address, see listing for Russell Peterson.)

Charles H. Southwick is a professor of biology at the University of Colorado–Boulder, who has research interests in population ecology and animal behavior. He has conducted more than fifty overseas field trips to Asia, Africa, and Latin America and is author of about 120 scientific papers and six books, including *Global Ecology* (see entry 318).

Wallace Stegner has written on environmental subjects for at least fifty years, never as a full-time activist, but always as a convinced believer that unless we save the habitat—ours and that of the other creatures—we cannot save ourselves. He is recipient of the John Muir Award from the Sierra Club and the Robert Marshall Award from the Wilderness Society. During his career, he has produced about fifteen novels and a dozen works of nonfiction, including *Beyond the Hun-*

dredth Meridian: John Wesley Powell and the Second Opening of the West (see entry 86); and *The Sound of Mountain Water* (see entry 483). An overview of his work can be found in *Collected Stories of Wallace Stegner* (Random House, 1990).

John Steinhart is a professor of geophysics and of environmental studies, and is chair of the Energy Analysis and Policy curriculum at the University of Wisconsin–Madison. He is coauthor with Carol Steinhart of *Blowout: A Case Study of the Santa Barbara Oil Spill* (Duxbury, 1972); and *Energy: Sources, Use, and Role in Human Affairs* (Duxbury, 1974).

Jonathan Stoke is chair of the Sawtooth Group of the Sierra Club in Haily, Idaho.

Harriett S. Stubbs is a research associate professor at North Carolina State University–Raleigh and is executive director of the Acid Rain Foundation. Address: Acid Rain Foundation, 601 Blenheim Dr., Raleigh, NC 27612.

Apichai Sunchindah is a project officer with the Swiss Development Cooperation (SDC) Regional Coordination Office in Bangkok, Thailand, who manages a portfolio of development and humanitarian assistance projects funded by the SDC in Thailand, Myanmar, Laos, Cambodia, and Vietnam. He has worked for the Asian Institute of Technology, the Australian Center for International Agriculture Research, and the U.S. Agency for International Development.

Meredith Taylor is chair of the Wyoming chapter of the Sierra Club in Dubois, Wyoming.

C. Dart Thalman is former director of the Quebec-Labrador Foundation (QLF) /Atlantic Center for the Environment in Ispwich, Massachusetts. (For organizational information and address, see listing for Kathleen Blanchard.)

M. Pugh Thomas is director of the Environmental Resources Unit at the University of Salford in Salford, England, and managing editor of the *International Journal of Environmental Education and Information.*

Jennifer Tichenor is with the Environmental Action Coalition, a nonprofit educational organization with special knowledge and resources concerning conservation of the urban environment. Address: Environmental Action Coalition, 625 Broadway, New York, NY 10012, Tel. (212) 677–1601.

Peter Timmerman is a researcher with the Institute for Environmental Studies at the University of Toronto in Ontario, Canada.

Yi-Fu Tuan is Vilas professor of geography at the University of Wisconsin–Madison. He is author of several books, including *Topophilia: A Study of Environmental Perception, Attitudes and Values* (see entry 489); *Space and Place: The Perspective of Experience* (University of Minnesota Press, 1977); and *Landscapes of Fear* (Pantheon, 1979).

B. L. Turner, III is a professor of geography at Clark University in Worcester, Massachusetts, and is director of the George Perkins Marsh Institute there. He is coeditor of *The Earth Transformed by Human Action: Global and Regional Changes in the Biosphere over the Past 300 Years* (see entry 92).

Tom Turner is staff writer for the Sierra Club Legal Defense Fund, which is an independent, nonprofit environmental law firm that represents environmental organizations and individuals in legal and administrative proceedings all across the country. The headquarters is in San Francisco, with offices in Washington, D.C., Denver, Seattle, Honolulu, and Juneau. Turner is author of *Sierra Club: 100 Years of Protecting Nature* (see entry 332). Address: Sierra Club Legal Defense Fund, 2204 Fillmore St., San Francisco, CA 94115, Tel. (415) 567–6100.

Thomas Urquhart is executive director of the Maine Audubon Society, an independent statewide environmental organization focusing on advocacy, education, and wildlife conservation. Current priorities include conservation of the northern forest, protection of coastal water quality, pesticides, and protection of wildlife habitat and endangered species. Address: Maine Audubon Society, Gilsland Farm, 118 U.S. Rt. 1, Falmouth, ME 04105, Tel. (207) 781–2330.

Thomas R. Vale is a professor of geography at the University of Wisconsin–Madison. He is editor of *Progress Against Growth: Daniel B. Luten on the American Landscape* (see entry 438), author of *Plants and People: Vegetation Change in North America* (Association of American Geographers, 1982) and coauthor, with his wife Geraldine, of *U.S. 40 Today: Thirty Years of Landscape Change in America* (University of Wisconsin Press, 1983) and *Western Images, Western Landscapes: Travels along U.S. 89* (University of Arizona Press, 1990).

Jack R. Vallentyne is a senior scientist at the Canadian Centre for Inland Waters in Burlington, Ontario. He is a founding member of the World Council for the Biosphere and travels and lectures widely on global environmental topics under the guise of "Johnny Biosphere." He is author of *The Algal Bowl: Lakes and Man* (Ontario Department of the Environment, 1974).

Stephen Viederman is president of the Jessie Smith Noyes Foundation, which is among the largest philanthropic foundations supporting environmental and reproductive rights activities in North America and Latin America. In particular, the foundation supports grassroots activities at the intersection of the environment and social justice. Viederman has a special interest in ecological economics, and in the process of changing individual and institutional environmental behaviors. Address: Jessie Smith Noyes Foundation, 16 East 34th St., New York, NY 10016, Tel. (212) 684–6577.

Ken Voorhis is director of the Great Smoky Mountains Institute at Tremont, which is a residential environmental education center in Great Smoky Mountains National Park dedicated to educating people about and developing awareness of the natural and cultural resources of the park. Address: Great Smoky Mountains Institute at Tremont, Rt. 1, Box 705, Townsend, TN 37882.

Fred Waage is an associate professor of English at East Tennessee State University in Johnson City and editor of *Teaching Environmental Literature* (Modern Language Association, 1985).

Mark C. Wagstaff is executive director of the Wilderness Education Association (WEA), which is a nonprofit membership organization whose mission is to promote the professionalization of outdoor leadership, and to thereby improve the safety and quality of outdoor trips and enhance the conservation of the wild outdoors. The WEA promotes wilderness education and preservation through wilderness leadership training. Address: Wilderness Education Association, 20 Winona Ave., P.O. Box 89, Saranac Lake, NY 12983, Tel. (518) 891–2915.

Charles Walcott is executive director of the Cornell University Laboratory of Ornithology in Ithaca, New York.

Brian Walker is president emeritus of the International Institute for Environment and Development in London, England.

Jay Walljaspar is editor of the *Utne Reader,* which is a bimonthly digest of alternative press based in Minneapolis, Minnesota. Address: 1624 Harmon Place, Suite 330, Minneapolis, MN 55403, Tel. (612) 338–5040.

Arthur H. Westing is a senior research fellow and adjunct professor of ecology at the Stockholm International Peace Research Institute. He is author of several books on environment and peace issues, including *Warfare in a Fragile World: The Military Impact on the Human Environment* (Taylor & Francis, 1980).

Walter Westman was a senior researcher at Lawrence Berkeley Laboratory and at the National Aeronautics and Space Administration (NASA) Ames Research Center in California. He was a professor of environmental planning and geography at the University of California–Los Angeles, and author of *Ecology, Impact Assessment, and Environmental Planning* (see entry 496). He is since deceased.

Roger J. Wheater is director of the Royal Zoological Society of Scotland in Edinburgh. The society is responsible for maintaining animal collections at Edinburgh Zoo and the Highland Wildlife Park. It has committed its collections to the conservation of species through scientifically-based and coordinated captive breeding programs, conservation education, research, and recreation. Address: Royal Zoological Society of Scotland, Edinburgh Zoo, Murrayfield, Edinburgh EH12 6TS Scotland, United Kingdom, Tel. (031) 334–9171.

Joyce Williams hails from Leeds, England, and is affiliated with the National Association for Science, Technology and Society. She is a visiting scholar in the Science, Technology and Society program at Pennsylvania State University in Pennsylvania. (For organizational information and address, see listing for Eugene Bazan.)

Elissa Wolfson is managing editor of *E Magazine*. The magazine was formed as a clearinghouse for information, news, and commentary on environmental issues for the benefit of the general public, with sufficient depth to involve dedicated environmentalists. Address: *E Magazine*, 28 Knight Street, Norwalk, CT, Tel. (203) 854–5559.

Donald E. Worster is Hall Professor of American History at the University of Kansas, in Lawrence. He indicates that he is a historian "interested in how we humans, in modern times, have driven ourselves to try to dominate the earth and what that drive has meant in ethical and social terms." He is editor of *The Ends of the Earth: Perspectives on Modern Environmental History* (see entry 348); and is author of *Nature's Economy: A History of Ecological Ideas* (see entry 100); *Dust Bowl: The Southern Plains in the 1930s* (see entry 347); and *Under Western Skies: Nature and History in the American West* (Oxford University Press, 1992).

Joseph Wright is an environmental education consultant to the Department of Education in Indianapolis, Indiana.

Michael Zamm is director of environmental education for the Council on the Environment of New York City. Address: Council on the Environment of New York City, 51 Chambers St., Ste. 228, New York, NY 10007, Tel. (212) 566–0990.

Nancy Zuschlag is an extension agent for natural resources with the cooperative extension program of Colorado State University in Fort Collins. She is president of the Colorado Alliance for Environmental Education, a nonprofit organization dedicated to fostering an environmental literacy of Colorado citizens through cooperation among education, business, agriculture, and government agencies. Address: Colorado Alliance for Environmental Education, 15200 W. 6th Ave., Golden, CO 80401.

Appendix: Sources for Further Reference

During my research, I came across several magazine articles, reports, and books that identify important environmental literature in particular areas. For the reader who would like to review additional references or would like to see how others have ranked books on nature and the environment, I have described here the sources I found most informative. One soon discovers, of course, that a single source leads to hundreds of other sources, and each of those in turn leads to hundreds more.

An annotated list of nature writings appears in Herbert Faulkner West's book *The Nature Writers: A Guide to Richer Reading* (Stephen Daye, 1939), which contains references to works written primarily in the nineteenth and early twentieth centuries. Around the same time, the great naturalist William Beebe assembled a collection called *The Book of Naturalists: An Anthology of the Best Natural History* (Knopf, 1944).

Edwin Way Teale selected 100 volumes for a nature library in an article called "The Great Companions of Nature Literature" in *Audubon* magazine 46, no. 6 (1944). He later compiled selections from these writings in *Green Treasury: A Journey through the World's Great Nature Writing* (Dodd, Mead, 1952).

Several recent magazines and scholarly journals have carried articles that review environmental literature. In the Autumn 1986 issue of the literary journal *Antaeus* are lists of favorite nature books by several prominent nature writers, including Annie Dillard, Gretel Ehrlich, Robert Finch, John Hay, Edward Hoagland, Barry Lopez, and Thomas Lyon.

Sierra magazine has printed two articles, one entitled "Leaves of Green" (May/June 1986), and the other called "Visionaries and Cassandras" (July/August 1991), that are particularly useful. The first cites one example each, from two dozen environmentalists, of what they consider to be influential or memorable books. The second article was written by Kathleen Courrier, director of publications for the World Resources Institute, and presents the author's roster of books that she feels have built the environmental movement.

The editors of *Not Man Apart,* the newspaper of Friends of the Earth, published "The Environmental Books Hall of Fame" (November 1973), which was an article in that newspaper that listed the nominations of several well-known environmentalists.

The *Earth First!* journal has recorded book selections in articles such as "A Smattering of Books" (December 21, 1982), by Dave Foreman; and "The Books of Deep Ecology" (August 1, 1984), by Bill Devall and George Sessions. Foreman is cofounder of Earth First! and now operates Ned Ludd Books, which is an environmental bookstore in Tucson, Arizona. He also publishes *The Big Outside Catalog* with his selected favorites.

During the spring of 1990, coinciding with the twentieth anniversary celebration of Earth Day, several magazines carried articles listing recommended readings: "The Essence of Environmental Thinking" in *The Ecologist* (July/August 1990), by Sandy Irvine; "Getting Down to Earth: 20 Years Later," two columns in *The Washington Post Book World* magazine (April 1, 1990), by William Howarth and Kathleen Courrier; and "An Earth Day Reader" in *Smithsonian* (April 1990), by T. H. Watkins.

During the 1970s, *Library Journal* carried in its April issue an overview of the best environmental literature of the year. Michael Huxley, who operates a bookselling firm that specializes in natural history, prepared an article titled "Landmark Books for an Environmental Collection" for *Cite AB* (April 8, 1991). And an article on "The Essential Volumes of a Wildlife Professional's Library" was published in *Wildlife Society Bulletin* 15, no. 4 (1987).

Several professional organizations have sponsored the compilation of annotated bibliographies. A 1985 book, *Teaching Environmental Literature: Materials, Methods, Resources,* published by the Modern Language Association of America, includes recommendations of noteworthy books on nature and the environment from several educators.

In 1978, the Association of American Geographers (AAG) published a collection of articles in *Sourcebook on the Environment: A Guide to the Literature* (University of Chicago Press), in which well-known geographers surveyed the most important books on specific topics of environmental studies. A subsequent book published by the AAG and the National Geographic Society, *A Geographical Bibliography for American Libraries* (1985), has a chapter devoted to conservation and environmental management.

Thomas J. Lyon, an associate professor of English at Utah State University, has edited a collection of American nature writing called *This Incomparable Lande* (see entry 238), in which he presents an extensive annotated bibliography of nature writing. Island Press of Covelo, California, also published in 1991 a book called *In Praise of Nature* (see entry 259), by Stephanie Mills, which contains reviews of about 100 books that Mills considers important.

　　　　Several Bibliographies on environmental ethics and philosophy have been published during the 1980s. *Ecophilosophy: A Field Guide to the Literature* (see entry 373), by Donald Edward Davis, includes annotations for some 280 books on ethics, religion, and philosophy related to the environment. Similarly, two bibliographies by Mary Anglemeyer and Eleanor Seagraves were published earlier in that decade by Smithsonian Institution Press. They are: *A Search for Environmental Ethics: An Initial Bibliography* (1980), sponsored by the Rachel Carson Council; and *The Natural Environment: An Annotated Bibliography on Attitudes and Values* (1984), sponsored by the Global Tomorrow Coalition. In 1976, philosopher Loren Owings prepared *Environmental Values, 1860–1972: A Guide to Information Sources,* which covers the historical development of attitudes toward nature.

　　　　Owing's bibliography is volume 4 of the *Man and the Environment Information Guide Series* published by Gale Research Company, a series that includes other bibliographies on air pollution, environmental design, environmental economics, environmental education, environmental law, environmental planning, environmental politics and administration, environmental toxicology, human ecology, noise pollution, wastewater management, and water pollution.

　　　　In recent editions of such general reading guides as the thirteenth edition of *The Reader's Advisor: A Layman's Guide to Literature—Volume 5, The Best in the Literature of Science, Technology and Medicine,* edited by Paul T. Durbin (Bowker, 1988), and the twenty-third edition of *Good Reading: A Guide for Serious Readers,* edited by Arthur Waldorn, Olga S. Weber, and Arthur Zieger (Bowker, 1990), there are chapters on ecology and environmental science, biology, natural history, and other related topics.

　　　　In addition, there are several specialized bibliographies on particular topics or aspects of the environment: *A Bibliography of Animal Rights and Related Matters* (University Press of America, 1981), by Charles Magel; and *International Development and the Human Environment: An Annotated Bibliography* (Macmillan, 1974), by M. T. Farvar.

　　　　Joan S. Elbers has prepared an annotated bibliography, *Changing Wilderness Values, 1930–1990* (Greenwood, 1991), which contains 324 entries for books and articles about the wilderness, wilderness experiences, and issues.

　　　　Scores of brief topical bibliographies have been prepared by Vance Bibliographies for its *Public Administration* series. See particularly the exhaustive treatment of "environmental hazards" prepared by E. Willard Miller and Ruby M. Miller, which includes bibliographies on *Air Pollution, Industrial and Toxic Wastes, Liquid Wastes, Radioactive Materials and Wastes, Solid Wastes,* and *Water Pollution,* all published in 1985. The Council of Planning Librarians publishes a bibliography series, of which many of the books are on environmental topics. Examples include: *Jobs and the Environment* (CPL Bibliography #116); *Deep Ecology and Environmental Ethics* (#185); *Environmental Mediation* (#189); *Environmental Consciousness—Native America Worldviews and Sustainable Natural Resource Management* (#214); *Groundwater* (#261); and *Wetlands* (#265).

David Orr, education editor of the journal *Conservation Biology*, presents a list of essential readings in his book *Ecological Literacy* (see page 225).

Finally, I have found the bibliographic essays in the following works to be exceptionally useful: *The Ends of the Earth: Perspectives on Modern Environmental History* (see entry 348), edited by Donald E. Worster; *The American Environment: Readings in the History of Conservation* (see entry 266), edited by Roderick Nash; and *Ecology and the Politics of Scarcity* (see entry 266), by William Ophuls.

Author Index

This index includes all authors mentioned in the guide: those identified in entries 1 through 500; those mentioned in the various annotations as authors of supplemental or related books; and those listed in the introduction, in the biographical notes about the respondents to the questionnaire, and in the appendix. The authors are listed alphabetically, followed by the title of the book and the page number on which the citation is found. When there are two or more authors for a book, they are listed separately and designated by "(jt. author)" for joint authorship. Listings in boldface identify *The Environmentalist's Bookshelf* Top 40 Books (see pages 7–9).

243

Title Index

This index includes all titles mentioned in the guide: those identified in entries 1 through 500; those mentioned in the various annotations as supplemental or related books; those listed as additional recommended books for particular authors; and those mentioned in the introduction, in the biographical notes about the respondents to the questionnaire, and in the appendix. The titles are listed alphabetically, followed by the author of the book and the page number on which the citation is found. Listings in boldface identify *The Environmentalist's Bookshelf* Top 40 Books (see pages 7–9).

Subject Index